THE CORE EXECUTIVE IN BRITAIN

BARNSLEY COLLEGE
EASTGATE
LEARNING CENTRE

BARNSLEY COLLEGE

00086670

6497

TRANSFORMING GOVERNMENT

General Editor: R. A. W. Rhodes, *Professor of Politics, University of Newcastle upon Tyne*

This important and authoritative new series arises out of the seminal ESRC Whitehall Programme and seeks to fill the enormous gaps in our knowledge of the key actors and institutions of British government. It examines the many large changes during the postwar period and puts these into comparative context by analysing the experience of the advanced industrial democracies of Europe and the nations of the Commonwealth. The series reports the results of the Whitehall Programme, a four-year project into change in British government in the postwar period, mounted by the Economic and Social Research Council.

Published titles include:

Martin J. Smith
THE CORE EXECUTIVE IN BRITAIN

Kevin Theakston
LEADERSHIP IN WHITEHALL

Patrick Weller, Herman Bakvis and R. A. W. Rhodes
THE HOLLOW CROWN:

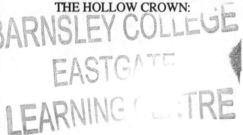

BARNSLEY COLLEGE
EASTGATE
LEARNING CENTRE

Transforming Government
Series Standing Order ISBN 0–333–71580–2
(*outside North America only*)

You can receive future titles in this series as they are published by placing a standing order. Please contact your bookseller or, in case of difficulty, write to us at the address below with your name and address, the title of the series and the ISBN quoted above.

Customer Services Department, Macmillan Distribution Ltd
Houndmills, Basingstoke, Hampshire RG21 6XS, England

The Core Executive in Britain

Martin J. Smith
Professor of Politics
University of Sheffield

Published in association with the
ESRC WHITEHALL PROGRAMME

E·S·R·C
ECONOMIC
& SOCIAL
RESEARCH
COUNCIL

First published in Great Britain 1999 by
MACMILLAN PRESS LTD
Houndmills, Basingstoke, Hampshire RG21 6XS and London
Companies and representatives throughout the world

A catalogue record for this book is available from the British Library.

ISBN 0–333–60515–2 hardcover
ISBN 0–333–60516–0 paperback

First published in the United States of America 1999 by
ST. MARTIN'S PRESS, INC.,
Scholarly and Reference Division,
175 Fifth Avenue, New York, N.Y. 10010

ISBN 0–312–21905–9

Library of Congress Cataloging-in-Publication Data
Smith, Martin J. (Martin John), 1961–
The core executive in Britain / Martin J. Smith.
p. cm.
Includes bibliographical references and index.
ISBN 0–312–21905–9 (cloth)
1. Great Britain—Politics and government. 2. Cabinet system—
–Great Britain. 3. Executive power—Great Britain. I. Title.
JN405.S64 1999
320.441—dc21 98–35013
CIP

© Martin J. Smith 1999
Foreword © R. A. W. Rhodes 1999

All rights reserved. No reproduction, copy or transmission of this publication may be made
without written permission.

No paragraph of this publication may be reproduced, copied or transmitted save with
written permission or in accordance with the provisions of the Copyright, Designs and
Patents Act 1988, or under the terms of any licence permitting limited copying issued by
the Copyright Licensing Agency, 90 Tottenham Court Road, London W1P 9HE.

Any person who does any unauthorised act in relation to this publication may be liable to
criminal prosecution and civil claims for damages.

The author has asserted his right to be identified as the author of this work in accordance
with the Copyright, Designs and Patents Act 1988.

This book is printed on paper suitable for recycling and made from fully managed and
sustained forest sources.

10   9   8   7   6   5   4   3   2   1
08   07   06   05   04   03   02   01   00   99

Printed in Hong Kong

To Jean

Contents

List of Tables, Figures and Boxes

TABLES

FIGURES

BOXES

Foreword: Transforming Government

There are enormous gaps in our knowledge of the key actors and institutions in British government. We cannot do simple things like describing the work of ministers of state, permanent secretaries, and their departments. Also, there have been large changes in British government during the post-war period, such as: the growth of the welfare state; the professionalism of government; the consequences of recession; the effects of New Right ideology; the impact of the European Union; the effects of new technology; the hollowing out of the state; and the new public management, with its separation of policy and administration. We do not know how these changes affected British government. And we cannot understand the effects of these changes by focusing only on Britain. We must also analyse the experience of the advanced industrialised democracies of Europe and the Commonwealth.

To repair these gaps in our knowledge and to explain how and why British government changed in the post-war period, the Economic and Social Research Council mounted the Whitehall Programme on 'The Changing Nature of Central Government in Britain'. This series on 'Transforming Government' reports the results of that four-year research programme. The series has five objectives:

- Develop theory – to develop new theoretical perspectives to explain why British government changed and why it differs from other countries.
- Understand change – to describe and explain what has changed in British government since 1945.
- Compare – to compare these changes with those in other EU member states and other states with a 'Westminster' system of government.
- Build bridges – to create a common understanding between academics and practitioners.
- Dissemination – to make academic research accessible to a varied audience covering sixth-formers and senior policy-makers.

The books cover six broad themes:

- Developing theory about the new forms of governance.
- The hollowing out of the state in Britain, Europe and the Common-wealth.
- The fragmenting government framework.
- The changing roles of ministers and the senior civil service.
- Constitutional change.
- New ways of delivering services.

Martin Smith's book on the British core executive is a major addition to the series.[1] He redefines conventional accounts of the British executive by developing three arguments:

- It is misleading to focus on personality and on the role of the Prime Minister and key ministers. There are many actors with complex interdependencies in the core executive. All control some resources. No one actor can succeed without exchanging resources. Power is everywhere.
- Actors are central but so are structures. We must understand the structural and historical context in which the core executive works.
- Power is relational, based on dependency not domination. We must focus on the context, resources, structures and the choices of actors in the core executive. These structures of dependence take the form of overlapping policy networks.

Chapter 2 assesses critically the Westminster model of British govern-ment, arguing that it omits too much and explains too little. It then develops the power–dependency model of the core executive. Chapter 3 places the core executive in a wider socio-economic and historical context, exploring the changing pattern of dependencies in the nine-teenth and twentieth centuries. Chapter 4 deconstructs the conven-tional analysis of the power of the Prime Minister and cabinet. Chapter 5 explores the roles and relationships of minister and civil servants, again stressing their mutual dependence. Chapter 6 analyses the weakness, not the strength, of the core executive, especially its diffi-culties in developing a coordinated, strategic approach. Chapter 7 critically appraises the reforms of the 1980s and 1990s, documenting the seemingly endless and fruitless search to strengthen central cap-ability. Chapter 8 explores the impact of the EU and other interna-tional interdependencies on the core executive. Chapter 9 draws the argument together and should show even the casual reader the swingeing implications of Smith's analysis.

The core executive has changed in six ways in the post-war period. There has been a shift from bureaucratic to decentralised management. The core executive sets the overall policy direction, avoiding detailed intervention. The public sector is smaller. Economic interest groups have been excluded from the policy process. There is less consensus between politicians and officials. The centre manages networks rather than controlling bureaucracies. So, Smith's conclusions about the capability of the British centre are dramatic. For example, he argues that the core executive is increasingly concerned with governance rather than government. The core executive is no longer sovereign (if it ever was) but is at the centre of networks of different organisations, which it does not directly control. Fragmentation is pervasive. Co-ordination is elusive. The cabinet is now almost universally accepted as nothing more than a rubber stamp; it has become almost a dignified part of the constitution. And that constitution has not kept pace with the changes that have occurred in government.

One of the challenges facing everyone on the ESRC research programme was to build bridges between the academic community and research users. Smith takes the present-day analysis of the British executive out of the academic journals and makes it accessible to a larger audience for the first time. I expect the book to change the way in which we discuss the power of the British executive. Gone forever are the hoary old clichés of prime-ministerial power, replaced by a recognition that power is everywhere and understood through the language of dependence, networks, governance and choice.

R. A. W. Rhodes

Director, ESRC Whitehall Programme, and
Professor of Politics, University of Newcastle

Note

1. The ESRC Whitehall Programme had published six books by April 1998.

   J. Bradbury and J. Mawson (eds), *British Regionalism and Devolution*. London: Kingsley, 1997.

   P. Day and R. Klein, *Steering but not Rowing? The Transformation of the Department of Health: a Case Study*. Bristol: Policy Press, 1997.

   R. A. W. Rhodes, *Understanding Governance: Policy Networks, Governance, Reflexivity and Accountability*. Buckingham: Open University Press, 1997.

   R. A. W. Rhodes and P. Dunleavy (eds), *Prime Minister, Cabinet and Core Executive*. London: Macmillan, 1995.

P. Weller, H. Bakvis and R. A. W. Rhodes (eds), *The Hollow Crown*. London: Macmillan, 1997.
J. Seargeant and J. Steele, *Consulting the Public. Guidelines and Good Practice.* London: Policy Studies Institute, 1997.

For further information about the Programme and its publications contact Professor R. A. W. Rhodes, Department of Politics, University of Newcastle upon Tyne, NE1 7RU. E-mail address: r.a.w.rhodes@ncl.ac.uk.

Acknowledgements

I have been overwhelmed by the number of people who have been prepared to help with the writing of this book, not least by the large number of officials and politicians who were willing to speak candidly about the operations of the core executive. Rod Rhodes not only initiated the ESRC Whitehall programme that has provided the framework and finance for this project (ESRC award no. L124261005), but has also given freely of his advice and offered constructive criticism. Dave Marsh and Dave Richards have been very generous in allowing me to use material from our shared project (ESRC award no. L124251023) under the Whitehall Programme, and have continually discussed the themes of this book and Whitehall in general. Jim Buller assisted in gathering some of the interview material in Chapter 7. My postgraduate students, Helen Butler, John Chapman, Matthew Flinders and Francesca Gains, have all been working on related policy areas, and through their projects have helped to clarify my own thinking. The Department of Politics at the University of Sheffield has provided a supportive atmosphere for research and my colleagues have grumbled little at my two-year absence from the fray of teaching and administration. Thanks to Andrew Gamble, Petr Kopecky, Steve Ludlam and Tony Payne, who have at various points read draft chapters or papers. Matt Flinders, Jean Grugel, Steven Kennedy, Rod Rhodes, Dave Richards and an anonymous reader all read a draft of the whole book and offered many useful views on how it could be improved. Dave Richards, in particular, was prepared to discuss all aspects of the book on numerous occasions. He spotted, and helped me to sort out, a number of problems and I am very grateful for his contribution. Dave also proved an entertaining and sociable companion on our many research trips to London. Finally, Jean Grugel carefully read the complete manuscript in great detail, discussed on many occasions a range of issues and pushed me over the final hurdle. Without her support the whole experience of writing this book would have been less pleasurable. It is to her that the book is dedicated.

Martin J. Smith

1 Introducing the Core Executive

The core executive is at the heart of British government. It contains the key institutions and actors concerned with developing policy, coordinating government activity and providing the necessary resources for delivering public goods. The aim of this book is to examine, and to analyse, the British core executive in a way that goes beyond the traditional and oft-repeated, and unhelpful questions: has prime-ministerial power replaced cabinet government? Who is dominant, ministers or civil servants? And does Parliament control the executive?

The starting-point is that all actors within the core executive have resources, with no actor, or institution, having a monopoly. These resources, which include information, authority, finance, and control of an organisation, provide the potential for achieving goals (see Rhodes 1988). Actors are individuals within an institutional setting who can exercise choice. In the core executive this means prime ministers, ministers and civil servants. Because no actor or institution controls all the resources necessary to achieve their goals (for example, although the Prime Minister may have authority, he or she does not have all the information necessary for policy-making), actors within the central state depend on each other. The political process is about exchanging resources, and through controlling the process of exchange a range of actors can influence policy outcomes. In addition, the extent to which actors depend on each other varies. Not all actors or institutions have equal resources, and the degree of dependency and the way resources are exchanged are products of the particular context that actors face and the specific tactics they develop in using their resources. In certain ways this approach is a reflection of some post-modern notions that power is everywhere, and not hidden away in a particular institution such as Number 10 or the civil service.

The core themes of the book are:

- All actors within the core executive have resources.
- In order to achieve goals resources have to be exchanged.

1

- Notions of prime-ministerial government, cabinet government or presidentialism are irrelevant, because power within the core executive is based on dependency not command.
- In order to understand the operation of the core executive we need to trace the structures of dependency.
- These structures of dependency are often based on overlapping networks. Frequently these networks do not follow formal organisational structures, and this can lead to fragmentation and conflict over responsibility and territory.
- Even resource-rich actors, such as the Prime Minister, are dependent on other actors to achieve their goals. Therefore, government works through building alliances rather than command.
- Actors operate within a structured arena. Traditional approaches to central government have placed too much emphasis on personality. Prime ministers, officials and ministers are bound by external organisation, the rules of the game, the structures of institutions, other actors and the context. Therefore, the nature and form of the core executive do not change with personality.
- The degree of dependency that actors have on each other varies according to the context. As the political and economic situation changes, actors may become more or less dependent. Economic success may provide the Chancellor with more freedom, or electoral success may provide the Prime Minister with greater room for manoeuvre. Economic failure means the Chancellor needs more support from the Prime Minister. Political failure means the Prime Minister needs more support from the cabinet.
- Because of the distribution of resources, the strength of departments and overlapping networks, the core executive is fragmented and central coordination is extremely difficult.

The relationships between ministers, between ministers and officials and between ministers and the Prime Minister do not primarily depend on personality. They are structured relationships, which are shaped by the rules of the Whitehall game, the institutions of government, past policy choices and the external political and economic context. Asking whether there is prime-ministerial government does not take us far in understanding the operation of central government. Rather, the crucial questions are:

- What sort of relationships do prime ministers develop with their colleagues?

- How do prime ministers and ministers build alliances?
- How quickly do these alliances change?
- What sort of networks do the Prime Minister, ministers and officials have in Whitehall?
- How does the wider political context affect these relationships?
- How are the relationships between ministers and officials structured by departments and the values of Whitehall?

APPROACHES TO CENTRAL GOVERNMENT

As we will see in the following chapter, the traditional focus of central government has been very narrow. It has sought to identify the site of power within the central state. Such a narrow approach derives from a number of distortions and simplifications. In particular, it results from the way in which the constitution and its attendant notions of parliamentary sovereignty and ministerial and cabinet responsibility have shaped both perceptions and analysis of the central state (see Greenaway *et al.* 1992). A number of studies have attempted to get away from highly personalised accounts of central government and to question the traditional constitutional and institutional approaches. In the 1960s and 1970s authors such as John Mackintosh (1963 and 1977b) started to question some of the implications of the traditional assumptions concerning the Prime Minister and cabinet. However, despite much innovative and interesting work by commentators such as Mackintosh, George Jones (1975) and Anthony King (1985), their terrain was still framed largely by the traditional constitutionally defined agenda.

In recent years more analytical accounts of the core executive have been developed. Bruce-Gardyne and Lawson (1976) carried out a number of detailed case-studies of key issues in British public policy. Their studies highlighted the strength of departments, and therefore the limited role of the Prime Minister and cabinet, and the importance of interdependence, in the policy making process. They concentrated not on personalities but on the complexities of the institutional arrangements in the policy process and examined how institutions affected policy outcomes (see also Greenaway *et al.* 1992). In addition, some of the best political memoirs (see for example, Donoughue 1987, Healey 1990, Howe 1994, Lawson 1994) demonstrate an awareness of the complex nature of core executive relationships.

More recently, Burch and Holliday (1996: 5) have suggested an approach that recognises:

cabinet system actors operate within a series of limits which are both internal and external to that system. Internal limits comprise abiding organisational patterns and established ways of working. They shape behaviour, and provide the immediate context within which opportunities to exercise individual initiative arise . . . External limits comprise the economic, social and political context within which all cabinet system actors operate . . . In our way of looking at things, the role of the individual is conditioned by and secondary to these limits and constraints.

As will emerge below, there have also been important developments in the application of rational choice models to central government (Dunleavy 1991, Dowding 1995).

Perhaps most influential in reassessing the approach to central government has been Dunleavy and Rhodes's call for a more systematic research agenda for core executive studies (Dunleavy and Rhodes 1990; Rhodes and Dunleavy 1995). They suggest we can improve our understanding of the core by widening the focus of central government studies and applying a range of conceptual and theoretical approaches. Taking up the challenge, this book uses the notion of the core executive in order to develop an approach to central government that is consciously analytical and concerned with the wider context of central government policy-making (see Box 1.1 and Figure 1.1).

THE CORE EXECUTIVE

It follows that in order to understand the central state it is important to examine the core executive not only as a set of formal institutions but also as number of overlapping and interconnecting networks through which various actors exchange resources. The concept of policy networks is based on the idea that organisations are dependent on each other for resources and they have to exchange resources in order to achieve their goals (Rhodes 1981). Within the core executive we can see that there are a range of institutions that are connected by their mutual dependence. Departments need the Prime Minister's authority in cabinet while the Prime Minister needs departments to develop and implement policy. The impact of the Prime Minister, a cabinet minister, or an official on policy depends on the structures of dependency (or networks) linking them to other actors and the resources that each of these actors control. This structure of relationships provides the framework within which the actors of the core executive operate. But it does not determine policy outcomes, or who 'wins'. The effectiveness of actors within the core executive depends, in large part, on the tactics, choices and strategies they adopt in using their resources. Ministers and Prime Ministers can build alliances, and officials can withhold information or call on other departments to support their arguments.

BOX 1.1
What is the core executive?

Rhodes (1995a: 12) provides a definition of the core executive and outlines its importance:

> The term 'core executive' refers to all those organisations and procedures which coordinate central government, and act as final arbiters of conflict between different parts of the government machine. In brief, the 'core executive' is the heart of the machine, covering the complex web of institutions, networks and practices surrounding the prime minister, cabinet, cabinet committees and their official counterparts, less formalised ministerial 'clubs' or meetings, bilateral negotiations and interdepartmental committees. It also includes coordinating departments chiefly the Cabinet Office, the Treasury, the Foreign Office, the law officers, and security and intelligence services. The label 'cabinet government' was the overarching term for (some of) these institutions and practices but it is an inadequate and confusing because it does not describe accurately the effective mechanisms for achieving coordination. At best it is contentious, and at worst seriously misleading, to assert the primacy of the cabinet among organisations and mechanisms at the heart of the machine.

I have also included departments in the definition of the core executive for two reasons: they are the core policy-making units within central government (Smith *et al.* 1993); and they are headed by ministers who are key actors within the institutions of the core executive (see Figure 1.1).

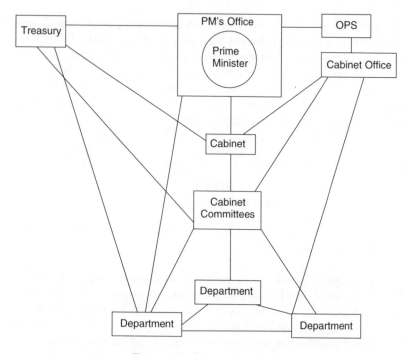

Figure 1.1   The core executive

It is not always those with the most resources or the actors who are the least dependent who win. The choices of actors do have an affect on the outcome of policy. Nevertheless, as Burch and Holliday (1996) indicate, these choices are made within a set of structured relationships and institutions.

Moreover, the freedom of actors to use their resources will depend on the particular context. For example, after an emphatic election victory a Prime Minister is usually less dependent on his or her cabinet than when the government is behind in the polls and the Prime Minister is an unpopular leader. Therefore we can assume that following success the Prime Minister has more freedom to use resources than at other times. Nevertheless, the Prime Minister is nearly always constrained by the structures of dependency.

In sum, unlike traditional approaches to central government, one of the central themes of this book is that it is impossible, and indeed fruitless, to try and identify a single site of power within the core executive, because power is everywhere. The structures of dependency and the distribution of resources mean that all actors can have some success. No single actor can achieve what he or she wants without exchanging resources, and therefore compromise is built into the structure of government.

To understand power in the core executive we need to:

- trace the structures of dependency – in other words analyse how different networks link various parts of the core executive and examine who has to exchange resources to achieve their goals;
- evaluate the resources of actors;
- look at the context within which dependent actors and/or institutions exchange resources;
- examine the strategies and tactics of actors.

It is important to remember that while relationships of dependency and the distribution of resources may be structural, they are not permanent and fixed. The resources of actors and their relationships to each other change across time. The relationship of the Treasury to departments has been in constant flux in the twentieth century, and the post-war period has seen the Prime Minister accrue more resources with the development of the Prime Minister's Office. Therefore, in addition to a contextual approach, it is important to develop a historical account in order to examine how relationships have developed over time and how actions at one particular time can create the structural context for later actors. One clear example of this effect is the way in which the reforms to central government that are discussed in Chapter 7 have provided the context for the new Labour government and created a whole new set of structured relationships between departments and the Next Steps agencies.

Finally, there is a strong tendency in studies of central government to see it as a hermetically sealed unit: the constraints on the Prime Minister are the constraints of the cabinet and Parliament and not the outside world. However, it is apparent that the core executive exists in a set of structured dependencies with external institutions. Traditionally, Parliament has been the focus of constraints, but there are constraints that derive from the economic system, international institutions and, particularly in recent years, the European Union.

In sum, this book aims to shift analysis away from the focus on personality and institutions in accounts of central government that have tended to dominate this area of political science. The intention is to develop an analytically driven account of the core executive in order to examine the interactions that occur between structures and agents in the policy process. To this effect, the book begins by analysing the weaknesses of the traditional approach to central government. It then develops an alternative framework, which is used in the course of book. The book proceeds to place the core executive in historical context, reviewing the changing structures of dependency throughout the nineteenth and twentieth centuries. Chapter 4 examines the relationship between the Prime Minister and the cabinet, demonstrating that the division between cabinet and prime-ministerial government is a false dichotomy. Chapter 5 concentrates on the operation of departments and highlights the dependent relationship between ministers and officials. Chapter 6 examines the coordination of the core executive, highlighting the problems of developing a strategic approach to government when there appears to be no single coordinating body. Chapter 7 looks at the reforms to the core executive and government more generally that occurred during the 1980s and 1990s, and examines how these changes have affected the structures of dependency in the core executive. Chapter 8 examines the impact of the outside world on the core executive. Chapter 9 looks at the implications of the book for understanding the state and the constitution.

2 Analysing the Core Executive

Traditionally, analysis of central government has been dominated by the 'Westminster model'. This chapter will describe this model, outline its problems and propose an alternative framework for analysing the core executive. Through the lens of the Westminster model, Britain is generally perceived as having a hierarchical and unified political system, with power concentrated in the central institutions of the state. This view of the political system has influenced both politicians and political scientists examining British politics. In this chapter I will argue that such a perspective offered a partial reflection of the British political system, but was oversimplified as a form of analysis because of its crude definition of power. Consequently, I will examine a number of more sophisticated analytical frameworks that pay attention to the value systems of government, informal institutions, policy networks and resource dependency. Finally, I will outline the framework that will be used to examine the core executive in this book. I will demonstrate that the core executive is not based on command, but on resource exchange and dependency. Therefore, to understand the core executive, it is important to trace the structures of dependency that link the actors and institutions of the central state. I will suggest that the nature of such links can be understood only in the context of structure, tactics and the prevailing political circumstances.

THE WESTMINSTER MODEL

The study of British central government has been dominated almost throughout the twentieth century implicitly and explicitly by the Westminster model. Although from the 1960s onwards political scientists began to question the Westminster model through behavioural and institutional studies, they remained very much within its paradigm. Institutional and behavioural analysis did not question the fundamentals of the Westminster model, but corrected some of its simplicities. The Westminster model is essentially an 'organising perspective' that defines an area of study and indicates some of the questions to be asked

(Rhodes 1997a: 5). It is built on the assumption that there is parliamentary sovereignty (Gamble 1990, Judge 1993): all decisions are made within Parliament and there is no higher authority. Legitimacy and democracy are maintained because ministers are answerable to Parliament and the House of Commons is elected by the people. Decisions are taken by cabinet and implemented by a neutral civil service. This view is derived from the Whig notion of the constitution being in self-correcting balance (Tant 1993: 63). The cabinet could effectively take decisions, but any abuse of power could be checked by Parliament and ultimately the electorate (Mackintosh 1977a).

This model was also perceived as providing for the best system of government. It was normatively good because it was able to combine government responsibility – and a strong notion of governmental autonomy – with democratic control through accountability and elections. 'Britain's success in maintaining economic advance, overseas expansion and political stability was credited to the excellence of British political institutions' (Gamble 1990: 407). Consequently, the model became a prescription of what government should be and was exported in particular to colonies and ex-colonies (Payne 1993, Norton 1991a).

The Westminster model prescribed both what government did (or does) and the way it was examined. It also provided the agenda for the focus of empirical work on central government. The model framed the beliefs of both politicians and political scientists; to varying degrees they accepted the Westminster model as representing reality (Judge 1993: 132–3). The Westminster model did reflect, to a significant extent, the nature of the British political system. Power was concentrated within the parliamentary system, the exercise of power was hierarchical and the system was relatively closed to outside influences. This view reflected a belief that this system is the way things *should* be, and subsequently led to misconceptions about both the nature of power and the location of the focus of research. The normative presumptions of the Westminster model underpinned empirical analysis of central government. While this approach may have reflected, to some extent, political reality – particularly pre-war – it was always too narrow in its focus.

In the 1960s and 1970s many analysts developed critiques of the Westminster model through questioning the power of Parliament, the neutrality of the civil service and the relationship between the Prime Minister and the cabinet (see for example, Mackintosh 1977a and b, Walkland and Ryle 1977, Kellner and Crowther Hunt 1980). Although this material questioned the Westminster model's notion of where power was located, it did not question in principle the view of power being within the parliamentary arena, nor the implicit assumptions in the model's definition of power. It accepted the constitutional prescriptions and still analysed power in a behavioural fashion. As Leys (1989: 7) points out, this conception led to power being seen as residing solely within the system and, particularly, within the interface between cabinet and Prime Minister. In this sense, despite criticism of the Westminster model, it continued to be used as the organising principle – as the paradigm within which the central state was examined.

Weaknesses of the Westminster model

Nearly all research on central government has either derived, explicitly or implicitly, from an analysis of the Westminster model. Either it has developed the model (Jennings 1966) or it has attempted to reassess the model (Mackintosh 1977a). In either accepting or rejecting the claims of the pure Westminster model, most analysis of central government has operated within the agenda it created. As a consequence, analysis of central government is, generally, institutional, behavioural and constitutional.

The Westminster model is institutional in its concern for the workings and power of particular institutions. Where studies of central government have been theoretically underpinned, they have been predominantly behavioural. In other words, they have focused on the actions of individuals: powerful actors are those who are successful in achieving their goals even though they may have reached them through luck or the impact of external events (Dowding 1996). They see power as observable – and in some cases measurable and therefore not something that resides in the values and institutions of the system. It has also been largely constitutional accepting the constitutional conventions concerning where power lies and who are the important actors. The combination of institutionalism, behaviourism and constitutionalism has to led to the notion that central government is hermetically sealed, and it has produced oversimplified questions and answers concerning the distribution of power within the central state.

A core underpinning of the model is parliamentary sovereignty. The implications of this principle are twofold. First, as a result of party discipline and the growth of government, the majority of key decisions are made within the executive – parliamentary sovereignty in reality is executive sovereignty. Reinforced by a deferential political culture, secrecy, and élitism, the key sites of political decision-making are the higher echelons of the civil service, the cabinet and the Prime Minister. Second, the link between parliamentary sovereignty and national sovereignty means decisions are made within the confines of the nation-state. Within the 'Westminster model', the Crown-in-Parliament is 'absolutely and inalienably sovereign' and so 'British governments cannot share power with other tiers of government, sub-national or supra-national' (Marquand 1988: 9). Other actors such as pressure groups, local authorities and international organisations like the European Union are recognised as having an input (Middlemas 1979, Beer 1982), but the arena of their activity is Parliament and the academic interest is concerned with their impact on Parliament (Raison 1979, King 1975, Hailsham 1978).

The democratic legitimacy of parliamentary sovereignty was maintained by the notion of ministerial responsibility. Ministers are responsible for making decisions within their departments, but they are then accountable and answerable to Parliament for those decisions (Woodhouse 1994). Through Parliament there is a system of democratic control. However, as Judge (1993) points out, this conception of accountability results in a very hierarchical system, with power being situated at the apex of government departments in the form of the minister.

This notion of sovereignty as the monopolisation of power in increasingly limited places results arises from a narrow conceptualisation of power. For Mackintosh (1977a: 35):

> In analysing a system of government, the student of politics seeks to find out who wields power, how the machinery for the exercise of power operates, what are the constraints on those with power and why society is prepared to accept these arrangements.

More explicitly, Mackintosh maintained (1977a: 36) that: 'In terms of estimating which persons or institutions are most powerful within the government, the issue is who decides what the government tries to do, irrespective of whether satisfactory or sensible results are achieved.' This conception of power is widely used in studies of central government. Concern is largely with the individuals involved in policy decisions who succeed in influencing the outcome. What occurs beyond cabinet or the executive is to some extent irrelevant.

Within this conception of power there is almost no discussion of the theoretical assumptions that it contains in relation to the executive. It focuses solely on the behaviour, motivations and interests of individuals. Although the context of the individuals is institutional – that is, actors are studied within the context of cabinet, department or Prime Minister – little consideration is given to how these institutions affect their behaviour. The result is a conception of power that is observable and pluralist. As Norton argues, 'there has been some centralisation of power in central government', but 'the political system remains highly pluralist' (Norton 1991b: p. 153). The focus is on who is seen to succeed with the emphasis often being on their personality or their tactics, and without reference to the ideologies and structures that may have framed particular outcomes.

Within this behavioural and pluralistic framework, power is conceived as an object. It is something that belongs to a particular actor or institutions – power is in the cabinet or the Prime Minister or the civil service. It is attached to the office and as a result the power relationship is a zero-sum game, where there is a winner and a loser. Power belongs to one institution or another, and has shifted from Parliament to the executive to the Prime Minister. Those analysts involved in the prime-ministerial–cabinet debate are attempting to develop and reassess the Westminster model, but they do not question the theoretical assumptions of the approach. While providing important empirical material, their analysis remains within the framework of the constitution and they fail to explicate their definition of power. Consequently, the conception of power is both crude and static. Power is ascribed to an institution or person and fixed to that person regardless of the issue or the context. Power may move from the Prime Minister to the cabinet over time, but it is not seen as fluid within a particular situation. Moreover, there is almost no consideration of how actors relate to their structural situation nor how relationships vary across time.

Common to this approach is a high degree of emphasis on personality and individual volition. Many traditional approaches to central government see the distribution of power as relying heavily on the personality of the Prime Minister (Madgwick 1991). The power of the Prime Minister does not develop out of the complex relationship between the prime-ministerial office, the institutions of the core executive and the outside world. Often it is the style of the Prime Minister which determines the shift from prime-ministerial to cabinet government (Hennessy 1986, Kavanagh 1990, Madgwick 1991). This leads to a view that the volition of the Prime Minister changes the nature of government (King 1985, Wilson 1976, Foley 1992). Commentators and politicians continually saw Margaret Thatcher as a strong personality who was a dominant leader, while Major was portrayed as a ditherer who could not provide sufficient leadership. Little attempt is made to account for the completely different structural situations. Major was leading a divided, exhausted and unpopular government. However strong or weak his personality, it would have been difficult to lead. Of course, I am not suggesting that the personality or style of the Prime Minister does not matter. Undoubtedly the personality and style does affect both the policy process (see, for example, the issue of coordination in Chapter 6) and decisions, but it is only one factor among many. Personality is not the predominant explanation of the operation of the core executive.

Despite a number of analyses implicitly acknowledging the variability of the Prime Minister's power and his or her dependency (see Barber 1991, Jones 1975, King 1985), until recently there has been almost no theoretical development in the analysis of central government (see Rhodes 1993, 1995a, 1996a, 1997a, for a discussion). Consequently, the focus has been on a very limited number of institutions, in particular the cabinet and the Prime Minister (Smith *et al.* 1993). Accordingly, the analysis of British central government has been sterilised and simplified into a number of either–or questions. Norton (1991a: 5) asks:

> Has not cabinet government in Britain now been finally and irrevocably displaced by prime-ministerial government? Is not the much vaunted independence of the Judiciary under threat? Is not Parliament incapable, even more so now than before of influencing government?

These debates are repeated endlessly, never to be resolved.

Such a restricted scheme emphasises the limited notion of power that has dominated the analysis of central government, simplifying the relationships within the core executive, the nature of decision-making and the nature of modern government. It fails to place departments, ministers and the cabinet in context. The focus of research cannot be solely on institutions, but needs to examine relationships and the contexts of institutions. It is necessary to examine the range of actors that are involved in a decision, the relationships they have to each other and the resources that they can use. Power has to be seen as fluid and relational, not static. In that sense, power does not lie anywhere within the system because it is everywhere – all actors have resources, and outcomes need to be negotiated. In recent years, as a response to both the failings of the Westminster model to describe reality and a number of changes in the real world, a number of approaches have developed more analytical means of viewing central government. I will now review these alternative perspectives.

ALTERNATIVES TO THE WESTMINSTER MODEL

The notions underpinning the Westminster model, such as prime-ministerial and cabinet government, reflected a world in which the state was perceived as sovereign and sovereignty was located in the executive and legitimised by Parliament. As a response to new issues such as the reform of government, membership of the European Union (EU), and increasing internationalisation there was a growing perception that the Westminster model was failing to meet political and economic problems. The acceptance of the market as a solution to economic and political problems developed as a result of the apparent failure of Keynesian economics and state-delivered services. The new faith in the market occurred partly because of changes in the international economy that have made it increasingly difficult for states to control their economic fortunes. The apparent failures of the state combined with market ideology have assisted the development of a new public management that is based on a belief in injecting market criteria and management principles into the public sector. These ideas have produced a range of reforms that have resulted in a shift from a directive state to a more fragmented one. Such changes have influenced notions of *governance* as a flexible form of control rather than *government* as direct control. As a response to these changes, analysts have developed a number of new approaches to the problems of government and the policy process, including the core executive, policy networks, rational choice, globalisation and governance. I will now review these approaches and outline how they can contribute to a fuller analysis of the central state.

The core executive and policy networks

Rhodes and Dunleavy (1995) and Rhodes (1995a and b, 1997) have proposed a new framework of analysis – the 'core executive'. Unlike the 'Westminster model' paradigm, the core executive approach suggests that a range of institutions are important in the operation of central government, that the distribution of power may be horizontal rather than vertical, and that power is not concentrated in a limited number of institutions. Rather than offering a simple model of government, it implies that there are no firm boundaries to central government and that an important focus for research is the complexity of interactions between different elements of the core executive (see Lent 1997). Rhodes (1997a: 3) emphasises the shift from a hierarchical political system to the 'differentiated polity':

> So the strong executive, the tradition of 'leader knows best', encapsulated in the 'Westminster model', founders on the complex, multiform maze of institutions that makes up the differentiated polity. Interdependence confounds centralization. More control is exerted, but over less. Services continue to be delivered, but by a network of organizations which resist central direction.

The focus of analysis becomes the range of actors within the core executive and how they interact, not how a single actor or institution dominates the system.

Similar themes have been developed by Burch and Holliday (1996) in their analysis of the cabinet system. They outline the formal powers and resources of actors but also 'investigate the ethos, conventions and codes which proscribe how individuals holding cabinet system positions should act' (Burch and Holliday 1996: 6). They distinguish between the formal and informal aspects of the cabinet system, and are concerned with how the structures and processes of the system affect political behaviour. Consequently, they extend their focus beyond formal institutions and examine the rules and structures of the cabinet system. Unlike authors taking traditional approaches, Burch and Holliday recognise that positions within the core executive do not have power, but create the potential for power and, therefore, 'An individual's impact on policy outcomes depends in part on circumstances, which are conditioned by a range of external factors. When circumstances are right, opportunities to act expand' (1996: 7).

What Burch and Holliday (1996) and Marsh and Smith (1995) also emphasise is the role of networks in understanding Whitehall. Following Marsh and Rhodes (1992) networks are defined as a meso-level concept that stress the importance of organisational rather than personal relationships. These relationships are based on information and communication exchanges, which create 'resource dependencies'. The intensity of these relationships can vary from closed policy communities to open and unstable issue networks. They are structural relationships, because they: define the roles that actors play within networks; prescribe the issues that are discussed and how they are dealt with; have distinct sets of rules; and contain organisational imperatives – at the very least maintaining the network.

Networks within the core executive, as opposed to those between Whitehall and outside groups, have a number of specific features:

- The absolute boundary of who is included is relatively limited.
- Members of networks will often be institutionally defined. People with specific roles will have tasks that include them in particular networks. However, at the same time, some networks may be interpersonal and break down or change greatly with the removal of a particular individual.
- Many networks will be informal, and will exist in order to overcome the rigidities of formal hierarchies.
- If networks are more often informal, then the institutionalisation of power will occur through cultures and values rather than through institutional forms. Thus, as Heclo and Wildavsky (1981) suggest, it is important to understand the actors' perceptions of the organisational forms that face them. It is also important to understand the way actors recreate those organisational forms (Giddens 1986).

Hence, networks within the state will vary from formal and institutional to informal and cultural. Within broad limits, who is involved will be clearly defined. However, within the Whitehall universe membership of networks will depend on a number of factors. In some cases it will be institutional – an official from the Department of Transport is unlikely to be involved in the details of social security policy, whereas an official from the Treasury may. There is also likely to be formal inclusion and exclusion based on lines of authority and hierarchy. At other times membership may be negotiated. In the development of a new policy, inclusion could depend on discussion, upon knowing what is going on, or, perhaps, upon particular personal contacts. Networks will be both personal and institutional. Finally, membership may be cultural, historical or contextual. There may be specific values that have developed over time concerning who should be involved in particular decisions (Dunleavy and Rhodes 1990, Smith 1994). In contrast, the particular political, economic or social context within which a decision is made may affect those included and excluded.

Consequently, following Anderson's (1983) view of nations, it is important to realise that these networks or communities are not based just on personal connections; rather, they are 'imagined', because members of the community do not necessarily know their fellow members, 'yet in the mind of each lives the image of their communion' (Anderson 1983: 15). Within networks there is a shared world-view, a common culture. Using Anderson and Geertz (1973), Norgaard (1994) points to how individual behaviour is guided by culture and historical patterns of meaning. Thus we need to understand how the culture of a community patterns behaviour, how it is reproduced and how it changes.

Networks are important because:

1. Much policy-making and intra-organisational contact in central government is not through formal institutions but through contacts of informal networks. Therefore it is important to understand how these networks operate and affect policy outcomes.
2. They involve the institutionalisation of beliefs, values, cultures and particular forms of behaviour. They are organisations. Organisations shape attitudes (Perrow 1970) and behaviour. Networks result from repeated behaviour and, consequently, they relieve decision-makers from taking difficult decisions. They simplify the policy process by limiting actions, problems and solutions (see Berger and Luckman 1967). They define roles and responses. In doing so they are not neutral, but reflect past and present distributions of resources and conflicts. Thus, when a decision is made within a particular network, it is not made on the basis of a rational assessment of all the available decision, but will reflect past practices, past conflicts and the culture and values of the decision-makers. In other words, networks are important because they affect policy outcomes. They are the structuration of organisational power and of past conflicts. By examining networks we are looking at how power relations are institutionalised.

Departments are dependent on each other for different expertise, authorities and capabilities in service delivery when they are developing policy that cuts across departmental boundaries. As Figure 2.1 demonstrates, there are numerous connections and overlaps between different networks. Some networks are relatively permanent, for example, the connections between Prime Minister, cabinet and department,

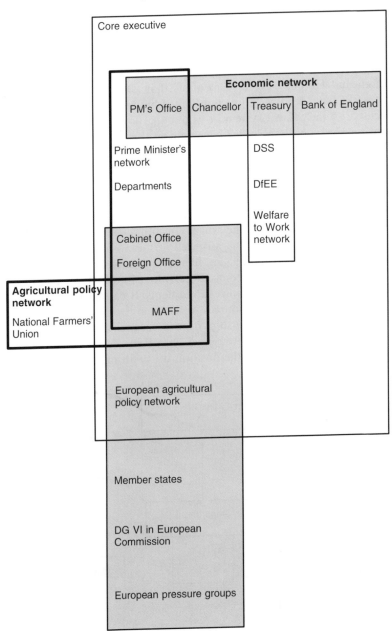

Figure 2.1   Examples of overlapping networks in the core executive

while other exist for the lifetime of a particular policy, such as Welfare to Work.

Some departments will have automatic access to particular networks, while others may join according to the views of the Prime Minister. Burch and Holliday (1996: 106) argue that 'During our period, our networks have become more coordinated, more regularised and more focused on the cabinet system.' I would question this view, suggesting that there is considerable flexibility in core executive networks, which have a tendency to change rapidly and often to operate outside of the immediate sight of the centre. For example, departments often develop networks with organisations outside the core executive (see Marsh and Rhodes 1992a, Smith 1993), which provides an alternative set of resources for fighting battles within Whitehall.

Figure 2.2 demonstrates the range of institutionalised connections of each department. Within the auspices of these relatively permanent networks are a whole range of temporary networks, some formal through cabinet or official committees, others informal through meetings between officials in various departments. Because various parts of the core executive have resources, officials and ministers have to be involved in continual relationships of resource exchange. Some of these resources are structurally determined – the Prime Minister has certain resources that derive from the position of the Prime Minister – while

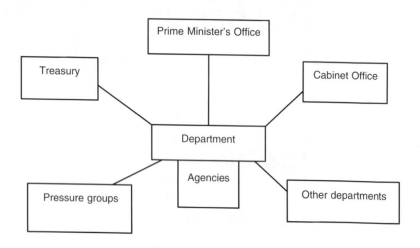

Figure 2.2   Departmental networks

others vary according to particular circumstances. For example, authority is an important resource. Authority varies with the success of a minister, the degree of support he or she has in the party and, sometimes, personality. Hence, networks are both structural and causal, and we need to understand how actors interpret these structures.

Public choice

The notion of governmental overload in the 1970s, the idea that government was expected to do too much and was draining resources from the private sector, increased the legitimacy of New Right ideology, particularly as adopted by the British Conservative Party. Combining elements of liberalism and traditional Conservatism, it on one hand suggests the Westminster model was failing while on the other it calls for the reassertion of parliamentary sovereignty. The New Right offered a particular critique of the state based on notions of overload; budget maximisation; the dominance of professions; threats to individual freedom and the continual growth of public expenditure undermining private investment (Pollitt 1984). The New Right solution to these threats is to cut back the role of the state and, where possible, introduce competition to prevent budget maximisation. However, Thatcher was strongly committed to parliamentary sovereignty and central to her project was the reassertion of executive authority in the face of intermediate institutions, the civil service and the European Union. Consequently, in many areas, rather than the state being 'rolled back', power was centralised and increased (Gamble 1988).

The New Right perspective on the state challenges many of the assumptions of the Westminster model. It views government and the civil service not as neutral and electorally responsive but as more concerned with the maximisation of personal utility and with attending to the claims of special interests. The result is an overextended state, which takes too great a share of national wealth and is inefficient at producing public goods. Consequently, parliamentary accountability is not seen as an effective mechanism for controlling the behaviour of either politicians or bureaucrats. Indeed, much of the New Right project has been concerned with introducing new forms of accountability – such as markets and managerialism – into government (see Stone 1995).

New Right ideology has also influenced a theoretical challenge to the study of central government in the form of public choice theory. Public choice is the application of economic theory and methods to politics, and it has strongly influenced New Right thought. Niskanen uses this approach to suggest that bureaucrats will maximise their budgets in order to best serve their own personal welfare. In addition, the state is a monopoly supplier and therefore public services are over-supplied at higher than market cost, producing Pareto-inefficiency (Niskanen 1971 and see Dowding 1995).

One of the most interesting developments in public choice theory is Dunleavy's bureau-shaping model. Bureau-shaping theory attempts to provide a more specific and meso-level explanation of why the reform of government should have occurred so rapidly in Britain. Taking a public-choice perspective, it questions the view suggested by writers such as Niskanen that as self-interested utility maximisers bureaucrats are necessarily budget maximisers. Dunleavy (1991) argues that the interests of bureaucrats are rarely served by budget maximisation (as they do not directly receive the benefits). Rather, 'collective strategies of reshaping their bureaux into different agency types can best advance senior officials' interests' (Dunleavy 1991: 174).

Indeed, their interests can be served by reducing the size of their bureaux. Bureaucrats 'try to reshape their departments as small staff agencies, removed from the lines of responsibilities and hence more insulated from adverse impacts in the event of overall spending reductions in their policy area' (Dunleavy 1989a: 252). Dunleavy suggests this is possible because there are different types of budgets, and senior officials will on most occasions be concerned with max-imising the core budget, which is the part of the budget spent directly on the agencies operation. Therefore, privatisation and the hiving off of agencies constitute rational behaviour by bureaucrats. By placing routine managerial and implementation functions in the hands of agencies, high-level officials can concentrate on more fulfilling policy work (James 1995: 451). This approach challenges the idea that states are neutral tools for politicians or that they are uniform, Weberian line bureaucracies (Dowding 1995).

The bureau-shaping model does have some intuitive appeal, but there are a number of problems with the approach. First, it ignores the political and historical processes that have led to reform and to particular types of reform, and instead focuses on the interests and behaviour of officials (and assumes that top officials have common interests). It also has a tendency to over-emphasise the power of officials, suggesting that it is they rather than politicians who shape the structure of government (Smith *et al.* 1998b).

Second, how does this model justify the assumption that the interest of senior officials is in policy work rather than management? It seems that the reforms of recent years have resulted not in more policy work but in greater managerialism (Pollitt 1990). Increasingly, the role of permanent secretaries is one of managing rather than policy-making. Sir Terry Heiser (1994: 23) has pointed out that among senior civil servants: 'the importance of "management" as opposed to "policy" is much more easily recognised, and the professionalism of civil service management, especially in the rising generation, is greater than ever in my time'. Recent reforms do not seem to have coincided with increased status for civil servants. According to Barberis (1994:35), 'there has been much talk about the loss of influence exercised by top civil servants; about their subordination within the policy process; and about their role becoming more managerial'.

Third, the model seems to accept the idea that the creation of Next Steps agencies leads to a clear separation of 'policy' and 'operation'. It is apparent, however, that many agencies have a distinct policy role (Massey 1995). More than routine and managerial functions are being divested into agencies.

Fourth, James (1995: 453) argues that this model can explain the latest reform, market testing, as a reassertion of Treasury control. It seems that the impetus behind market testing was political. It was partly a result of the government wishing to do something to continue the process of reform as one of its few policy successes, and it was a way of continuing the privatisation programme. Finally, the model cannot explain the why the Fundamental Expenditure Review (FER) reduced core budget and directly challenged the interests of senior officials by removing their jobs.

In sum, the bureau-shaping model has a tendency to ignore politics. There is little examination of what goes on in particular departments and how that might have affected the process of reform. Radcliffe (1991: 41) believes that Dunleavy's study is 'strongly non-political in that ministers themselves and the political environment in which departments operate are largely absent'. Despite the problems with rational choice theory, it does force us to think about how individuals act within structured situations and how changes in those situations affect the choices people make. Unlike most approaches to central government, it has a theory of action that is not based on personality.

Globalisation

The post-war period has seen an exponential growth in the level of foreign trade, foreign exchange dealing and transnational companies. Internationalisation means the increasing interconnectedness, politically and economically, between states, and generally refers to increased bilateral relations. The 1970s and 1980s in particular saw the growth of foreign exchange markets, euromarkets in credits and bonds and the growth of multinational banks (Hirst and Thompson 1992). 'Perhaps the main development of the 1980s was the growth of international markets in bonds and equities, and the growth of cross-border dealing in derivative instruments such as options, futures and swaps' (Hirst and Thompson 1992: 39). In addition, the growth of information technology and communications have greatly reduced the relationship between space and time. As Camilleri and Falk (1992: 5) argue:

> Within these global communication webs, territorial boundaries, which once represented natural barriers to communication, now become increasingly artificial. Organizations, communication, cultural and economic interchange and political strategizing extend over new communication territories which pay little or no attention to what may seem to be the increasingly ephemeral boundaries of nation and state.

Throughout social science there is an increasing interest in the impact of globalisation as a response to increasing dependence and integration in the international arena. The importance of globalisation is that it recognises, unlike either domestic state or international relations theory, the permeability of the relationships between the domestic and international spheres. According to Waters (1993: 3), globalisation is: 'A social process in which the constraints of geography on social and cultural arrangements recede and in which people become increasingly aware that they are receding.' Globalisation is in a sense a stage beyond internationalisation, with global forces replacing nations. For politics, the impact of these changes seems to be a shift of power to transnational actors, whether intergovernmental organisations like the European Union or transnational corporations, and the subsequent loss of national sovereignty. Part of the process of globalisation is that new public management has become the global form of public administration (see Hood 1995 and Dunleavy 1994).

Interestingly, globalisation is identified as the source of government reform by the former Permanent Secretary at the Treasury, Sir Terry Burns. He argues that globalisation has caused an information revolution, increased difficulties in countries isolating themselves, and made markets less susceptible to government influence. These changes have led to the reform of the governmental process, with a shift away from 'highly discretionary control from the centre in favour of a more decentralised approach'. Consequently, the Treasury should clearly define its core activities, and other functions have to be either privatised or transferred elsewhere in government; the Treasury's organisation should become flatter; its objectives should become clearer; and the organisation of the management structure should be related more closely to objectives (Burns 1995). The modernist, Keynesian project of Treasury control of both expenditure and the economy is over, at least to the degree envisaged by either Keynesian or socialist planners. The economy cannot be controlled and public expenditure is best contained through decentralisation with more discretion allowed further down the governmental hierarchy.

However, the globalisation-of-government thesis underestimates the importance of the nation-state. On one hand, advocates of globalisation tend to be ahistorical. They assume that in the past there were sovereign nation-states and that sovereignty is now gradually being eroded. Yet, is it true that the British government had more sovereignty during the sterling crises of 1947, 1967 and 1976, or the crisis of 1992? Nation-states remain the site, to a large degree, of both political demands and political goods. For Hall (1994: 210), 'State power continues to structure the political economy of the advanced world' and even transnational companies are based in, and dependent on, nations and national law (Hutton 1995). Actors within nation-states are concerned with retaining control over the policy process and are still faced with national political demands. Although they undoubtedly face international constraints, it needs to be established whether they are less or greater than in the past. Even the EU is highly dependent on the support and resources of nation-states (Hirst and Thompson 1992). Cerny (1990: 234) makes an important point when he argues: 'The role of state actors will change, but their critical location in the increasingly interpenetrated transnational structured field of action will actually increase the impact of state structures in complex ways.' Relations between states and transnational organisation and between states and states will change, but nation-states will continue to control important resources, allowing influence, to varying degrees, on policy outcomes.

Consequently, national policies have to be understood in their national as well as international contexts. Policy may be influenced by international trends, but the nature of that policy is more likely to be determined by national factors than by globalisation. Explanations of reform that focus solely on exogenous factors may be useful in pointing to some of the pressures for reform, but they are limited as explanatory tools. Nevertheless, it is important to pay attention to the external context in which the core executive operates. Hitherto, much analysis has seen the centre as hermetically sealed because of the focus on parliamentary sovereignty. External forces impacting on national governments are not new. What is relatively new is the attention that is paid to these forces and the attempts that are made to conceptualise their impact.

Governance

Governance has been suggested as a way of conceptualising the new forms of government that have resulted from a combination of reform, globalisation and loss of sovereignty. Governance is governing without government (Rhodes 1996a). For Rosenau (1992: 13), 'It is to search for order in disorder, for coherence in contradiction, and for continuity in change.' The complexity of new forms of government and the fragmentation of services delivery raise the question of how it is possible to achieve political goals. No longer is government confined to the nation state, but it can involve a range of institutions, public and private, from the supra-national to the national to the local to the neighbourhood. Consequently, governance is not about command, but rather about control or steering 'without presuming the presence of hierarchy' (Rosenau 1992: 14). Rosenau is concerned with governance at the global level, where, he suggests, there is no single emergent order around which communities converge.

The notion of governance has also been applied at the national level. Jessop maintains that certain notions of governance are an attempt to break away from the 'conceptual trinity of market-state-civil society', and to see governance as alternative forms of organisation based on 'relational contracting, "organized markets" in groups, enterprises, clans, networks, trade associations and strategic alliances' (Jessop 1995: 310). In this sense it is similar to the idea of self-government that arises at the international level. Through networks, various interests involved in a particular policy areas regulate themselves by developing their own rules and sanctions. As a process of self-regulation and mutual adjustment, it allows governing without government as a single, overriding authority. There is increasing interest in political cooperation that crosses the public–private divide and is concerned with networks rather than hierarchies (Jessop 1995: 310–311). It is a mode of social coordination, 'the ways in which disparate but inter-dependent social agencies are coordinated to achieve specific social (economic, political, etc.) objectives' (Jessop 1995: 317) Governing is increasingly a concern with balancing and coordinating a range of public and private interests and organisations (Kooiman 1993).

It may be possible to conceive of policies in Britain being determined at the EU level and implemented by agencies or private sector bodies. However, does multi-level interaction mean that the state has forsaken control? Such a change would indicate, that in Britain, 'the new state' has not forsaken governing, but its role is to coordinate the myriad of public, private, departmental and non-departmental agencies involved in the delivery of services. However, this perspective is undermined by two contradictory arguments. On one hand, British *central* government has been weakened by reforms that make it increasingly unlikely that there is a coordinating centre strong enough to pull together the range of bodies that may be involved in the delivery of services. In the language of Osborne and Gaebler (1992), the role of the government is to steer not to row, but it is not clear that there is a single pair of hands on the rudder. The reforms have created a 'policy vacuum', with steering being based on 'crisis management and blame avoidance', which results in a lack of coordination and a confusion of roles (Rhodes 1997a: 24).

Alternatively, while government may not be very effective at co-ordination, it does not necessarily mean it has abandoned the desire to control. One of the problems of the 1979–97 Conservative governments was contradictory goals. The Thatcher and Major governments wanted to improve efficiency and reduce costs, and they believed it could be achieved through delegation, privatisation and market testing. How-ever, the wish for economy overrode the desire for efficiency, produ-cing some unwanted goals. The reforms made central control more difficult. At the same time, the Conservatives attempted to reassert a traditional conception of parliamentary sovereignty and in a range of policy areas they reimposed central control, for example, in education, health and prisons (Jenkins 1996). It is nevertheless still the case that the government has policy goals that are determined at the state level that it wants implemented. Governance is not a balancing act: it involves leadership and developing new forms of implementation.

Reform may have made control more difficult, but in a sense this loss of control is an unintended consequence of the introduction of new public management, and it seems unlikely that the Conservative governments of 1979–97 were less concerned with control than any previous government. Decisions may be made in Europe – but they are made by states, and are delivered by private or semi-public agencies which continue to be licensed and funded by the state. It is unlikely, at least within the British context, that new forms of governance are self-reproducing. If the notion of governance is to be used at the domestic level in Britain then it cannot be governing without government. Rather central government, or more particularly, departments have to be seen as one of many competing centres of authority, and this fragmentation increases the difficulties of government control (Rhodes 1996b). What is crucial to remember about the core executive is that it is differentiated (Rhodes 1997a) and that it has very little executive control. In order to deliver policy, actors within the central state have to build alliances with a whole range of bodies including agencies, regulatory bodies, voluntary groups, the private sector, local authorities and more.

Despite the problems of public choice, governance and globalisation, these approaches indicate the need to take account of structure, context and action and so help to develop notions of the core executive. Globalisation illustrates the constraints of the international system, governance emphasises how the context of state action has changed the mode of governing, and public choice, while offering a theory that is flawed, at least highlights the need to develop a theory of action beyond simple notions of personality. All these perspectives demonstrate both how we can study the core executive in a way that breaks out of the constitutional and institutional constraints and how to analyse it in a theoretically informed way. The core executive has to be conceptualised as a set of actors and institutions that are connected because of resource dependency. The connections occur through a range of formal and informal networks, and they are governed by 'rules of the game' and shared values. To some extent, these values derive from the constitution and they govern the relationships between actors and institutions. Nevertheless, there is considerable room for interpretation in these rules.

The basis of this book is that all actors within the core executive have resources, and in order to achieve their goals they have to exchange them. The process of exchange occurs through networks and alliances, which develop because of mutual dependence. Because no actor has a monopoly of resources, power cannot be located within a single site of the core executive. Who succeeds will depend on the circumstances and the alliances that develop at a particular time. Clearly, some actors have more freedom in using their resources than others, but their degree of freedom will often depend on the support they have within the core and the external context. Consequently, there cannot be prime-ministerial government, because the Prime Minister will always depend on other actors. What the Prime Minister can do is increase his or her resources and in certain conditions have a greater ability to exercise those resources. In Burch and Holliday's terms, he or she can increase his or her 'potential power', but the actual power will depend on circumstances. To understand the core executive, we have to recognise its complexity and the way structure, resources, agency and context affect power.

COMPLEXITY IN THE CORE EXECUTIVE – RECONCEPTUALISING POWER RELATIONS IN THE CENTRAL STATE

The theoretical and empirical challenges to the 'Westminster model' have made even non-academic analyses aware of the complexity in the modern British core executive:

> British government is like a dance, a quadrille in which the partici-pating groups exercise figures in the middle of the floor but never entirely give up their independent identities. British government is a competition in which, one side never finally gaining complete mastery, the contending forces advance and retreat (Dynes and Walker 1995: 15).

The question is, how do we theorise this complexity? To understand the modern British state it is important to take into account structure, agency, resources, context and the nature of power. Complexity means we must avoid simple causal explanations of power relations (Lent 1997) and look at the intricate relationships between exogenous and endogenous factors.

Structure

Structure is the limit of action, but the nature of that limit will depend on the level of analysis and the nature of the actors. One person's agency is another person's structure (Hay 1995, Ward 1987). A decision by a powerful actor will constrain the actions of the powerless. Within the central state there are various levels of structure faced by different actors and departments. Civil servants are constrained by rules governing their behaviour, authority and sphere of influence. Ministers, likewise, are constrained by their status and functional responsibility, and indeed the state as a whole may be constrained by financial markets, international agreements and the nature of its armed forces. All these structures are the result of human agency and therefore subject to change. What structure does, at least from a critical realist perspective, is to 'condition agency' and 'define the range of potential strategies that might be deployed by agents (whether individual or collective) in attempting to realise intentions' (Hay 1995: 199). By analysing the core executive through the prism of structure and agency, it is possible to examine the state in a way that is not static. Both structures and agents are in flux, and so we can introduce an important temporal element to the understanding of central government.

In the discussion of the core executive structure enters in three ways. First, and most obviously, are the limits placed on the state's actions by Britain's position in the world economy and polity. Britain is constrained by transnationalism, the size of the currency markets, the strength of the world economy and membership of intergovernmental bodies such as the EU. The impact of these constraints was demonstrated by the forced exit of Britain from the European Exchange Rate Mechanism (ERM) (see Thompson 1996b).

Second, structure exists in the formal institutions and less formal networks of central government. Departments or agencies, and their networks, are sets of rules, norms and values that reflect past decisions and past conflicts. They limit what departments do, how problems are perceived and what actions they take. For a department to undertake a particular policy initiative, and whether it is successful, may depend on perceptions of the department's role and whether it has the administrative machinery to implement the policy.

Third, structure influences the distribution of resources within the state. Who has the authority to undertake particular actions is often structurally determined. The Chancellor of the Exchequer derives

BARNSLEY COLLEGE

EASTGATE

considerable authority from the post, has the resources to make key decisions concerning the economy almost autonomously and has a great deal of control over economic policy. The field of command of the Minister for Culture, for example, is obviously much less.

Consequently, all actors in the core executive are faced with a particular structural situation, which depends partly on their position within the executive but also on the core executive's relationship to the outside world. Consequently, central government cannot be understood primarily in terms of the personality of office-holders. Personal perceptions of structures will affect how actors choose to deal with the constraints they face, but they do not have a free choice in how they act.

Resources

Central to the understanding of central government is the idea that all actors have resources, and therefore all actors have something with which they can bargain in core executive interaction. The strength of their bargaining position will depend on the resources they hold and how much other actors need their resources. But resources do not equal power, and power is rarely, if ever, based directly on command. Power depends on how resources are exchanged, and hence it is about dependence not control (see Jessop 1990; see also below).

Resources are determined in part structurally, because they are related to the roles of actors, but they may also be derived personally. Some ministers have more authority or political support than others. For instance, Ernest Bevin had much more autonomy in foreign policy than Michael Stewart (Butler 1998). To an extent it is possible to specify some of the resources held by actors within the core executive. Civil servants have time, information, operating procedures, and control over implementation. Ministers have their departments, political authority in a specific area, support from elements of the party and control of a particular policy. (See Table 2.1.)

Although some actors have more resources than others – the Prime Minister has more than a single minister – those with the most resources do not necessarily have the most power. Resources do not equal power: capabilities in deploying resources and the strategic settings are critical to understanding who influences outcomes. As Dowding (1991) points out, examining resources is not enough, 'for those resources will only allow actors to bring about outcomes in particular circumstances'. Therefore to understand power we need some understanding of agency and context.

Table 2.1   Resources of prime ministers, ministers and officials

Prime Minister	Ministers	Officials
Patronage	Political support	Permanence
Authority	Authority	Knowledge
Political Support/party	Department	Time
Political support/electorate	Knowledge	Whitehall network
Prime Minister's Office	Policy networks	Control over information
Bilateral policy-making	Policy success	Keepers of the constitution

Agency

While there are constraints, there are also intentions. Actors have resources, which may or may not be structurally determined, but the exercise of power depends on intention: how resources are used and goals achieved. Hay (1997) has emphasised the need to avoid both intentionalism (the idea that individual will is the key determinant of outcomes) and structuralism (the idea we are determined in our actions by wider social forces). Rational choice theory is one attempt to resolve this issue by examining how actors make choices with an institutionally determined set of preferences. The theory presumes individuals act within structured situations; to quote Dowding (1996: 19),

The game (in game theory) is thus a description of the structure in which each individual finds him or herself. The expected result occurs because rational individuals, knowing their own preference ordering and the structure of the game, will play to achieve the best payoff given these circumstances. In this sense, game theoretic explanation is structural. It is also individualistic: the payoffs occur because of the actions of individuals and not because of some other cause.

Rational choice theory can analyse actors within structured situations. In certain circumstances, actors can see their situation and make a choice about which actions suit their interest. However, it is not always the case that actors know their preferences, or that what they choose to do is what is best. Sometimes choices and actions cannot be separated in that interests are constituted in action. Indeed, Dowding (1996) acknowledges that preferences change because of action, and that we do not necessarily try to achieve our best preference. The problem with rational choice notions of agency is they attempt to model behaviour, and so are forced to focus too much on the role of individuals, once they have established the existing preferences, while paying little attention to where those preferences come from or how context can shape action. Consequently, the theory's assumptions about action are a necessarily crude focus on the utility-maximising motivations of actors (Hay 1997). This leads, according to Hay and Wincott (1997), to an 'unhelpful dualism of structure and agency'.

We need to conceive of individuals as strategically calculating actors, whose strategies are 'informed by [strategic] calculation, the strategic context within which actions takes place and . . . the shaping of perceptions of the context in which strategy is conceived of in the first place' (Hay 1997). Actors have strategies that affect outcomes, but those strategies are formed within a particular situation and a belief system. Consequently, actions are not derived from a set of purely free choices by actors. Actors are constrained by their values, their perceptions of their roles, what they see as the limits of their actions and it is within this context that they develop strategies for achieving goals. We need to understand their perceptions of the world and its rules (see Garfunkel 1967) in order to understand why they make particular choices.

Ministers and officials have a range of strategies (see Table 2.2). Strategies may be seen as the overall style for achieving goals, whereas tactics are the means to achieve strategic goals within particular situations. Strategies and tactics are infinite. The Prime Minister may choose to be a collectivist or dominant in cabinet, but when faced with a particular situation he or she may decide that the best tactic is to build an alliance with a particular minister. The choice of tactics and strategy will depend on the particular situation. As we will see in Chapter 4, Thatcher probably chose the wrong strategy and tactics when she was challenged for the leadership in 1990. It is also true that the tactics or strategies of ministers will depend on their structural situation. For example, a threat to resign may be a good tactic for the Chancellor, but probably not for the Minister of Sport. Even so, resignation threats to resign will have little impact if the Chancellor is unpopular, or has threatened to resign before. Tactics and structural position cannot be removed from ever changing contexts, and therefore models that simplify the relationships between actors give us little but relatively trivial information about tactics.

Agency is crucial in any understanding of power, because it explains how an actor with limited resources can defeat an actor with greater resources. Ministers can choose a range of tactics from threats of resignation, to building coalitions, to leaks of information to defeating the Prime Minister or the Chancellor. A leak from the Heritage Ministry in 1996 suggesting that the Treasury was attempting to use lottery money to replace established spending forced the Chief Secretary to the Treasury to deny that he had that intention in the public expenditure round. However, the sorts of tactics used will depend to a large extent on context. Public choice offers a theory of action seeing actors as self-interested utility maximisers. However, its problems arise in being unable to deal with the socialisation process and exogenously changed preferences, and its failure to give any substantial account of the relationship between agency and structure (see Harris and Kelly 1995, Hay 1995, Hay and Wincott 1997). A more complete theory of agency accepts that actors are located within structural situations, which affect the choices they make. As structures are the result of human actions, actors are subject and object; they are part of the structure and to some extent above it, and therefore able to make changes in certain circumstances (Giddens 1986). Their interests cannot be separated from the structure or context.

Table 2.2   Examples of strategies and tactics of prime minister, ministers and officials

	Prime Minister	Ministers	Officials
Strategies	Dominant Collective Interventionist Coordinator Cabinet adjudicator	Autonomy Interdependence Coalition building	Control information Isolate minister Dominate particular decision-making areas
Tactics	Threats to resign Threats to sack Promises of jobs Bi-partisan or multi-partisan alliances in Cabinet Appealing over cabinet Divide and rule	Alliances with other ministers or Prime Minister Threats of resignation Using overall political support Using international fora to say little choice	Informing other departments Withholding information Saying other departments will object Networks with other departments

Context

Context is in a sense a catch-all term, which contains elements of structure but is often contingent. It contains at least three elements: the political, the historical and the institutional. Contextual analysis means that the decision-making process has to be disaggregated. Power relations between the actors within a particular policy-making area depend on the particular historical development of the institutions within that arena and the way past decisions are institutionalised. However, overlying the more structural, historical and institutional context are the political circumstances of the time: the political support and popularity of the ministers involved and the economic conditions of the time. The degree of policy success or failure within government will affect the level of dependency between ministers, between ministers and civil servants and between ministers and the Prime Minister.

Power

The notion of power deriving from this model is one based on resource dependency (Rhodes 1981). All actors within the core executive have resources, but no actors have a monopoly of resources, and therefore they cannot develop policy on their own. Ministers need civil servants for information, advice and assistance with implementation. It also helps if they have the support of other ministers. They are placed in a particularly strong position if they have the support of the Prime Minister. Even the Prime Minister relies heavily on the support of ministers, both in a political sense and in the sense that it is ministers who will develop the majority of policy. Therefore, to exercise power there has to be an exchange of resources. Because prime ministers need ministerial support, they often do not get their own way. Thatcher was forced from office because she lost the support of her cabinet (Smith 1994, Jones 1995).

Dependency has important implications for conceptualising power. First, it means that power is relational and not an object. Power depends on relationships between actors and not on command. Frequently, outcomes can be a positive-sum game rather than a zero-sum one. In order to achieve goals, actors have to negotiate, compromise and bargain. Consequently, power does not just exist in conflicts between cabinet and Prime Minister but, as Foucault suggests, it is in every situation and relationship as actors develop belief systems, strategies and alliances in order to exchange resources and achieve goals. There is no need to adopt a discourse or post-modern approach to see the core executive as a field of micro-politics, where power is exercised through a multitude of agencies and coherence imposed through the 'adoption of shared vocabularies' (Murdoch 1995: 189; see also Foucault 1980).

Power, then, is fluid and the core executive is complex. This complexity suggests that outcomes are unpredictable and causes difficult to determine (Owen 1995). Cause and effect cannot be discussed in a simple linear fashion (Lent 1997). When considering the decision-making process in the core executive, many causes and interactions will affect outcomes. Power within the core executive cannot be characterised as prime-ministerial or cabinet power, because capabilities to affect decisions are spread widely throughout the political system. The power of various actors and institutions will vary according to the policy, the context and the tactics of those involved.

This model of power is a way of taking account of structure, agency and complexity. Structure both constrains the action of various actors and provides them with certain resources. Some actors have more resources than others, and if they are able to use those resources then they will have a greater impact on events. The use of resources depends on context and strategy. If an actor with fewer resources has a good strategy for achieving her or his goal then she or he may be able to have power over an actor with more resources. Thus, we have room for agency within a structural conception of the distribution of resources. Actors can choose strategies. The likelihood is that actors with the most resources will win most of the time. Nevertheless, few actors have all the resources they need to act and to achieve their goals, and so most power relationships within the core executive are based on an exchange of resources. It is important to remember that some actors can change the resources of other actors, and that one person's actions may be another person's structural constraint.

CONCLUSION

The Westminster model, and the analysis that developed as a reaction to it, was a partial reflection of the British political system. However, it always oversimplified the analysis of central government because of its crude assumptions about the nature of power; its tendency to see power in false dualities; its view of the executive as having a monopoly of power and its exclusion of external forces. These simplicities have been challenged by new ideologies, policies and circumstances, which have led to significant theoretical developments. These developments have created a need to reconceptualise central government and to take account of two factors in particular. One is that the core executive is complex: simple notions of power that are hierarchical and zero-sum are not adequate for an understanding of how policy-making occurs. Second, analysis of the core executive needs to take account of structure, context and agents. All actors within the core executive have resources, but how they use them will depend on their tactics (agency); tactics, however, depend on the particular political and economic context and the limits of action as defined in the structures and processes of institutions. In this book I will use this framework to examine the operation of the core executive, starting in the next chapter with how this has developed historically.

3 The Core Executive in Historical Perspective

This chapter examines the evolution of the British state, from the mid-nineteenth-century night-watchman state to the modern, interventionist, bureaucratic state. The twentieth century has seen the central state take over an increasing number of policy areas. This chapter will examine the relationship between the increasing functions and role of the state and the development of the core executive. It will highlight that, as the state grew, there was a greater need for central coordination. The chapter will investigate the reasons behind state expansion and evaluate the impact its development has had on the state's capabilities and internal power relations. In other words, it will examine how the growth of the state has affected the nature of the core executive. It will outline how the state has grown between the nineteenth century and 1979, and will demonstrate how this growth has impacted on the development of the core executive.

The period between the 1850s and the 1940s saw the establishment of the modern state in Britain. This growth was a process of what Weber saw as bureaucratic rationalisation, resulting from 'the availability of well-developed and firmly entrenched skills and habits of meticulous and precise division of labour, of maintaining a smooth flow of command and information, or of impersonal, well-sychronized coordination of autonomous yet complimentary actions' (Bauman 1989: 15). In the era of modernity, rational procedures and bureaucracy became the dominant form of state organisation. They provided the state with the capacity to intervene in every aspect of society, and to order it according to a uniform set of principles within a given territory. The state developed the capabilities to make and implement policies that could be imposed on citizens.

While Palmerston read and answered all his letters and dispatches (Mueller 1984), and Peel even spent his Christmas Day making official appointments, the contemporary minister has civil servants to answer letters, to draft replies to parliamentary questions and even to make thousands of routine decisions. But they do so according to set rules and procedures that allow ministers to know that, most of the time, decisions are made and letters answered within the confines of standard operating procedures (SOPs). Rationality and bureaucracy have provided the organisational capability for the state to intervene in countless new areas, and so the expansion of the state is to a large extent about the development of 'infrastructural power' (Mann 1984) – the ability to intervene in society without the use of coercion.

THE GROWTH OF THE STATE 1850–1979

During the nineteenth century, British government and society was dominated by the notion of *laissez-faire,* or libertarianism. The role of the government was limited to: maintaining order; maintaining the market economy and property rights; ensuring and protecting the freedom of individuals; and protecting citizens from external threat (Greenleaf 1983a; McEachern 1990). However, even at the high point of liberalism in the mid-nineteenth century, the state was never solely a night-watchman. The poor laws had existed since Elizabethan times, and as early as the 1840s factory, education and health legislation gave the state a social role (Mueller 1984). Nevertheless, relative to Continental European states and the twentieth century British state, the degree of state intervention in the mid-nineteenth century was limited (McEachern 1990: 50–51) and much of the social legislation was implemented half-heartedly (MacDonagh 1958). Before 1890 it was almost universally accepted that 'the level of government expenditure was kept at the minimum consistent with the provision of adequate protection against the Crown's enemies and of the maintenance of order' (Peacock and Wiseman 1967: 35). Indeed, between 1841 and 1890, public expenditure declined in relation to the size of the economy, from 11 per cent of GNP in 1841 to 9 per cent in 1890 (Peacock and Wiseman 1967).

As Figure 3.1 indicates, although government expenditure did increase in real terms in the nineteenth century, it was relatively stable as a percentage of GNP. Public expenditure increased in real terms, but in terms of the size of the economy it was relatively static, at least from 1841. As expenditure grew in absolute terms so did the size of the civil service (see Figure 3.2). Hogwood (1992: 130) emphasises how: 'In 1851 public employment was only 2.4 per cent of employment and by 1890 it was still less than 4 per cent. There was a sharp rise to 6 per cent by 1901.'

Even by the end of the nineteenth century, the state was relatively limited in what it did, how much it spent and how many people it

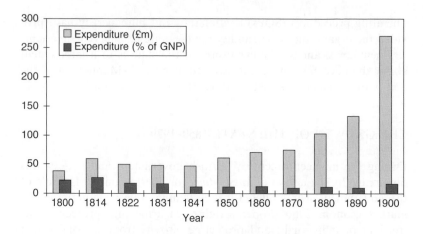

Source: Data from Peacock and Wiseman (1967: 37).

Figure 3.1   Government expenditure, 1800–1900

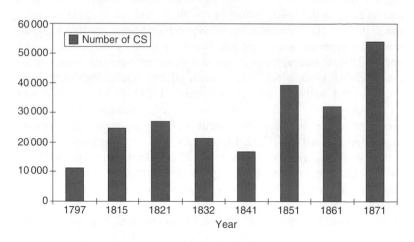

Source: Data from Mueller (1984: 174).

Figure 3.2   Size of the civil service

employed. It was only in the twentieth century that it started to expand. For reasons that we will discuss in the next section, the state in the twentieth century undertook an increasing number of functions. As early as 1906 the state increased its role in the provision of welfare through health and unemployment insurance and old-age pensions.

During the inter-war years the government became increasingly involved in the economy and the 'onward march of social policy' (Peden 1991: 105). During and after the Second World War, the role of the state both in the economy and in social policy substantially increased. The Labour government of 1945 continued the work started by the wartime coalition and established the welfare state, which provided free education, health care and a comprehensive welfare benefits system. On the economic front, the government committed itself to providing full employment, at least initially, to planning the economy and, through nationalisation, to taking control of large numbers of key industries. In addition, the government committed itself to Keynesian demand management, so accepting responsibility for the aggregate level of demand within the economy (see Pollard 1992). Individuals were no longer responsible for their own welfare, nor was the economy left to the market. These economic and social responsibilities were more or less maintained by all governments until 1979.

The greater economic role obviously increased the size of the state and public expenditure. In absolute terms the increase in state expenditure during the twentieth century has been massive (see Figure 3.3), but even as a percentage of GNP it has increased from 11 per cent in 1910 to 52 per cent in 1979 (see Figure 3.4). As Figure 3.5 highlights,

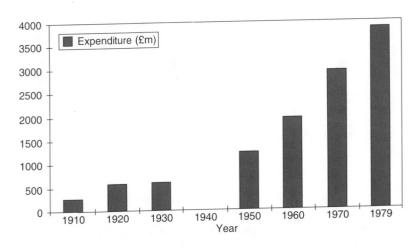

Source: Data from Greenleaf (1983: 33)

Figure 3.3   Public expenditure, 1910–79

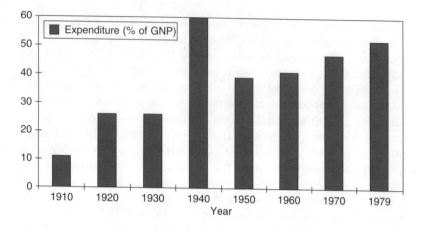

Source: Data from Greenleaf (1983: 33)

Figure 3.4   Public expenditure as a percentage of the GNP, 1910–79

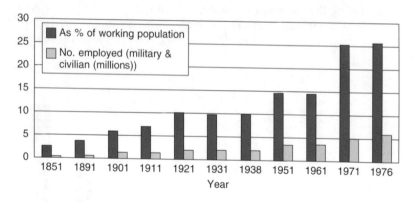

Source: Data from Greenleaf (1983a: 36)

Figure 3.5   Level of public employment

this increase in expenditure was accompanied by an increase in public employment. The expansion of the public sector required the development and institutionalisation of the core executive. In the mid-nineteenth century, Britain was governed by a core of departments revolving around the Treasury, the Foreign Office, the Board of Trade and the Home Office. During the twentieth century, departments (and a myriad of non-departmental and quasi-governmental boards) were created in welfare areas such as health, education and labour, and in economic areas, for example, energy (in different guises), industry, transport and aviation. Corresponding with the growth of new departments there has been an increasing formalisation of rules and procedures. This process of institutionalisation has increased the capability of state actors to intervene in society (Greenleaf 1983a).

The increased numbers and powers of departments required the strengthening role of central coordination. The Cabinet Office, the Treasury and the Prime Minister have had to formalise their operations and introduce new techniques to control the numerous departments and agencies. The following section examines explanations of state growth.

EXPLAINING THE GROWTH OF THE STATE

The state grew significantly from the end of the nineteenth century until the 1970s. There are six main factors behind the broad development and growth of the state:

The impact of war

The greatest increases in the size of the British state have occurred at the time of war. This is even true of relatively small wars such as the Crimean and Boer Wars, which highlighted the need for social reform in health and education and, in the case of the Crimean War, increased pressure for the reform of state organisations. However, state expansion is a consequence particularly of the industrialised, total wars of the twentieth century. As Tilly (1990: 14) notes, 'state structures appeared chiefly as a byproduct of rulers' efforts to acquire the means of war; and . . . relations among states, especially through war and preparation for war, strongly affected the entire process of state formation'.

War impacts on the state in a number of ways. It forces the state to undertake an increased range of functions and therefore state actors have to develop the capability to intervene more effectively in society. The state has to organise production and distribution as well as the military campaign. These requirements led to the establishment of higher levels of administrative capability, greater taxation and the legitimation of increased state intervention. Frequently, war affects perceptions concerning the range of state action that are acceptable; for example, during war increased taxation, redistribution, nationalisation, control over distribution and intervention in the privately owned economy entered the political agenda.

In Britain in the twentieth century, war was particularly important in destroying the vestiges of the *laissez-faire* state. The First World War undermined the 'fiscal and conceptual constraints on state expansion' and displaced the bureaucratic conservatism that had been dominant (Cronin 1991: 70). The Great War presented problems that could not be solved by the market and, in order to cope with the shortage of munitions, difficulties in food supply, the problems of securing adequate supplies of transport for troops and ensuring the continuation of production, the government created new ministries (Greenleaf 1983a). Increasingly, government regulation increased to 'the point of virtual nationalisation' (Greenleaf 1983a: 59).

The First World War completely changed the conception of what the state could and should do. It was accepted that certain problems could not be solved by the market, and the administrative capabilities developed during the war demonstrated the state had the ability to resolve some of these problems. Cronin (1991: 71) believes that by the end of the First World War, 'there had arisen a new state in Britain enlarged by the novel tasks superimposed upon it and entangled in society and economy to an unprecedented degree'. Despite these changes, there was some reaction against the growth of the state in the 1920s, and it was effectively the Second World War that saw the establishment of the modern collectivist state (Dunleavy 1989b).

With the Second World War, 'The grip of government was not only tighter and more extensive but also applied sooner and more deliberately and systematically' (Greenleaf 1983a: 61). The state developed the ability to intervene in every aspect of British society, from economic production and the supply of labour to the rationing of food. The degree of economic control in Britain was in fact greater than in Nazi Germany (Dunleavy 1989b: 278). However, more significant in terms of state expansion was the way many of the wartime controls and the acceptance of state intervention continued into the post-war period. For Dunleavy (1989b: 278),

> The perpetuation of the system into peacetime was not simply the result of inertial momentum. It also reflected a leap in social learning a recognition of the value of managed social effort for achieving specific and predictable economic and logistical effects.

It was accepted that the *laissez-faire* state had failed during the inter-war depression (see above). War proved how state organisation could achieve important societal goals. It changed capabilities and attitudes, and the rise of Labour and the development of Keynesianism gave ideological and theoretical support to the notion of greater state intervention.

Social and economic change

War had a ratchet effect on the growth of government; at the end of war the state never declined to its pre-war size. However, war did not cause the growth of government, but accelerated and consolidated growth that had already been occurring. A significant factor in the growth of the British state was economic and social change that occurred as a result of industrialisation. Skowronek (1982: 4) claims that for the United States, 'the expansion of national administrative capacities . . . was a response to industrialism'. A similar claim can be made for Britain. Industrialisation presented problems previously unknown to politicians and administrators.

Population growth led to an increasingly specialised division of labour and greater differentiation of society (Skowronek 1982). This increased complexity created a range of new social problems. Urbanisation and the concomitant social and economic dislocation that resulted were particularly important. With intensive living arrangements, new problems of sanitation and social order developed. Simultaneously, communications heightened awareness of new social problems. This social and economic change produced what Hall and Schwarz (1985: 9) refer to as a crisis of the British state, because state regulation 'could no longer be produced by means of liberal policies, practices and objectives'.

From a different perspective, MacDonagh (1958: 57) also emphasises the impact of industrialisation on the nature of the state because of the social problems that arose from industrialisation, the concentration and mobility of the population and the potential solutions that derived from mass production and new developments in transport. The state was faced with new problems that the liberal order was unable to solve. Gradually, legislation and institutions developed to deal with new situations. As new institutions and administrators were employed, there was an increased appetite for regulation because, 'The executive officers and their superiors now demanded, and to some extent secured, legislation which awarded them discretion not merely in the application of its clauses but even in the imposition of penalties and the framing of regulations' (MacDonagh 1958: 60).

Technology and the spread of information also affected the nature of the state. First, technology and transportation reduced the division of time and space. Events had an impact on a greater number of people more quickly, which increased the pressure on politicians for action (Giddens 1985, Greenleaf 1983a). Moreover, technology increased the ability of the state to intervene in civil society. As we shall see, as the state grew it became increasingly professionalised and specialised: 'It was indeed the civil servants, the state's own representatives of expert efficiency and the professional ideal, who took the initiative in suggesting the extension of state control and in creating the mechanism to carry it through' (Perkin 1989: 189). It was only through technology that the 'administrative unity of the nation-state' could be consolidated (Giddens 1985: 172). If states are to expand their ability to intervene in society then they need the mechanisation of transport, the development of means of surveillance, the expansion of the collection of data and the ability to create administrative organisations (Giddens 1985). Greenleaf (1983a: 49–50) highlights how the combination of war and technology encouraged the growth of the state. Technology changed the nature of war and created the total war, which required the state to mobilise the whole of society.

The impact of class pressure

War, social and economic change and technology affected people's relations to the means of production. In other words, industrialisation changed the class position of individuals and changed the relations of classes to each other. There are a range of commentators, Marxist and non-Marxist, who see the growth of the state as a response to class conflicts and class pressures.

Two key approaches exist to the class analysis of the British state. One view sees the aristocracy as being remarkably successful at maintaining its dominant position despite industrialisation (Anderson 1987). The second view maintains that the state grew in response to the changing nature of capitalism and the growth of working class pressure (McEachern 1990, Middlemas 1979).

Anderson argues that the British agrarian class had the 'longest consecutive history as a capitalist stratum proper' (Anderson 1987: 28). The divorce of producers from the means of production occurred much earlier in Britain than elsewhere in Europe. The consequence was that the British agrarian class became extremely wealthy and their fortunes 'towered over those of the most successful industrialists' (Anderson 1987: 31). As a result, the aristocrats, rather than the industrialists, had the necessary resources for political involvement. For Anderson, this class blocked the development of 'a modern state in England'. Industrialisation did not alter the parameters of the state, and rather than intervene to encourage its development state actors merely created buffers to some of its side-effects (Anderson 1987: 38). The aristocracy managed to maintain control of the state, ensuring that it never became large and interventionist: 'piecemeal reforms of suffrage or administration, in homeopathic doses, slowly modified the structures of traditional power and privilege, without ever redrawing them at a stroke' (Anderson 1987: 48). While the remainder of Europe saw a transition of élites, in Britain the aristocracy managed to hold on to power.

Consequently, even the Northcote–Trevelyan Report on the civil service (see Box 3.1, p. 54), which appeared at first sight to be a move towards creating a modern bourgeois state, was in fact no such thing. For Gowan (1987: 18):

> Not only were the reformers under no pressure from the rising urban middle classes to open up the civil service: they believed and hoped that the reform would weaken the capacity of this group to penetrate the upper reaches of the service, thereby strengthening the hold of the landed classes on administrative power.

The reforms of the mid-nineteenth century were in fact mechanisms for keeping the aristocracy in power. The shift from a system of patronage to one of selection would ensure that the civil service was drawn from Oxbridge, which was still under aristocratic dominance (Gowan 1987).

There are a number of problems with Anderson's thesis, and especially with its view of the Northcote–Trevelyan reforms. First, it assumes that the aristocracy had the ability to act as a coherent class, with an awareness of its interests and of how to protect them. Regarding Northcote–Trevelyan as a mechanism for maintaining aristocratic power overestimates the ability of political actors to see into the future. How could Gladstone, Northcote or Trevelyan have known that the rejection of patronage would protect rather than threaten the power of the aristocracy? Second, such a view cannot explain why there was so much opposition to the reforms. Indeed, the reforms only began to be implemented in the 1870s, and were not fully implemented until the First World War. Moreover, the main opponents of the Report were the Home Office and the Foreign Office, the most highly aristocratic of the government departments. Third, Northcote–Trevelyan can be seen as part of a process of reforms starting with the 1832 Reform Act which were part of an overall reform of the state in response to middle-class pressure. These reforms might have attempted to incorporate the middle class rather than transfer power to them, but the long-term effect was to whittle away the power of the aristocracy. Fourth, Anderson seems to deny that Britain became a relatively successful capitalist state.

It is difficult, in fact, to deny both the growth and modernisation of the British state in the late nineteenth century and that much of this growth was in response to the successful pressure of the working and middle classes. The state did become involved in the regulation of capitalism, at least from the middle of the nineteenth century. Undoubtedly, the bureaucracy was not the size of that of France or Germany, but it had no need to be; at this point British capitalism was highly successful without state intervention.

A more fruitful class analysis is to regard the growth of the state as a response to class pressure from 'subordinate' classes. For McEachern (1990: 45–6):

> The rise of capitalism destroyed the certainties of the feudal economic and social order. With industrialisation, capitalism transformed the entire economic and demographic character of society. The forces that gave coherence and legitimacy to the old order were destroyed and the question was sharply posed of how the new kind of society would combine class rule, the secured domination of the new and rising class, the bourgeoisie or capital, with dynamic economic growth and accumulation.

With the rise of capitalism, classes formed and developed organisations that pressurised political actors and led ultimately to the collapse of the nineteenth-century liberal order (McEachern 1990). Similarly, Middlemas (1979) maintains that from the First World War the class organisations of labour and capital became so politically significant that they had to be incorporated into the state in order to maintain social order. They became 'governing institutions', which at the same time both pushed the state towards taking greater action and assisted it in implementing policy. Much of the growth of state intervention in welfare and the economy can be seen as a response to working-class pressure. For example, the reforms of the 1906 Liberal government resulted, to some extent, from the larger electorate, the growth of the trade union movement and the rise of the Labour Party (Peden 1991: 18–19).

The impact of international competition

A key factor in the growth of the state is international competition. As Skocpol (1979) points out, the state has to be 'Janus-faced'. It looks both inwards to the domestic polity and outward to the international system. International factors often have a major impact on the success or failure of the ruling élite, and the international system is a shaper of the states within it (Tilly 1990). In the middle of the nineteenth century the British state was almost never threatened by international competition, either economic or military. The main Continental competitor, France, had been defeated in 1815 and Germany was not unified until 1870. Most of the Continent was still struggling with the aftermath of the 1848 revolutions. Economically, Britain was far ahead of any competitor in terms of production and world trade, and it or Britain had the economic and political strength to enforce favourable trading conditions. According to Kennedy (1988: 193–4):

> Around 1860, which was probably when the country reached its zenith in relative terms, the United Kingdom produced 53 per cent of the world's iron and 50 per cent of its coal and lignite and consumed just under half of the raw cotton output of the globe . . . It alone was responsible for one-fifth of the world's commerce, but for two-fifths of the trade in manufactured goods. Over one-third of the world's merchant marine sailed under the British flag, and that share was steadily increasing.

However, the impact of industrialisation was to shift the global balance, as other nations started to develop the techniques of modern capitalism (Kennedy 1988). The spread of industrialism was to present Britain first with economic competition and then with increased military competition.

Throughout the nineteenth century the US economy was growing rapidly and the civil war turned it into a large military power. Likewise, the unification of Germany led to an industrial and technological boom (Kennedy 1988). As late as 1880, both Germany and the United States had much lower levels of industrialisation per capita than Britain. By

1913 the United States had overtaken Britain, and Germany was catching up. Britain's industrial and commercial dominance declined as its relative share of world output declined (Kennedy 1988).

Britain's industrial and political élites were confused and threatened by Britain's apparent economic decline (Hall and Schwarz 1985). 'The rise of competing industrial nations exposed the vulnerability of a British economy, which was dependent on the fortunes of the world market as never before' (Schwarz 1985: 81–2). This increased economic competition created greater pressure for the state to intervene in the economy. Indeed, the growing campaign for tariff reform was largely a result of the increased international competition (Greenleaf 1983a: 107). As other economies industrialised, it became apparent, at least to some, that the liberal state was no longer an appropriate model.

Moreover, as foreign economies grew and became increasingly successful, they also presented more of a military threat. As early as the Crimean war, the difficulties of a liberal state fighting a war became apparent (Kennedy 1988: 226). With the further problems of the Boer War and then the threat of total, industrialised war in 1914, military competition forced the state to increase taxation and intervene more in order to prepare for military threats. Britain's economic base was fundamental to its military capacity, and as Britain's capacity declined the capacity of other states increased.

The role of ideology

A common explanation for the growth of the state is the increasing influence of collectivist ideology. For Fry (1979: 45), by the end of the nineteenth century *laissez-faire* ideology was increasingly challenged by the collectivist vision of the new liberals. The most important was T. H. Green:

> When one takes into account Green's theory of rights, his theory of positive freedom, his theory of property, and the extent to which he built on utilitarianism, Green can be seen as the intellectual pro-genitor of the welfare state (Fry 1979: 45).

Hall and Schwarz (1985: 21) see the crisis of liberalism as deriving partly from the development of 'three dominant collectivist currents . . . imperialist, new liberal and Fabian'.

Explanations of change based on ideas (idealism) posit that the revolution in government that occurred in the nineteenth century would not have happened 'without allowing for the part played in it by contemporary thought about political and social organisation' (Parris 1960: 35). In particular, Bentham and Benthamism are seen as revolutionising the conceptions of the British state and public policy (Parris 1960; MacDonagh 1958).

There is always a problem of the chain of causality with idealist notions of change. Parris seems to suggest that the key explanatory variable is the ideology. Yet as Perkin (1977: 108) emphasises: 'the process of reform is never a one-way influence of ideology upon practice, or of the empirical "pressure of facts" upon ideology, but a continuous interaction of the two, in which both are continually modified'. Nevertheless, ideas and ideologies are a reaction to material circumstances; they offer ways of understanding the world and coping with new problems. The undermining of *laissez-faire* ideology was a result of the failure of the paradigm to deal with the problems of social and economic change, war, social pressures and international competition. This failure created the space for the development of new ideas.

State-centred explanations of growth

The five explanations of state growth discussed above are generally society-centred. State growth is seen as a response to pressures from society or from forces outside the state such as social and economic changes, class conflicts or even competition from other states. However, these explanations can provide only a partial picture of the factors that led to the expansion of the state; the way state actors have responded to the forces they face has also affected the way the state has developed.

The élitist, or state autonomy, perspective views the state as having the resources to enable it to act independently from forces within society. This perspective sees state actors as having interests – in political goals, policy issues and certain institutional outcomes – that are more than self-interest, and which affect the way they make policy (Weir and Skocpol 1985). From this perspective, the growth of the state is as a result of the state actors increasing their infrastructural power – their ability to intervene in the society – by developing new administrative mechanisms that enable them to achieve their goals (Mann 1984). Consequently, political change is not simply a reaction to social factors, but can occur within the state as a result of the interest and actions of state élites.

The growth of the state is the result of state actors developing the capabilities to deal with new situations: 'State building is a process basic to any nation's political development. Government officials seeking to maintain power and legitimacy to try to mould institutional capacities in response to an ever changing environment' (Skowronek 1982: 10). From the end of the nineteenth century, the British state faced new problems that the night-watchman state could not solve – it lacked the administrative capability. Therefore, the growth of the state is a consequence of developing the organisational means for intervention. During the nineteenth and early twentieth centuries, state actors were concerned with concentrating and centralising authority within national government and developing the ability to penetrate civil society (Skowronek 1982). Reforms, such as Northcote–Trevelyan, were not solely a response to class pressure but also derived from state actors desiring the administrative capabilities to deal with new problems. The impact of industrialisation, urbanisation and war was to create the need for a specialised and professional civil service, so that politicians would be able to develop and implement programmes of intervention.

There is nothing inevitable about the way states respond to social change. The development of the British state was not an automatic reaction to social pressures but depended on the perceptions, abilities, choices and actions of state actors within a particular structural context of social pressure, war, political ideologies and internal and external economic conditions. Certain nations – Tilly (1990) gives the examples of Portugal and Romania – can fail to develop the ability to deal with the problems of industrialisation and industrial war. In examining the growth of the state and the development of the core executive, we need to analyse the growth of its infrastructure for intervening in society (Mann 1986).

THE DEVELOPMENT OF THE CORE EXECUTIVE

This chapter has traced the growth of the state in absolute terms from the middle of the nineteenth century, and we have seen that there was no single cause of state development. As the state grew it became necessary to develop the organisational and administrative capabilities necessary to run the core executive, and so departments developed with the resources to develop and implement significant social programmes. This required the development of coordinating machinery in order to control departments. The growth of state functions and expenditure led directly to the bureaucratisation and expansion of the core executive. We now need to examine how state growth affected the development of the core executive and the administrative capability at the core of the machine.

Establishing the core executive

Before the 1850s, central government operated very much on an *ad hoc* basis. Cabinet was informal, central coordination was weak, and government was unbureaucratic. In addition, the core executive had limited functions. Faced with new social problems – industrialisation, war, and class conflict – state actors had to develop the mechanisms and administrative capability to deal with these problems. The first significant development was the Northcote–Trevelyan reforms of 1854, which laid the foundations of a modern professional civil service (see Box 3.1).

The Northcote–Trevelyan reforms established a professional, expert and permanent civil service which had a degree of independence from its political masters. This was important. With the increasing size and responsibilities of the state, politicians were unable to make all the decisions and control all the operations of a department. They needed advisers they could trust. Officials had to sift, organise and provide ministers with information on key problems, and the available policy options. Ministers also needed high-quality staff who could take decisions independently in an ever-expanding number of fields. There was also a need for the administrative machinery to implement decisions in an increasing number of areas of civil society. The reforms of government in the nineteenth century 'created a series of mechanisms by which the central machinery of the state could make its decisions locally effective' (Cronin 1991: 19). What is striking is how this new civil service was informed by the parliamentary state. Ministers had to remain accountable, but they were no longer taking all the decisions. Therefore, they had to establish a bureaucracy in which officials could be trusted to act in their name. This idea of trusting officials who are loyal to ministers has remained a key value in the British civil service up to the present day (see Richards and Smith 1998). The Northcote–Trevelyan reforms can be seen as a process whereby state actors – Northcote, Trevelyan and Gladstone – recognised the need to improve the efficiency of the state in order to increase its capabilities to intervene in society.

BOX 3.1
The Northcote–Trevelyan Report

It is clear from the first page of the Report that Northcote and Trevelyan were concerned with the need to deal with the growing demands on government:

> The great and increasing accumulation of public business, and the consequent pressure upon the Government, need only be alluded to; and the inconveniences which are inseparable from the frequent changes which take place in the responsible administration are matter of sufficient notoriety. It may safely be asserted that, as matters now stand, the Government of the country could not be carried on without the aid of an efficient body of permanent officers, occupying a position duly subordinate to the Crown and to Parliament, yet possessing sufficient independence, character, ability, and experience to be able to advise, assist, and to some extent, influence those who are from time to time set over them (Northcote and Trevelyan, 1954: 1).

The main recommendations of the Report were: civil servants should be appointed by examination rather than patronage; promotion must be on merit; the civil service should have a unified structure; and routine clerks should be separated from administrators (Northcote and Trevelyan 1954: 16). The aim was to establish a more meritocratic, efficient and effective civil service. For Hennessy (1990: 31), 'the Northcote–Trevelyan reforms and their gradual implementation *were* the greatest single transformation the British Civil Service has ever undergone . . .'

Nevertheless, there was much opposition to the Northcote–Trevelyan reforms and it was not until 1870 that open competition was introduced. Even then, the Home Office and Foreign Office resisted reform for a number of years (Greenleaf 1987). Moreover, the reforms were evolutionary rather than revolutionary (Hennessy 1990) and did not undermine the night-watchman state. They did, however, establish the basis of the modern civil service, which enabled the creation of a bureaucratic, administrative state. The aim of the reformers was not to expand the state, but to make it more economical and efficient (Greenleaf 1987, Hart 1972). Increasing its capabilities was in a sense a side effect. By abolishing patronage and creating a class of what later became known as policy advisers, the reforms enabled the development of a more effective civil service. With the development of a professional civil service, the embryo of departmental resources was established. Departments were beginning to develop the expertise and organisational capability to enable them to control the policy process. With the strengthening of departments there was a need for the strengthening of coordination.

During this period the cabinet became increasingly formalised, and power relationships within it changed. From the middle of the nineteenth century, 'most government tasks came to be formalised under the effective responsibilities of ministers' (Daalder 1963a: 18). In order to coordinate the work of ministers, the cabinet grew and became much more formal in its structure (Daalder 1963a). According to Mackintosh (1977b: 143), the cabinet was now 'the centre of power', where policy was determined and conflicts were resolved.

The cabinet was also an important organisation for balancing the various factions and parties within government. Party discipline was much weaker in the nineteenth century, and so the Prime Minister was dependent on senior figures to maintain governing coalitions and was less able to sack ministers as he pleased (Mackintosh 1977b). However, there was some increase in prime-ministerial resources. It became increasingly the case that it was the Prime Minister alone who could summon cabinet. Moreover, with a developing hierarchy of ministers voting became a less appropriate means of assessing cabinet feeling. Consequently, it was left to the Prime Minister to sum up cabinet discussions, which increased his influence over the final decision. Finally, as the amount of business conducted within government increased, there was a tendency for ministers to concentrate on departmental affairs. With other ministers lacking adequate information, the role of the Prime Minister in coordinating government and determining strategy took on greater importance, and there was a gradual shift towards inner cabinets, especially on issues of foreign policy (Mackintosh 1977b).

With the growth of a more effective civil service to provide ministers with information and administrative capabilities, the division between ministers and backbenchers became greater. This increased the role and importance of the cabinet as it formalised its decision-making structures and increasingly controlled the key decisions. Within cabinet the balance of resources also changed, with the Prime Minister taking on more of a leading role and having the resources to overrule ministers.

This period also saw the emergence of the Treasury 'as the department crucial to the central control of administrative efficiency and financial accountability' (Thane 1990: 9). Again, as departments strengthened, the need for financial control became more important, and Gladstone in particular created the capabilities for effective control of departmental expenditure. He set up the Public Accounts Committee in 1861, and with the Exchequer and Audits Department Act 1866 he tied together the procedures of Estimates, Appropriations, Expenditure and Audit and created the office of Comptroller and Auditor General (Rosevere 1969) and established Treasury primacy (see Box 3.2).

Wright (1972) questions the extent of Treasury primacy. First, Treasury control was negative and, therefore, if a department did not demand increased money then the Treasury had very little control over its expenditure. Second, powerful cabinet ministers need not automatically accept the decisions of the Treasury. Third, controls of Admiralty and War Office expenditure were almost non-existent. Fourth, 'the Treasury attempted nothing in the way of systematic and continuous review of either the estimates (civil and military) or expenditure generally' (Wright 1972: 200). For Wright, the degree of Treasury control depended on the particular circumstances and relationships that existed between the Treasury and each department: 'In many respects negotiations between a department and the Treasury resemble a very formal and elaborate game, the rules of which were well known to both contestants but never openly discussed between them' (Wright 1972: 222). The fact departments played this game placed some restraint on what was spent.

Although the Treasury had problems exerting control, to which the dramatic increase in public expenditure at the end of the nineteenth century is testament, it did become progressively more influential towards the new century. It established the basic mechanisms for assessing government expenditure and entrenched, in principle, a system for controlling the level of increase. Rosevere (1969: 152) avers: by 1888 'The Treasury had become an exclusive élite', and it presumably had some impact on departments because the Prime Minister, Lord Salisbury, complained in 1900 that the Treasury has the power of the purse, and by exercising the power of the purse it claims a voice in all decisions of administrative authority and policy. I think that much delay and many doubtful resolutions have been the result of the peculiar position which, through many generations, the Treasury has occupied (quoted in Rosevere 1969: 183).

BOX 3.2
Treasury primacy

'By creating the first effective machinery for a retrospective, annual audit of government expenditure it put a willing Treasury on its mettle to enforce the strictest standards of financial propriety among the departments.' (Rosevere 1969: 141). For Thane (1990: 27), 'Treasury primacy was recognised in 1867 when its permanent secretary was granted seniority over the heads of other departments.' The basis of this primacy was Treasury control which meant, according to a minute by Sir Reginald Welby, Permanent Secretary at the Treasury 1885–94:

1. That the Chancellor of the Exchequer, who has to find the money, is to know how it is going. This is essential, but the duty of the Treasury in this respect would be fulfilled if we merely kept a register.   2. But the Chancellor is not content to be a mere Register, and that, further, has not in my opinion been the view taken by political authorities of his functions. He requires to be satisfied that demands are really necessary. Many things may be desirable but not imperative. The imperative ought to have precedence, and the Chancellor of the Exchequer practically decides for which of the services urged upon him he can afford to provide.   3. Someone in a great service like that of the public must watch over a certain uniformity of pay and regulation, and this duty falls to the Head of the Treasury, i.e., the Chancellor of the Exchequer (quoted in Hamilton 1955: 14).

The basis of Gladstonian finance was that public money should be spent only when it was absolutely necessary, and it was the role of the Treasury to determine what expenditure was essential. The Treasury's role was to determine the limits of government through the overall coordination of spending and policy.

By the end of the nineteenth century the number of departments had increased to eighteen and included agriculture, health and the Ministry of Works (Willson 1955). Consequently, departments were also developing their own bureaucratic techniques for gathering information, raising their policy expertise and improving the machinery for implementing policy (Savage 1996). Decisions could no longer be made by individual ministers. They increasingly relied on their civil servants, which affected the balance of resources between ministers and civil servants. With increased departmentalism there was a need for a more formal cabinet, and this formalisation increased the importance of the Prime Minister. The second half of the nineteenth century laid the foundations of the modern state and established some of the lines of dependence that are still present in today's core executive. Nevertheless, it was the social legislation of the early twentieth century and the First World War that established the modern core executive.

The First World War and the core executive

The Liberal government of 1906 used the machinery established in the nineteenth century to extend the role of the state in the provision of welfare. In 1908 Asquith was responsible for the introduction of a minimal old-age pension, and in the following four years Churchill and Lloyd George pushed through a range of social legislation. Although there was no coherent plan to create a comprehensive welfare system, the combination of pensions, labour exchanges and national insurance established the basis of the modern welfare state and 'created a great surge in state power in personal life and the national economy' (Hennessy 1990: 57–8).

Nevertheless, these social reforms occurred within the context of the nineteenth century state, which was constrained both by bureaucratic conservatism and by opposition to state expansion. Significant change 'was propelled by a series of qualitative transformations in the relationship between state and society prompted by war and the dictates of war mobilisation' (Cronin 1991: 30). It was war which dissolved the limits on state expansion and led to significant changes in the core executive.

The state, as it existed in 1914, could not cope with the demands of a modern total war. 'The 1914 system was really suitable for the Britain of 1905, not 1914 . . .' (Clarke 1975: 66). Scandals such as the shortage of shells in May 1915 demonstrated that a *laissez-faire* state was not effective for industrialised war (Hennessy 1990). The response to this crisis was the establishment of the Ministry of Munitions, through which the state took over completely the production and distribution of ammunition (Harris 1990; Hennessy 1990). The questioning of state capabilities derived partly from wider problems, with shortages of men, machinery and production bottlenecks compelling the government 'to intervene to determine the proper distribution of increasingly scarce resources' (French 1982: 8). The government became involved in transport, production, the labour market, agriculture and the financial markets. In a range of areas the state took on functions that had been left to the private sector, and as a result the cabinet and the Treasury acquired 'powers and developed the procedures which subsequently enabled these two institutions to oversee and to control the central government machine itself' (Burk 1982a: 1).

Significant changes in the core executive occurred during the First World War. Between 1914 and 1919, the cabinet was transformed 'from a political committee into a complex administrative machinery' (Turner 1982: 57). Under Asquith's premiership there had been problems of organisation, political conflicts and conflicts of responsibility. Lloyd George, who became Prime Minister in 1916, sought to clearly define the lines of responsibility by creating a small war cabinet of five members that was to determine the main lines of policy (Mackintosh 1977b: 371). As the majority of departmental ministers were not included in the war cabinet, the recording and distribution of decisions became essential. For the first time, a cabinet secretariat was established that kept and distributed cabinet minutes. In addition, small *ad hoc* committees were established to deal with particular problems, and war cabinet members chaired standing committees that coordinated policy between departments (French 1982). During the war a formal system of cabinet government was established, with an institutionalised system of committees serviced by a cabinet secretariat. These developments 'undoubtedly lowered the status of departmental ministers. Their work was coordinated from above. They had to execute decisions in which they were never consulted' (Daalder 1963b: 46).

Additionally, the war resulted in an increased role for the Treasury but, ironically, a reduction in its influence. The Treasury established control over the stock exchange, become involved in overseas finance and took over exchange rate policy from the Bank of England (Burk 1982b). But, while the absolute power of the Treasury may have increased, its control over staffing and expenditure was greatly weakened relative to the departments as they became increasingly autonomous and declared extra expenditure necessary for victory (Burk 1982b, Rosevere 1969). In effect, the Treasury lost its primacy during the war as the demands of the situation lifted the constraints on state expansion (Cronin 1991).

Such was the impact of the war on government that the government set up the Haldane Committee in 1917 to investigate the machinery of government. In its report, the Committee outlined the main functions of the cabinet:

> a) the final determination of the policy to be submitted to Parliament; b) the supreme control of the national executive in accordance with the policy prescribed by Parliament; c) the continuous co-ordination and delimitation of the activities of several Departments of State (*Report of the Machinery of Government Committee*, Cd 9230 1918: 1).

The Committee recommended that the cabinet should, consist of twelve members at most, meet frequently and have a proper provision of information. In the event, the impact of the Haldane report was limited (Daalder 1963b). Yet, crucially, Haldane did establish the crux of the relationship between ministers and officials, defining them as inextricably linked rather than hierarchical (Richards 1997). One of Haldane's recommendations, that the position of the Treasury should be strengthened, was implemented because with the end of the war there was a backlash against increased government spending (Hennessy 1990). The Bradbury Committee on the civil service recommended Treasury control be increased, and in 1921 the Geedes committee recommended a cut in government expenditure of £87 million, of which only £57 million was implemented (Cronin 1991).

In sum, the First World War saw a substantial expansion of the state as a direct result of the need to fight a total war. This had a significant impact on the core executive. New departments were created, cabinet government was formalised and the Treasury lost its control over departments but gained control, effectively for the first time, over key elements of the economy. The impact of the war on the post-war core executive was contradictory. The nature of the state had changed fundamentally in terms of both organisation and function. Nevertheless, the *laissez-faire* orthodoxy had not disappeared, and pressure developed on the state to decrease in size and for the Treasury to reassert its control. Although this happened to an extent, the state never regained its night-watchman status. Departments with significant social and economic responsibilities had been institutionalised, and were concerned to retain their functions. Consequently, the balance of resources was shifting between the centre and the departments, creating structural problems for the coordination process (see Chapter 6).

The First World War set the framework for the core executive for the next twenty years. However, there were some minor adjustments as a result of the economic depression. The inter-war years were a period of conflict over the role of the state, with many theorists and politicians rethinking the state's responsibilities for the economy and welfare. Initially the Treasury re-established dominance in the 1920s and reasserted the economic orthodoxy of limited government, the gold standard and balanced budgets. But with increasing economic problems, Britain abandoned the gold standard in 1931 and the National government introduced a degree of protection for the home market (Harris 1990). There was also a significant growth in economic intervention through the creation of a number of public corporations such as the Coal Commission and the London Passenger Transport Board (Fry 1979). The second Labour government (1929–31) also created a Committee of Civil Research to tackle unemployment, which was transformed into an Economic Advisory Committee (Hennessy 1990). Nevertheless, the reassertion of Treasury dominance prevented any major changes in the nature of the state during the inter-war period. However, as Savage (1996: 4) points out, this period did see the establishment of departments with some degree of independence from the centre as they developed their own expertise and sense of professionalism. Nevertheless, it was again war that forced a major change in the organisation of the state and the core executive.

The impact of the Second World War on the core executive

During the Second World War the nature of the state, and within it the core executive, were determined by the 'needs of a nation fighting for survival' (Middlemas 1986: 17). The war altered radically both the functions and the form of the state and the relationships between its key elements. As Peter Hennessy (1990: 88) emphasises, Hitler 'obliged the British Government to find new men and new methods overnight'.

The structure of wartime government was more clearly defined once Churchill became Prime Minister in 1940. He created a small war cabinet, which was responsible for overall coordination of policy but particularly in regard to the war effort. In 1941, Churchill's 'system of control settled into a fairly definite form. At the centre was the War Cabinet of eight to eleven members, most of whom had departmental duties' (Mackintosh 1977b: 492). The war cabinet was the final formal authority for home affairs, but most domestic matters were *de facto* dealt with by the Lord President's Committee, which also had sub-committees on Reconstruction and the Machinery of Government (Lee 1977; Mackintosh 1977b). Churchill preferred to work through a range of committees that 'were organised by function and cut across traditional departmental boundaries' (Cronin 1991: 145). The apex of government was dominated by a web of ministerial committees, with the Lord President's committee acting as the coordinator of domestic issues and the war cabinet of military issues (Middlemas 1986). The needs of war placed the war cabinet in a very strong position, and although at various times key offices of state such as the Home Office and Treasury were not included, ministers accepted the cabinet's authority and the confines of collective responsibility (Anderson 1946).

The core executive and the need for coordination also grew with the substantial growth in government departments that occurred during the war. New ministries were created for food, economic warfare, home security, shipping, and supply and production. The economic powers of government increased exponentially. The Ministry of Labour had almost complete control over the supply and distribution of labour (Middlemas 1979): 'The principle of manpower budgeting ensured that [Bevin's] Ministry would, for the rest of the war, be the principal department of state' (Middlemas 1986: 20). The Board of Trade planned and controlled exports and imports and the Ministry of Production oversaw the production programmes of various military and non-military departments and coordinated the supply of raw materials (Cronin 1991).

The needs of the military, production and manpower ensured, as in the First World War, that resources shifted from the Treasury to the key economic and military departments. Rosevere (1969: 273) highlights how: 'From 1939 until 1942 the Treasury was under a political shadow which not only diminished its customary prestige and authority but disqualified it from access to the new centres of deliberation.' Much economic planning was now within the new powerful economic ministries, negative limits on expenditure were no longer appropriate and, with the creation of the Central Economic Information Service and the Central Statistical Office, alternative sources of economic advice were created.

Nevertheless, the Treasury did not completely forfeit its traditional position. It retained the power of the purse and control over staffing.

The Treasury also determined exchange rate policy, price control and counter-inflationary policies. Moreover, both the Anderson Committee on the machinery of government and leading civil servants realised that in peacetime the Treasury would have to be the key actor in controlling public expenditure and economic management (Middlemas 1986, Rosevere 1969).

Once again, as the power of the Treasury declined during the war in relation to the core executive, its power in relation to civil society increased. The introduction of economic planning, and the acceptance, towards the end of the war, of Keynesian techniques, meant the role of the Treasury in the economy was much greater than had ever been envisaged in the inter-war period. The war vastly increased both the responsibilities and capabilities of the state. Under the auspices of Keynesianism, government accepted responsibility for maintaining full employment.

The extension of state activity resulting from the Employment Act 1944 was increased further by the Labour government's commitment to a comprehensive system of health provision and social security. Labour's welfare policy extended the reach of the state much deeper into civil society. Once the state was committed to providing welfare it had to provide the mechanisms for delivery. In health, elaborate networks were developed to incorporate doctors into the state in order to ensure they cooperated in providing free health care (Smith 1993). In social security, welfare expansion involved the development of state bureaucracy in order to dispense welfare payments at the local level. The infrastructural power of the state was increased overall but, more importantly, particular departments developed much greater policy responsibility, which increased their control over policy and expenditure. Welfare policy was generally demand-led and, consequently, very difficult for the Treasury to control. Although the responsibilities of the state were less than in wartime, they remained much greater than in the inter-war years. It had responsibilities for health, welfare, education, housing and the economy to a degree that would have been unimaginable in the twenties and thirties. The war created the organisation for an interventionist state and strengthened further the capabilities and resources of departments. Greater policy control, combined with popular support for welfare policies, further weakened Treasury control. Such was the extent of the loss of control that much of the post-war development of the core executive can be seen as a battle to reassert Treasury control and to modernise the state.

The core executive in the post-war era

Despite Britain winning the war and laying the foundations of the 'New Jerusalem', the post-war period has been one of relative economic and political decline. Britain ended the war both economically and politically subservient to the United States. However, the degree of this dependence was not recognised until the débâcle of Suez in 1956 and the increasing realisation in the late 1950s and early 1960s that Britain's economy was not growing as fast as its competitors'. According to Middlemas (1990: 153), by 1964 the changes in the international situation were such that it was difficult for the new Labour government to carry out its programme: 'Britain ceased to be an autonomous economic power . . . too much had been borrowed on too many understandings that were, in effect, mortgages for her government to disregard American opinion.' Despite economic and political decline, the new social and economic commitments of post-war government meant that the 'period between 1957 and 1964 saw [the state's] filling out and consolidation' (Lowe 1997: 602).

The combination of increased departmental autonomy and economic and political decline resulted, again, in attempts to reassert the control of the Treasury in order to reign in the ever expanding public expenditure programmes. These problems also produced attempts to modernise the core executive in order to resolve the crisis permanently. Efforts at modernisation occurred periodically from the end of the 1950s until the 1970s. They took two forms. The first was the rationalisation of the core executive through the creation of new and amalgamated ministries and the reform of the civil service. The second, and often related, was the attempt to increase the capabilities of the state in terms of economic management.

Harold Wilson's theme during the 1964 general election was the 'white heat of technology'. He saw state and economic modernisation as fundamental to Britain's attempt to break out of the cycle of relative economic decline and to put an end to the class nature of British society. The 1964 Labour government created five new departments: economic affairs (the DEA); overseas development; land and natural resources; the Ministry of Technology and the Welsh Office. In 1966 Wilson merged the Colonial and Foreign Offices and in 1968 he amalgamated them into the Foreign Office. In 1968 Wilson also created the Department of Health and Social Security (Fry 1981). Wilson was concerned with emphasising a change of priorities. He wanted to modernise Britain by withdrawing from Empire and moving towards Europe. He created new economic ministries such as Technology and the DEA in order to provide a counterbalance to the Treasury and, in so doing, to change the emphasis of economic policy away from finance and towards production. It was hoped these measures would break the constraints on British economic policy.

A corollary of reforming departments was the attempt to reform the civil service, which Wilson believed was essential for the modernisation of the state. The civil service was perceived by many as élitist and narrow. Wilson set up the Fulton Committee to examine 'the structure, recruitment and management, including training of the Home Civil Service' (quoted in Fry 1990: 175). The final report concluded that the civil service was too generalist and amateur, with a lack of skilled managers, scientists and technicians; there should be more transfers in and out of it; a new Civil Service Department should be created, which would take away responsibility for pay and management of the civil service from the Treasury; there should be a unified structure and more attention to career management and training; ministers should be allowed to use a small number of outside experts when necessary (Hennessy 1990, Kellner and Crowther Hunt 1979, HL 55 1997/8). However, many people believe that Fulton did not go far enough and that its criticisms were misplaced, while many of its recommendations, such as the unification of scientific and generalist grades, were not implemented (Hennessy 1990). Neither did it examine the nature of relationships between ministers and officials. Hence, most of the attempts at modernisation did little to change the nature of the core executive. Rather, they renamed old organisations and created new ones that met with similar problems to their predecessors.

The second goal of Wilson's reforms was to increase state capabilities, particularly in the area of economic policy. Many commentators (see for example, Zysman 1983, Hall 1986), argue that the reason for Britain's relative economic decline was the state's inability to intervene effectively in the economy, owing to a lack of economic capability. It has been argued that economic policy-making has been dominated by a Treasury concerned with controlling the aggregate level of demand, maintaining the value of sterling and controlling inflation (Pollard 1982). It was not prepared to intervene in any detailed way in the economy in order to modernise Britain's manufacturing base. Successive governments have recognised these criticisms, and have attempted to develop organisations with the ability to intervene.

As early as 1961, Harold Macmillan established the National Economic Development Council (NEDC) to provide a forum for tripartite discussion over the problems facing the economy. Through the so-called Little Neddys, the NEDC supplied fairly detailed reports on overcoming the problems of the British economy (Middlemas 1983). However, the impact of the NEDC has always been limited. It lacked any executive authority, and had no control over either the Treasury or British industry. Subsequently, it failed either to influence the making of economic policy or the behaviour of firms in particular sectors of the economy.

The 1964 Wilson government sought to go much further than NEDC and so created the DEA to develop a national plan for modernising the British economy and break out of the stop-go cycle. The DEA was to be superior to the Treasury in establishing Britain's economic priorities. In cooperation with industry, the NEDC and the other economic ministries, the DEA started to develop the National Plan. In addition, the Government established the Industrial Reorganisation Corporation with £150m to encourage mergers in British industry. However, the Treasury failed to cooperate with the DEA, and in principle followed a diametrically opposed policy of maintaining the value of sterling and deflating the economy. The result was that the optimistic National Plan was bound to fail and the DEA was finally wound up in 1970 (Brown 1972, Roll 1966).

Heath was concerned with developing a 'more strategic form of decision making' (Radcliffe 1991: 2) by undermining the departmentalism which he believed had hitherto characterised policy-making. Consequently, he created the large super-ministries to break down departmental boundaries in a number of areas. Heath was also concerned about the lack of support for the Prime Minister. He rejected the idea of a Prime Minister's Department, but did attempt to strengthen central coordination by establishing the Central Policy Review Staff (CPRS), which would examine and question the government's overall strategic objectives (Blackstone and Plowden 1988). The aim was to end the departmentalism that had come to characterise the governmental process. Heath hoped to introduce a new ethos of managerialism that would be concerned with achieving government objectives rather than departmental goals.

The Heath government, after its 1972 U-turn away from free market economics and disengagement, also attempted to extend the economic capabilities of the state. Through the Industry Act 1972, the Heath government substantially extended the mechanisms for intervention in the economy:

The Act provided for an Industrial Development Executive and Industrial Development Advisory boards with powers to make grants for regional development, and to give assistance to firms in the Assisted Areas, shipbuilding and off-shore construction. Section 8 gave such leeway to the Executive as to make it possible to assist any firm on more or less any pretext so long as the minister could define it as of benefit to the British economy (Middlemas 1990: 338–9).

In addition, these powers were used in the context of economic growth with the attempt of the Chancellor, Anthony Barber, to blast Britain out of the stop-go cycle through a relaxed fiscal policy. However, the policy collapsed because of a combination of the miners' strike, a loss of monetary control and, more particularly, the OPEC crisis, which quadrupled the price of oil and plunged the world into recession (Gamble 1981).

The succeeding Labour government built on the Heath government's mechanism for government intervention by creating the National Enterprise Board (NEB) and setting a system for planning agreements with private industry. However, the NEB was largely constrained to bailing out failing industries, and only one company – the bankrupt Chrysler UK – made a planning agreement. Again, Labour's attempts at economic modernisation failed in the face of international economic pressures and domestic economic crisis (Coates 1980, Grant 1982).

With the failure to sufficiently modernise the British economy in order to provide the necessary funds to provide for Britain's ever expanding welfare state, successive governments were forced into attempting to reinforce Treasury control in the hope of controlling public expenditure. In the late 1950s, the House of Commons Estimates Committee revealed that, despite common perceptions, the Treasury's control of expenditure was inadequate. It recommended an independent inquiry into Treasury control. As a consequence, the Plowden Committee reported in 1961 and concluded as follows:

What was needed was a more rational and efficient means of planning the use of public money and other wealth. The four elements of reconstruction proposed were: regular long-term surveys of the entire range of public expenditure and prospective resources in the contest of which decisions about future spending could be take; more stability of expenditure policy (that is no more stop-go); more tools of control (as by reform of the Estimates and the greater use of quantitative methods); and more effective machinery for ministers to take collective decisions (Greenleaf 1987: 275).

Following the report, the Public Expenditure Survey Committee (PESC) was introduced. Under this system, departmental ministers had to set out their long-term spending plans and provide a rationale that was used to convince, or not, Treasury officials (Middlemas 1990). But PESC was too complicated, and did very little to control public expenditure. By the mid-1960s it was already clear that expenditure was slipping out of control (Middlemas 1990). The age-old problem remained: departmental ministers would not place themselves in a 'financial strait jacket' (Lowe 1997: 613). The Heath government then introduced Policy Analysis Review (PAR), which was management by objectives: 'Department assessments of priorities were to be assessed *before* ministers made their bids and then combined later into an efficiency audit, to see if their attention had been achieved' (Middlemas 1990: 302). PAR allowed the Treasury and departments to review objectives and the efficiency of spending. However, political criteria continued to dominate in the making of spending decisions and, as a consequence, many of the PAR reports were ignored. Overall, there was a failure of any systematic attempt to control expenditure (Greenleaf 1987). It was only when faced with the demands of the International Monetary Fund (IMF) that the Labour government imposed absolute cash limits, which for the first time succeeded in reducing in real terms the level of government expenditure. Under the pressure of economic crisis and the demands of the IMF, in 1976 the Labour government abandoned Keynesianism and full employment, and opted for monetary control. As the commitment to reducing inflation and government spending as a proportion of GDP reasserted itself, the Treasury became increasingly dominant.

The weakening of Britain's economic position and the end of the post-war boom resulted in a significant shift of power in the core executive. With the Second World War and the subsequent commitment to welfare, the Treasury lost control to the spending departments. From the fifties until the seventies, departments worked on an inflation-plus formula and with Prime Ministers generally focused on political goals these demands for extra money frequently succeeded. Consequently, the alternative to restraint was to pursue a strategy of modernising the state and the economy. Macmillan, Heath and Wilson all attempted strategies of modernisation which for external and internal reasons had only limited success. The result of this failure was the IMF crisis in 1976 and the realisation that 'the party was over' (Whitehead 1985). An alternative strategy was to reassert the control of the Treasury. Throughout the sixties and seventies, government attempted half-heartedly to strengthen the Treasury, but it was not until the late 1970s that the economic imperative made economic restraint essential. As Middlemas (1991: 458) points out,

> the Treasury's emergence as the only department of state capable and willing to provide an overview, *but on a strictly financial basis* not a policy one, suggests that a new configuration of Whitehall has developed during the last fifteen years.

Following these developments, power has increasingly shifted to the Treasury in the areas of both economic policy and public spending (see Chapter 6). This tendency has been reinforced by the willingness of the Prime Minister to support the Treasury in opposition to other departments. As is illustrated in Chapter 6, the Prime Minister has also increased his or her resources by strengthening the Prime Minister's office and creating the Policy Unit, which has made him or her less dependent on outside advice. In addition, the Cabinet Office, combined more recently with the Office of Public Service (OPS), has expanded its role in coordination. The result is a strengthening of the centre, and the Treasury, at the expense of departments. Consequently, the centre – in the person of the Prime Minister – and the Chancellor in coalition make a formidable alliance. The state actors with the greatest resources have been unable to develop the resources and capabilities to control the economy or to achieve economic goals. As a result they have attempted an alternative strategy of controlling the other actors within the core executive. Whether this has been achieved will be seen in the course of this book.

CONCLUSION

The growth of the state was the result of a combination of factors, including economic change and social and class pressures, which were enhanced by the impact of war. These factors did not have any direct causal impact, but depended on how actors within the state perceived the situation they faced. These perceptions depended on their own beliefs, ideologies, organisational goals and organisational capabilities.

Faced with new problems and issues, the development of new administrative capabilities depends on the historical and institutional position of the state actors involved. Hence, it is very difficult to make any general statements about the growth of the state. The British state has developed for various reasons at different times. In the nineteenth century it grew to deal with the problems of urbanisation and industrialisation. In the 1920s and 1940s, state growth was a response to war and in the post-war period it was the result of class pressure, social change and economic crisis. What has occurred is that the state has become a modern state with the capabilities and mechanisms for dealing with the problems of the twentieth century: total war; rapid economic and social change; and the development of transitional economies and increasing international interdependence.

The pressures and the consequent growth of the state have had a significant impact on the key institutions within the state – the core executive. As the state grows and its environment changes, so the resources of various institutions change. As the core executive has developed, resource-rich departments have become institutionalised. Consequently, a tension has developed between on the one hand departments trying to retain control over their policy areas and on the other central coordinators attempting to retain financial control and strategic capability. As economic problems have increased, there have been a number of attempts to shift resources from departments to the centre. As the book will demonstrate, this conflict is an issue that has not been resolved.

4 The Core of the Core: Relations between the Prime Minister and the Cabinet

Discussions concerning Prime Minister–cabinet relations have rarely been elevated above the issue of whether prime-ministerial government or – more recently – presidentialism has replaced cabinet government (see Thomas 1998). It is hard to question Peter Hennessy's view (1994: 437) that the debate is one of most 'pronounced sufferers' of the malaise of 'premature staleness' that affects topics of academic debate. In fact, the debate is essentially irresolvable, because its participants believe that power can be fixed to the cabinet or the Prime Minister, and therefore fail to understand the complexities of core executive relations. This chapter will break out of the intellectual impasse, by not focusing on the personality of the Prime Minister. Rather, it will argue that:

- the Prime Minister operates in a context that is structured by institutions and outside political and economic factors;
- the Prime Minister has more resources than other actors but is dependent on other actors and resource exchanges to achieve goals;
- other actors and institutions within the core executive have resources;
- because the Prime Minister is dependent on other actors, his or her success depends to some extent on strategies and tactics.

Therefore, to understand the power of the Prime Minister we need to understand the situation within which he or she acts, the resources available, how they are deployed and the success of the Prime Minister in building the necessary alliances.

The traditional debate is well rehearsed (see King 1985a, Crossman 1972, Thomas 1998, Hennessy 1994, Madgwick 1991, Kavanagh 1990 for a discussion) and therefore in this chapter I will pay it only brief attention. In the 1960s Mackintosh (1963) and Crossman (1963) questioned the view that the cabinet was any longer the site of real power. For Crossman, 'Every Minister is in a sense the Prime Minister's agent' (Crossman 1972: 163). In the 1980s, Thatcher was presented as the apotheosis of prime-ministerial government, but Foley (1992) goes further, suggesting that Thatcher was not exceptional but an indication of a more general shift to presidentialism in British politics.

On the other hand, the cabinet government perspective questions the degree of prime-ministerial government and maintains that the two key powers of the Prime Minister, appointment and determining the cabinet agenda, are severely constrained. Wakeham (1994), a minister in the Thatcher government, argues that, despite her style, cabinet government continued. Prime ministers need the support of the cabinet, they are often greatly constrained by the party and the cabinet, and they are severely limited in the extent to which they can sack colleagues (Brown 1968: 35, Jones 1985: 209, Alderman 1976, James 1992: 117–24). As Lawson (1994: 444) points out, 'There is a limit to the number of resignations that a Prime Minister can wear sensibly.'

This debate, informed by the Westminster model, oversimplifies the nature of power in the core executive, the extent to which power is fluid, and the way structure and context affect the actions of individuals and institutions. The Prime Minister's style may affect decisions and processes, but it is not the key determinant. As Barber (1984: 96) highlights:

> Thatcher's powers have fluctuated during her premiership, although her personality remains constant. Whether she was at her most powerful following the Falklands campaign, or being forced to modify her demands for public spending cuts, there was no doubting her determination and willingness to browbeat her ministers into submission, but her success varies according to the circumstances.

In a sense, the debate accepts the constitutional myth of collective responsibility, which sees the cabinet as the central decision-maker in government. The reality is that the majority of decisions, most of the time, are made elsewhere. The Prime Minister and cabinet are also operating in a world of constraints, which includes economic and political conditions, lack of time and information, organisational limits and other key actors both outside and inside the state. Power cannot be conceived as an object that belongs to the Prime Minister or the cabinet.

The prime-ministerial versus cabinet government debate misconceives the nature of relationships within the core executive. Who has power varies constantly, and depends not only on what resources are available but how they are used in particular circumstances, the structural situation of other actors and the wider political context. The crucial question is, how do the actors with resources play the game in order to achieve their goals? Lawson's experiences of cabinet provides some recognition of this variability (1994: 441–2):

> I suspect that the power of the Prime Minister does vary from Prime Minister to Prime Minister, and perhaps it also varies according to the political strength that a particular Prime Minister has at a given time. What was certainly observable during Margaret Thatcher's very long period in office . . . was that there was a steadily widening gulf between her and her cabinet colleagues, which made the process of cabinet government more and more difficult to achieve in a satisfactory way.

A more subtle understanding of power relationships within the core can be delineated in the existing literature (see King 1985a: 6–7). Barber, in particular, suggests a much more flexible way to examine the relationships between Prime Minister and cabinet:

> (a) A Prime Minister's power is likely to be greatest when he handles a crisis well or at the beginning of a ministry, especially if he has led his party out of opposition. (b) The powers of the Prime Ministers fluctuate during his period in office. (c) Individual setbacks do not usually threaten the Prime Minister's position as the head of government, but they can reduce his powers within the government. (d) In exceptional circumstances, a series of failures following one another can undermine a Prime Minister's position beyond recall.

Therefore, in the remainder of the chapter, conscious of the variability of prime-ministerial and cabinet power, I will present an explicitly complex account of the power in the core executive by examining the structure, resources and dependencies of the Prime Minister. The crucial question is not who has power, the Prime Minister or the cabinet, but what strategies and tactics they use to exchange resources?

RECONCEPTUALISING THE PRIME MINISTER

Rejecting the simplicities of the cabinet government debate, Burch and Holliday point to the importance of the rules, values and practices that maintain the British cabinet system. They argue that while these are undoubtedly open to interpretation, they are 'an important constraint upon all individual initiative' (1996: 49). Burch and Holliday thereby imply that the nature of government is not simply open to prime-ministerial whim. It is necessary, therefore, to develop an analytical framework for examining prime-ministerial power. Following the discussion in Chapter 2, it is important to assess the resources and constraints of the Prime Minister and evaluate the changing tactics that are used to deploy those resources.

The Prime Minister has a set of resources that are partly personal, deriving from his or her style and authority, and partly structural, deriving from the office. The resources on their own are not sufficient for achieving goals, and therefore the Prime Minister is involved in processes of exchange, usually with ministers, but also with officials, advisors and to some extent MPs. The process of exchange also depends on the external context. If the political circumstances are favourable then the Prime Minister is less dependent on colleagues, but the extent of dependency will vary according to the resources controlled by ministers, which again depend on their context. Finally, the external context and the resources of ministers affect the tactics and strategies of the Prime Minister and the minister. The Prime Minister has to use the tactics that are appropriate to his or her degree of dependence. If a minister is in a weak position then the Prime Minister may be able to order a particular policy; if he is strong, the Prime Minister may have to build an alliance or co-opt the minister. At the same time, ministers have strategies that they can use to control the Prime Minister, including building coalitions, leaking information, threatening to resign or offering support for the Prime Minister. The crucial point is that the Prime Ministers operates in a structured context. It is structured by: the institutions of the core executive; the networks that relate the Prime Minister to the cabinet and officials; the rules of the Whitehall game; and the external political and economic

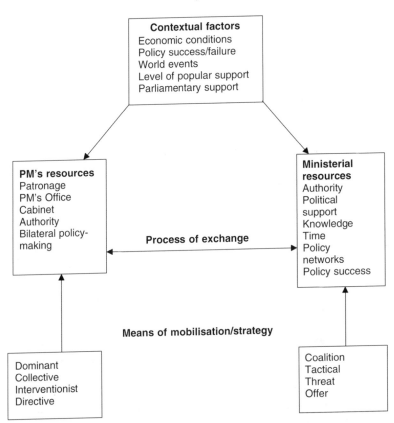

Figure 4.1   A model of prime-ministerial power

situation. Within these structures the Prime Minister makes choices. To some extent the choices may be affected by personality, but personality does not determine the nature of the Prime Minister's power.

Resources

In order to understand the role of the Prime Minister in the core executive and the basis of his or her relations with the cabinet, we have to outline the available resources. As we saw above, there are two types of resources – formal and informal. The formal resources of the Prime Minister are well illustrated by the traditional debate and cover: the powers of appointment; control, to some extent, of the cabinet agenda; appointment of the chairs and membership of cabinet committees; and the Prime Minister's office, which provides both administrative support and some ability to develop strategic oversight. Of course, these resources are only capabilities, not powers. The more informal resources of the Prime Minister include an overview of government, the ability to intervene in any policy area, and authority. This general oversight is particularly important, because of the segmented nature of British government, and it provides the Prime Minister with a holistic view of government unavailable to other ministers concerned with departmental interests.

Ministers are constrained from playing a collective role in government by a number of factors:

- Cabinet is confined largely to rubber-stamping decisions rather developing a strategic overview of government. Gilmour (1992) points out that in the first year of the Thatcher Conservative government there was no discussion of the government's economic policy, and Young (1989) reveals the absence of cabinet debate over either of the controversial budgets of 1980 and 1981. Hennessy (1986, 1998) highlights the decline in the amount of business that was decided at cabinet level under Thatcher, and how the decline has continued under Blair.
- Ministers often do not have the interest, time or ability to be involved in other areas of policy. Ministers are very much concerned with the work of their own departments, which is where they will succeed or fail. Consequently, most of their time and energy is focused inwardly. They do not read papers of other departments if they feel it has no implications for their own department (Headey 1974). Healey (1990: 326–7) reveals that when he was Defence Secretary he found the work all-consuming and that his colleagues were:

> content to let me get on with my job, so long as I did not interfere with theirs. So for a long time I played little part in Cabinet discussions about domestic issues in which my department was not directly concerned.

- According to Castle (1980), cabinet is not an arena for strategic decision-making but for fighting for departmental interests. Ironically, this can produce acquiescence rather than conflict. Ministers may be unwilling to speak out against proposals for fear that a colleague may later speak out against them (Crossman 1975: 47, 202).

These institutional constraints on collective action place the Prime Minister in a structurally advantageous position. The Prime Minister is at the centre of the networks that traverse the core executive and therefore he or she has access to all areas of government. He or she is able to define the strategic direction of a government and consequently to define what does not fit into that strategy. More importantly, it enables the Prime Minister to choose areas of policy involvement, indicating how style may affect policy. Wilson tended to set the broad parameters of policy (Kogan 1971, Wilson 1976), whereas Thatcher liked to work bilaterally with ministers in areas that she saw as important. Most Prime Ministers are involved in economic and foreign policy on a more or less continual basis. For example, economic policy and the budget are generally developed through a complex process of interaction between Number 10 and Number 11. Therefore, the Prime Minister has a view of government that is not available to other ministers.

The second informal resource of the Prime Minister is authority. This concept is difficult to define, and it is not always clear whether authority belongs to the person or the office. Authority can be seen as an acceptance of power without needing to exercise any formal capabilities. It is the voluntary submission to legitimate power (Wrong 1988). A crucial rule of the Whitehall game is that ministers and civil servants accept the authority of the Prime Minister which allows him to command actions. Ministers accept the Prime Minister's right to intervene in departmental policy and the Prime Minister's views are given greater weight than those of other ministers.

Nevertheless, unlike other resources that are fairly objective, prime-ministerial authority is largely relational and will depend on the position of the Prime Minister. In particular, the Prime Minister has greatest authority after an electoral victory, and particularly if it is an unexpected one:

Winning the general election against all expectations enormously boosted Heath's self-confidence . . . Not only was he prime minister but he was prime minister with no debts to anyone and a clear personal mandate to impose his new authority on those who had sniped at him for so long . . . His personal authority was actually greater than it would have been had he entered Downing Street a year or two earlier on the back of a sweeping and predicted Tory landslide (Campbell 1993: 289).

Thatcher's authority was greatest after the Falklands victory and the subsequent landslide election victory in 1983. These successes allowed her to remove most of her critics from cabinet, and according to King (1985b) allowed her 'to put her stamp on an extraordinarily wide range of policy decisions'. Major's problem in 1990 was a lack of authority. Although winning the Conservative leadership election in that year gave him some authority, he was not seen as his own man. His electoral mandate was won by Thatcher, and initially she constantly reminded the new Prime Minister that he was there to implement her agenda. This situation limited his cabinet and policy options. For a long period, Major was in a position of reacting to problems like the poll tax and ERM membership rather than setting his own agenda. Tony Blair's position is very different. Such was the size of Labour's victory in 1997, which was attributed largely to Blair, that the new Prime Minister has sufficient authority to force through new policies with little criticism. To some extent he is able to stand above some of the problems of his own government.

Despite the Prime Minister's formal and informal resources, it is necessary to examine resource exchange that results from dependency to understand prime-ministerial power. Even with an array of institutional resources and the authority of the office a Prime Minister can achieve nothing on her or his own. In order to translate capabilities into power she or he is dependent on others for advice, information, support, and assistance in making policy. Ministers and civil servants have their own resources. Perhaps, most importantly, ministers have their own sources of authority. For some senior ministers, their authority is such that it is almost impossible for a Prime Minister to dismiss them. For example, in the period around 1987–8 Nigel Lawson was in an exceptionally strong position. As Chancellor of the Exchequer he had significant institutional resources through control of the Treasury and of economic policy. He was seen as the architect of Britain's economic revival and consequently had tremendous authority within the Tory Party (Watkins 1991: 96). Moreover, as he had little ambition to be Prime Minister he could take political risks. Lawson's stock rose further with his radical, tax-cutting 1988 budget, which delivered a balanced budget and cuts in taxation. Consequently, despite major disagreements between Thatcher and Lawson, he was, in the

Prime Minister's word, 'unassailable'. Thatcher admitted to Kenneth Baker that she could not have sacked Lawson because 'I might well have had to go as well' (Thatcher quoted in Baker 1993: 315).

Not only is a Prime Minister confronted with ministerial resources, he or she is also highly dependent on the cabinet for his or her authority. Because it is based on legitimacy, authority exists only while it is recognised, and therefore a Prime Minister's authority can extend only as far as the cabinet will allow. This can be seen most starkly in the case of Thatcher's resignation, where the cabinet effectively removed the Prime Minister's authority. Thatcher would have gone on to a second ballot in the leadership contest had she not realised that cabinet support was slipping away. She admits in her memoirs that once she was convinced that she had lost cabinet support she decided not to stand in the second round:

> a Prime Minister who knows that his or her cabinet has withheld its support is fatally weakened. I knew – and I am sure that they knew – that I would not willingly remain an hour in 10 Downing Street without the real authority to govern (Thatcher 1993: 851).

Structure

The resources of the Prime Minister and their use are conditioned by the structural situation. Structure conditions in two ways: internally and externally. Internally, within the core executive, the resources of the Prime Minister and his or her relationship to other actors are conditioned by the rules and institutions of the central state. The position of the Prime Minister is located within a particular set of relationships to other actors and with a certain set of resources. However, these structures do not exist independently of actors and, therefore, the nature of these structures is determined by the perceptions of the Prime Minister and other key actors. Their choices affect the nature of the core executive relationships and the use of resources. Prime ministers can avoid making decisions in cabinet or cabinet committee, if the Prime Minister and other actors perceive other forms of decision-making as legitimate.

Thatcher also restructured the relationship between the Prime Minister and Parliament. Dunleavy and Jones highlight how Thatcher's interventions in Parliament declined rapidly as she tended not to participate in debates or make Parliamentary speeches. Although this behaviour was associated with Thatcher in particular, Dunleavy and

Jones (1995) conclude: 'Prime ministerial activity in the Commons has decreased overall and narrowed down to a few forms of participation' (pp. 295–6). Although Major may have made more interventions than Thatcher, he did not return to the activism of the 1950s and 1960s.

This reconstruction of the rules is what Giddens (1986) calls structuration. Individual behaviour has reconstituted the rules of the games and this reconstitution is reproduced by the behaviour of succeeding Prime Ministers. The resources of Prime Ministers are structurally determined, but Prime Ministers are reflexive agents who can change the rules of the game and reinterpret them. This capacity to implement changes was emphasised in May 1997, when Blair shifted question time to a once-a-week, half-hourly session on Wednesdays. However, there are obvious limits to the changes that are permitted. For instance, neither Blair nor Thatcher were able to stop attending Prime Minister's questions. Some rules, therefore, are extremely difficult to change. Moreover, Prime Ministers may be limited to changes that are acceptable to other actors with resources. Thatcher's rejection of cabinet government was not accepted by colleagues, and a number of sources reveal that it was when she stopped relying on senior cabinet ministers for support and advice, turning instead to her political advisers, that she began to lose cabinet support (Lawson 1994, Howe 1994, Young 1989). The bypassing of cabinet was not acceptable to her senior colleagues and was a major factor in her resignation (see p. 97 above). She attempted to change the rules but, in the end, was constrained by the structure.

Externally, the office of the Prime Minister is structured by a whole range of constraints such as the structure of the world financial markets, the limits of state intervention, the limits of taxable income, or what the voters sees as acceptable prime-ministerial behaviour. However, the nature of these constraints varies. For example, the world economy moving from a period of recession to one of expansion or vice versa will affect the options available to government, so that the British government was able to pursue a policy of full employment within the structure of the post-war boom, and has been prevented from pursuing such a policy since the collapse of that boom in the mid-1970s.

It is also important to remember that structures are not completely determinate. Structural constraints do not force a particular action, but shape a range of options. If foreign investors are selling sterling the government does not have to raise interest rates, but if they choose not to then it may have to pay the costs of ignoring the markets. More realistically, other countries have adjusted to new world economic conditions while maintaining full employment by making certain policy choices.

One of the best examples of structural limits on the behaviour of the Prime Minister is Wilson's decision not to devalue sterling in 1964–7. Stones (1990: 38) emphasises how:

> the pound's use as an international investment currency meant that Britain was tied into a network of vertical interdependence with overseas investors. These holders of sterling possessed the potential power to withdraw their investment and so cause a run on the pound.

The problem lay in Britain's liabilities, which were greater than the reserves. If there was a run on the pound then the government would have been forced into a massive deflation in order to meet its liabilities. As a consequence, despite economic problems, devaluation was not perceived as an option, because the loss of confidence would have caused such a run, leading to an uncontrolled devaluation. However, as Stones points out, devaluation was rejected not just because of the structural constraints but because the Labour government and Prime Minister believed in maintaining welfare spending and increasing demand to end the stop-go economic cycle (Stones 1990). The problem for the Prime Minister was how to maintain Labour's economic and welfare commitments while also ensuring the confidence of the financial markets. The problem

> placed the government in a dilemma because the deflationary conditions which were required by the international financiers in order that they should continue to support sterling were in direct conflict with the policy of sustained reflation which was at the heart of Labour's strategic ideals (Stones 1990: 41).

As Wilson explicitly states in his memoirs:

> until we were in surplus it meant that every action we took had to be considered against a background of the confidence factor, particularly against an assessment of what speculators might do. It meant, and this is not only inhibiting but humiliating for any Government, that things we had decided to do, right in themselves – for example, an increase in old-age pensions, even as late as 1969, when we were

moving into surplus – had to be timed in such a way as to minimize possible speculative consequences (Wilson 1974: 59).

The constraints on Wilson, therefore, resulted from a combination of his perception of what was normatively desirable and the pressures deriving from Britain's position in the international financial markets.

These structural constraints affect Conservative governments as much as they affect Labour ones. To some extent they are less of a problem for Conservatives, because the policies necessary to ensure confidence are often policies that they ideologically favour. Even so, the political goals of Conservative Prime Ministers are sometimes constrained by the currency markets. For instance, Thatcher was very keen to keep inflation down. However, she was often loath to accept that this required raising interest rates, because of the electoral consequences of higher mortgage repayments. Prime ministers are continually faced by competing constraints. Rose and Davies (1994:1) highlight how policy-makers inherit programmes, budgets and institutions from previous administrations, so that it is wrong to see government as carried out by 'individual decisionmakers who have as much freedom of choice as an individual in a shopping mall trying to decide whether to have a pizza or an ice cream cone'. Whatever the 'style' or personality of the Prime Minister, he or she operates within a structured situation which limits options. The prime minister is not free to choose according to personal whim.

An important constraint on the Prime Minister is the capability of the state machinery. There is a limit to what the state can do, thus constraining the policy options of a Prime Minister. Skocpol (1985) points out that states have capabilities that are related to financial, administrative and political resources and therefore policy goals that are beyond the state's capabilities cannot be achieved. British governments have had great difficulty in intervening in industry in order to achieve higher economic growth, because they have lacked the administrative machinery or the ability to control key economic groups (Hall 1986). In addition, there are biases within the state that mean it is better suited to fulfilling some tasks rather than others, and thus certain outcomes occur despite the intentions of the Prime Minister. Jessop highlights how (1990: 250) 'the instrumentality of the state can no longer be understood; it is necessarily "biased" or selective and can never be equally accessible to all forces and equally available for all purposes . . .' For instance, the Labour government is unlikely to consider nationalisation as a solution to an economic problem, because they are unlikely to be advised by civil servants that it is a viable option; there will be a lack of political support; and the financial costs of confronting the private sector are too high. After a long period of Conservative rule, the state is biased against nationalisation as a policy. This bias does not mean it is not an option (it is a bias) – the government was prepared to consider nationalisation in order to build the high-speed channel tunnel rail link – but choosing that option for most areas of private industry would involve high costs in terms of prevailing against the biases of the state machinery and most of the key actors within the core executive.

The impact of political constraints was illustrated by Thatcher's failure to reduce public expenditure. The 1980 Public Expenditure White Paper stated that 'The Government intend to reduce public expenditure progressively in volume terms over the next few years' (*The Government's Expenditure Plans*, Cmnd 7841 1980). Yet, according to Hogwood (1992: 41):

> Despite the commitment of the government to public expenditure restraint, expenditure growth continued after 1979, though at a decelerating rate before falling by 0.7 per cent in 1987 and 1.2 per cent in 1988. Public expenditure growth has subsequently resumed, with an increase of 2.9 per cent in 1989 and 0.2 per cent in 1990.

This failure to contain public expenditure lies in a combination of economic, political and state constraints. Economic recessions involved increased social security payments and reduced income from taxation. Political pressures made it difficult for the government to cut expenditure in a range of welfare services. Indeed, key members of the cabinet strongly objected to the size of the public expenditure cuts in the 1980 budget. Perhaps the greatest constraints were the policies embedded in the structures of the state, which increased expenditure beyond the control of government. For example, education and health policies are more or less demand-led and consequently expenditure would increase unless radical changes in policy occurred. The way external structural factors constrain governments is illustrated in the International Monetary Fund (IMF) crisis of 1976 and Britain's ejection from the European Exchange Rate Mechanism (ERM) in 1992 (see Boxes 4.1 and 4.2).

It is important not to see the events depicted in Boxes 4.1 and 4.2 as simple cases of structural determination. They highlight the complexity of power and the difficulty of identifying winners and losers. While,

during these crises, the power of the Prime Minister relative to policy
options was reduced, relative to the rest of the cabinet, the power and
autonomy of the Prime Minister increased. Callaghan used the IMF
crisis to assert his control over economic policy. He also used it as an
opportunity to force policies on the cabinet that he wanted to adopt
anyway. Ludlam (1992) believes that many of the policies explicitly
adopted as result of IMF intervention had already become part of the
Labour government's programme. The structural problems with the
British economy occurred before the events of 1976, and Healey and
Callaghan were already convinced of the need to reduce public
expenditure, public borrowing and inflation. The cover of the IMF
was an opportunity for forcing a recalcitrant cabinet, dominated by

---

BOX 4.1
**Structural constraints on government: the case of the IMF
crisis, 1976**

The IMF crisis was a culmination of pressures from a range of
structural forces. The inflationary shocks of the first oil price hike
in 1974 were still rippling through the British economy; labour
productivity was declining; the government was spending a dis-
proportionate amount of income on overseas defence and having
great difficulty in controlling public expenditure overall. In addition, 'sterling was still the world's second reserve currency, after
the dollar; so changes of sentiment in the foreign exchange
markets were often greatly exaggerated by the movements of
reserves into or out of Britain' (Healey 1990: 411). Consequently,
the 1970s witnessed a series of currency crises (see for instance
Haines 1977). In 1976 pressure was particularly intense, because in
order to restore the confidence of the financial markets, the
Labour government requested a loan from the IMF. The IMF
would provide the loan only if the government agreed to certain
conditions, initially a £2 billion cut in public expenditure in order
to reduce the public sector borrowing requirement (PSBR). The
final agreement resulted in the government selling shares in BP
and £1 billion of cuts. In order to maintain confidence, the party
had little option other than to abandon many of its policy
commitments (see Coates 1980).

Keynesians and the left, to adopt policies that they would otherwise have opposed. This example raises two important theoretical points: when faced by what are seen as irresistible structural forces, there is still room for manoeuvre; and structural forces provide opportunities as well as constraints (Giddens 1986). External pressures can affect the distribution of resources between actors and therefore may place certain actors in a different position and open up various new courses of action.

These factors arose again in the case of Black Wednesday (Box 4.2). The collapse of the pound might have been avoided had it been devalued earlier, but Lamont consciously chose not to make that decision. Indeed, there is some suggestion that Lamont was opposed to ERM membership and that he may therefore have used the crisis to precipitate the pound's exit from the system.

Context, dependency and tactics

Prime Ministers (and other actors within the core executive) have resources, and they are constrained by structures. The basis of prime-ministerial power within the confines of structural constraints is the process of exchanging resources. If a Prime Minister wants to exercise power then he or she is dependent on his or her colleagues. Ministers need the Prime Minister's patronage and support. A minister is much more likely to be successful *vis-à-vis* the cabinet and the Treasury if the Prime Minister explicitly backs him/her. Michael Forsyth, although only a junior minister, was successful at forcing reluctant departments to produce citizen's charters because the policy was closely associated with John Major (Hogg and Hill 1995).

Prime Ministers are also dependent on the support of the cabinet. Thatcher's appointment of her first cabinet highlights her awareness of the need to maintain support from key figures in the party. She had worked with Heathites in opposition and kept a number in cabinet. Moreover, in achieving her economic goals, Thatcher was highly dependent on her Chancellor and the Treasury team. It was Geoffrey Howe and Nigel Lawson who devised the medium-term financial strategy, and Howe was prepared to implement it, despite hostility from many quarters. Without the Chancellor's support it would have been unlikely that the cabinet would have accepted the economic strategy. Thatcher's relationship and exchange of resources with the Chancellor was extremely important in terms of the Prime Minister achieving her policy preferences.

BOX 4.2
Exit from the ERM, 1992

During, and following, the 1992 election the Prime Minister and the Chancellor, Norman Lamont, maintained that membership of the Exchange Rate Mechanism was a central pillar of the government's economic policy (Thompson 1996b). However, on Black Wednesday, 16 September 1992, the government was forced to leave the ERM because of a series of events that were beyond their control:

- The pound was in a structurally weak position. The rate of the pound within the ERM was £1 to 2.85 Deutschmarks (DM), which many considered too high. This was made worse by the deep recession affecting the British economy which, in a situation of free-floating exchange rates, would have ordinarily resulted in the pound being devalued.
- US interest rates were exceptionally low at 3 per cent and German rates exceptionally high at 10 per cent. The result was that investors moved from dollars to DM and as a consequence the DM rose relative to the pound.
- The events took place in the immediate run-up to the French referendum on the Maastricht Treaty, and a number of polls indicated the French would vote no. With a no vote the ERM would have collapsed. Dealers believed this would result in the end of tough, anti-inflation policies and split EC currencies between the weak and the strong. Sterling was perceived as weak and therefore would fall in value. Dealers, therefore, sold weak currencies to buy strong currencies.
- The Italian lira was perceived as particularly weak and there were strong indications that the lira would be devalued. Consequently, a large number of small investors bought DMs with lira, gambling on its devaluation. The sale of lira also had the effect of raising the value of the Deutschmark.
- The president of the Bundesbank made a statement indicating that he thought certain currencies within the ERM would have to be devalued. The markets believed this comment was aimed at sterling.

Shortly before Black Wednesday, the Bank of England had spent £10 billion trying to defend sterling, to no avail. The German and

French central banks were also buying sterling. On Black Wednesday itself, in order to stop sterling leaving the ERM, interest rates were initially raised by 2 per cent and the Bank of England was 'buying pounds at a rate of tens of millions every few minutes' (Stephens 1996: 149). But the Bank did not have the resources to compete with the international markets. Its foreign exchange holdings were only 10 per cent of the daily turnover of the foreign exchange markets, and speculators knew the pound would be devalued and that even within a few hours they would be able to buy back the sterling they had sold at a large profit (Stephens 1996). The government had no choice but to leave the ERM.

In this situation, a combination of events beyond the government's control, particularly the activities of the foreign exchange markets, forced the government into taking action that it opposed. Stephens suggests that, for the ministers involved in the events, 'the overwhelming emotion was of disbelieving impotence . . . Still later it was said that nothing could be done – that the government was no more than the victim of events' (Stephens 1996: 245). Decisions made in the US, Germany and France effectively resulted in the exit of sterling from the ERM.

Even with this support, the Prime Minister suffered significant defeats. Patrick Jenkin cleverly prevented the loss of £600 million from the social security budget and Pym reduced the proposed cut in defence spending (Wapshott and Brock 1983, Young 1989). In 1981 the cabinet demonstrated the limits of its tolerance when faced with a demand for more cuts in public spending even after the highly deflationary 1981 budget. Young (1989: 218) conveys how:

> After a swingeing budget, and against a backdrop of civil breakdown – even as the Cabinet met, the Toxteth district of Liverpool was recovering from another night of highly publicized violence between police and unemployed youths – [Howe] presented a paper which solemnly announced a preliminary demand that next year's spending should be cut by £5,000 million.

The response was a rebellion in the cabinet which spread beyond the Wets (the left within the cabinet) to Thatcher loyalists such as John Biffen and John Nott (Young 1989) and the paper was withdrawn.

This example highlights the importance of both context and tactics. The degree of dependency and the need to exchange resources will depend on the context. If the external context is favourable to the Prime Minister, in terms of economic policy or electorally, then the Prime Minister has less dependence on the cabinet. If the external context is less favourable then the Prime Minister requires more support.

Success in achieving policy goals for both ministers and the Prime Minister will depend on tactics. How resources are deployed is an important aspect of power. The tactical deployment of resource can allow minister, in certain situations, with relatively few resources to defeat the Prime Minister or more highly resourced ministers. The three most recent Prime Ministers have had very different strategies and tactics. Thatcher's strategy was generally interventionist, Major was more collectivist, and Blair's appears directive (see Table 4.1).

Thatcher wanted to intervene very closely in the working of departments. As Lord Young confirmed in an interview, Thatcher's impact on the department was:

> Absolutely enormous. I used to be in fear and trembling when I went to see her as she somehow knew more about my department than I did. She worked incredibly hard and had an incredible capacity for detail. It was very difficult to get anything over her, very difficult.

Patrick Jenkin also accepted that Thatcher had an enormous effect on departments, especially compared with Edward Heath. One former

Table 4.1   Strategies and tactics of Prime Ministers

	Thatcher	*Major*	*Blair*
Strategy	Interventionist	Collectivist	Directive
Tactics	Use of small groups of ministers to build support for her goals Bilateral meetings with ministers	Working with cabinet to build consensus Delaying decisions until support	Use of PM's Office and Cabinet Office to develop strategic direction Cabinet Minister to ensure ministers follow direction

official in the Department of Education said that 'There were occasions in my time in education when policy pronouncements emerged from Number 10 of which we were totally unaware.'

Thatcher adopted a highly tactical approach in achieving her policy goals. When she was in an ideological minority in her first cabinet, she achieved a largely monetarist economic policy by sidelining economic policy into a cabinet committee where her ideological comrades were in the majority. Thatcher's strength was based on a dry coalition in key cabinet committees, and through her alliance with Howe she was able to dictate the rules of the game in order to achieve her policy goals.

Later, when she found increasing opposition in cabinet, Thatcher's tactic was to operate entirely outside the cabinet system. She depended on her political advisers for support and influenced policy by operating bilaterally with ministers who were not in a position to resist her demands. In Lawson's view, after her the problems of the Westland Helicopter affair (see Box 5.2):

> The lesson that Margaret took from it was that her colleagues were troublesome and her courtiers loyal. From then on she began to distance herself from colleagues who had been closest to her – certainly those who had minds of their own – and to retreat to the Number 10 bunker, where the leading figures were Charles Powell and Bernard Ingham (Lawson 1992: 680).

In an interview Lord Wakeham offered a slightly different interpretation of Thatcher's tactics:

> She would have an idea, or somebody would, and she would talk to them. She would bring two or three people in for the second meeting and we'd discuss it a bit further and I was usually one of those who were pretty close to her for most of the time and the idea would be talked about. She and I would then identify those in the cabinet who had the most concerns about that policy and then they were talked to . . . so they were brought in and when you have built that you then have something that you can put to a cabinet subcommittee get it agreed and by the time it came to the cabinet it was a *fait accompli*.

Both Wakeham and Jenkin deny that this was overruling the cabinet, and both believe Thatcher was frequently defeated in cabinet. Former cabinet ministers and officials have admitted that Thatcher was prepared to back down on issues. Indeed, she realised that she could lose and so ensured that she had support before issues went to cabinet or cabinet committee.

Ministers have a strong incentive for working with the Prime Minister. If a minister is to be successful, it is useful to have the Prime Minister on his or her side. Nigel Lawson revealed in an interview that:

> The Prime Minister's main power is the veto and that was the main way that the Prime Minister exercises his or her power. The Prime Minister basically cannot force her proposal on a minister who is not prepared to go along with it but they have a very effective power of veto.

As a minister can be vetoed, it is important to secure the Prime Minister's support. But because the Prime Minister cannot force a policy on a minister, he or she needs to build an alliance to influence policy. Even a dominant Prime Minister, like Thatcher, was dependent on colleagues in order to intervene. In the first phase of her administration Thatcher was effective at building alliances in order to achieve her goals.

Thatcher's second tactic was to use the Deputy Prime Minister, William Whitelaw, and then John Wakeham, leader of the House of Commons, as conduits and negotiators between her and cabinet. Patrick Jenkin recalled that it was:

> often Willy's job to say, 'PM I think you have to accept that your colleagues are not with you on this'. She didn't like it but she had to accept it [and] sometimes he would go to his colleagues and say, 'look I realise that most of us do not agree with her but on an issue like this she is entitled to have her way so belt up'.

Whitelaw was very important to Thatcher, because he could judge what the cabinet would bear and would inform her accordingly. Likewise, Wakeham saw himself as 'a fixer' who could negotiate on behalf of Thatcher in order to achieve her goals.

Despite Thatcher's desire to intervene, she was adept at judging when to leave certain ministers alone. She realised that Whitelaw, as Deputy Prime Minster, was not very dependent on her, and so he had considerable autonomy in the Home Office. Similarly, although Peter Walker was Thatcher's ideological opponent he was allowed a high degree of autonomy, as he related in an interview:

The fact is that I was in a stronger position with her than others because she wanted me to stay in cabinet and she knew I was not someone who pleaded for office and would have happily left. I was independent of her and therefore I had a stronger position than somebody who was a keen supporter of all she was standing for who was hoping to please her.

Thatcher was more dependent on ministers like Whitelaw, Walker and, at certain times, Lawson, than they were on her, and so they had considerable freedom and, in Whitelaw's and Lawson's case, influence. Consequently, even a Prime Minister with a dominant style who wants to intervene needs to understand the lines of dependence and work out tactics accordingly.

Major was clearly in a very different structural position to Thatcher on becoming Prime Minister. He lacked an independent electoral mandate and the economy was in recession. Consequently he adopted a different strategy. Thatcher was removed from office because she would not listen and ignored her lines of dependency. Therefore the new Prime Minister was expected to be more collegiate and Major obliged. He was concerned with reasserting cabinet government. In Anthony Seldon's (1997: 738) assessment:

> Major by temperament and choice was a conciliator. Before he became Prime Minister, he had found Mrs Thatcher's style of 'macho leadership' personally distasteful. His chairmanship of Cabinet and Cabinet committees, in contrast, allowed ministers to express their views, and guided them to a conclusion in line with his intentions. Rather than have dissent in the Cabinet he preferred to delay decisions until he could reconcile differences.

This strategy derived not so much from Major's personality but was a response to the circumstances.

As Seldon (1997: 742) suggests, 'Major's leadership could be argued to have been exactly what was required for the times.' With the removal of Thatcher, it became clear that the party and the cabinet had competing visions of Conservatism, and Major had to try to keep the cabinet together. Baker records in his memoirs:

> John's style of chairing the cabinet was quite different from Margaret's. John encouraged discussion and elicited colleagues' views . . .

One of John's great talents is his skill in handling difficult meetings and teasing out a consensus (Baker 1993: 427).

Hogg and Hill (1995: 12–13) also recount how, in the Thatcher cabinet,

After the traditional tour of the Foreign Office horizon silence would have been the norm. Margaret Thatcher did not encourage discussion. But now [under John Major] Michael Heseltine spoke up, with a comment on Jordan . . . Then Tom King, as Defence Secretary, came in again . . . One minister said afterwards, 'Suddenly we are having our first real discussion for years.'

It is also apparent that Major was very dependent on his senior colleagues. In the early period, he depended on Chris Patten and later on Kenneth Clarke and Michael Heseltine, and throughout on Tony Newton (Seldon 1997). It would have been difficult for Major to ignore their views. Indeed, it appears that Major's dependence on Heseltine increased as his administration progressed. According to Jonathan Hill, 'The truth of their relationship has been that each realised their interdependence' (quoted in Seldon 1997: 602).

Nevertheless, one former cabinet minister suggested in an interview that Major's tactics were not very effective:

John Major tended to do things which I think hampered the decision-making process. One was the chairer, very good, but he would intervene too early. That made it difficult to have a rational discussion if the PM had put his cards on the table. Mrs Thatcher never did that, she was much cleverer in doing things than that. The second thing was that he would have a meeting, not made up of a little group to discuss it, like Mrs Thatcher did, but a bilateral meeting with the minister concerned and often agree to things without having thought the issues through, or had the arguments exposed to him, and the result was the Prime Minister then proceeded through the cabinet system with less caution than he should have had as they thought they had the Prime Minister on their side.

Major's problem was that he was too close to decisions, and so he was associated with policy failures. As the same ex-minister said:

John was superb at summing up a cabinet discussion and finding a consensus. John would find the point of equilibrium, agree it and support it . . . Margaret would find maybe the same equilibrium and turn to the minister and say 'OK we'll do it your way – but you had better be right'. In other words she kept the high ground for herself despite having reached a decision.

The problem for Major's collectivism was that his colleagues could blame him for the decision saying they would have done things differently. It was the cabinet, rather than the Prime Minister, which was disassociated from the decision.

Blair's strategy appears to be one of setting an overall policy direction with the cabinet – but very much under his leadership – and then ensuring that the departments follow the broad policy outline. This approach can be seen clearly in the area of welfare reform, where Blair set the broad parameters of policy and was centrally involved in selling it to the party and the public. Once the broad agenda has been set Blair has used Peter Mandelson, and to a lesser extent Lord Irvine, the Lord Chancellor, to ensure that departments are acting in the collective interest of the government. This strategy is useful for the Prime Minister, because he can seem not to be interfering directly himself and therefore is not blamed for policy problems. In July 1998 this coordination process was further institutionalised with the creation of a Cabinet post to act as an enforcer of collective decision-making located in the Cabinet Office.

However, it also appears that Blair is aware of his dependencies. Two ministers, Gordon Brown and John Prescott, are in well-established positions. Brown agreed not to challenge Blair for the leadership of the Party and so Blair owes his position, to some extent, to Brown, who at the time of writing is probably the one cabinet minister who could challenge Blair. As a result of Brown's support for Blair, he has been given control of the government's economic strategy (Draper 1997: 30) and this has given the Treasury a significant input into the welfare reform strategy. According to Draper (1997: 29):

> Blair knows that his relationship with Brown is a key factor when it comes to the government's success. It is much closer than the usual relationship for a Prime Minister and Chancellor, and the two heavyweights regularly discuss matters that go well beyond the Treasury remit.

Labour's position on membership of European Monetary Union (EMU) is very much a result of policy worked out between Blair and Brown. Indeed, it could be that Blair and Brown are more interdependent than most previous Prime Ministers and Chancellors. Blair can articulate and sell their vision of welfare reform, and Brown has the capability to provide the economic means of reform. However, Ken Livingstone proposes a counter view. He suggests Brown had no chance of winning the leadership contest and has not run the economy particularly well. As a result Blair is not dependent on Brown at all (*Independent on Sunday*, 7 June 1998).

Prescott is also in a strong position in relation to the Prime Minister. He was elected by the party as deputy leader and is seen as protecting the compassionate heart of 'old' Labour. He also provides a useful function for Blair in that he can often convince the party membership that key policy changes, such as trade union reform and not renationalising the railways, are not at odds with Labour's principles. Prescott has too much party support and is too important in that position for Blair to be able to remove him easily.

It is not only Prime Ministers who can win with astute tactics. One of the best examples of ministerial tactics was when, in 1996, the Minister for Overseas Development, Lynda Chalker was faced with a large cut in ODA expenditure. The department sent out a press release outlining how the proposed cuts in the budget would mean a 5 per cent cut in ODA expenditure and the lowest level of expenditure ever on overseas aid. Indeed, the department pointed out that with the Fundamental Expenditure Review the real cut in expenditure would be 16 per cent. The department then encouraged non-governmental organisations (NGOs) to lobby the Treasury and the Prime Minister, pointing out how many projects would be affected by these cuts. As a consequence of the lobbying, the cuts were restored.

Ministers are probably in the strongest position to tackle the Prime Minister when their authority is high and when they are less dependent on the Prime Minister. As we see below, in the period between 1987 and 1988 Lawson was almost impregnable as Chancellor, and so when Thatcher vetoed membership of the ERM, Lawson effectively bypassed the decision by shadowing the Deutschmark. He placed an unofficial ceiling of DM3 and a floor of DM 2.80, and instructed the Bank of England to buy and sell sterling accordingly. In her memoirs, Thatcher concedes that she would have been within her rights to sack Lawson but also recognises the strength of his position (Thatcher 1993: 703). Lawson's resources – in terms of his control over the Treasury and the Bank of England, and his political authority – enabled him to implement a policy that was directly counter to the wishes of the Prime Minister. Despite Thatcher's strength in 1987, she was still dependent on her Chancellor in the field of economic policy.

Finally, Thatcher did force Lawson to abandon the policy. However, this resulted in Lawson effectively forcing Thatcher towards the ERM by building an alliance with Geoffrey Howe. Stephens (1996: 114) illustrates how, despite widespread criticism of Thatcher's style and policies within the government, ministers rarely worked together to try to defeat her. However, Lawson and Howe, in the events surrounding the Madrid European Community summit in 1989, demonstrated how effective a coalition can be for ministers *vis-à-vis* the Prime Minister. They implicitly threatened to resign unless Thatcher made a specific commitment to join the ERM. Thatcher said nothing to them at the time, but in Madrid she did specify the conditions under which Britain would join the ERM (although in her memoirs Thatcher says they did not resign, even though she never met their demands). Thatcher was in a weak position and it is unlikely that she could have survived the resignation of two of her senior ministers, and her position was weakened further by the poor showing of the party in the polls. Even a dominant Prime Minister such as Thatcher could not resist the weight of such an alliance and she was forced to concede.

What is also apparent is that the tactics Prime Ministers use vary greatly and depend on their resources and their perception of their resources. Again, if we compare the ERM crisis with the IMF crisis, we see very different tactics were employed. Callaghan's position was difficult in that there were some authoritative figures, such as Denis Healey, Tony Crosland and Tony Benn, in cabinet. Moreover, a number of distinct coalitions evolved around alternative ways of tackling the issue. On the left, Benn, Peter Shore and Michael Foot argued that the cabinet should resist the IMF and instead introduce a system of import controls (see Benn 1989). A second group, based around Crosland and supported by Shirley Williams, argued the government should present a Keynesian defence against the IMF, arguing that severe cuts at a time of recession were the wrong policy option. The third group, centred around the Chancellor, Healey, and including Joel Barnett and Edmund Dell, acknowledged the need for large cuts in public expenditure in order to obtain the IMF loan and to restore confidence in the markets. Callaghan presented himself as neutral, but his tactic was to split the Keynesians from the left and to build a majority in the cabinet for accepting the IMF conditions. He was able to achieve his will by arguing that there was really no alternative and by getting the IMF to soften some of its demands, thereby reducing the necessary public expenditure cuts. What is interesting is that Callaghan and Healey saw it as important to build a coalition in cabinet for policy (Callaghan 1987; Healey 1989; Dell 1991). Callaghan effectively took control of economic policy by bringing his cabinet with him: 'hoping to satisfy – even exhaust – colleagues and to leave no dissenting ministers feeling so angry at the fact that discussion was stifled that resignation was the only way to voice a particular view' (Donoughue 1987: 88).

Policy-making around the ERM was conducted completely differently. At nearly all stages, decisions about entering and leaving the ERM were conducted by a small group of senior ministers and officials from the Treasury and the Bank of England. The decision to join eventually resulted from an alliance between the Foreign Secretary Hurd and Chancellor, Major, which forced Thatcher to accept membership when she was in a very weak position following the resignation of Lawson (Smith 1994, Thompson 1995). At that moment she was highly dependent on Major. She could not afford his resignation (Stephens 1996) and, as a consequence, she had to accept ERM membership. The final decision to join was not made in cabinet. Similarly, the decision to leave the ERM was taken by Major and Lamont without consulting even senior ministers. As Stephens (1996: 262–3) reports:

> There had previously been occasional allusions in cabinet to the pressure on sterling, but no real debate about the options. Even within the inner circle – Douglas Hurd, Kenneth Clarke and Michael Heseltine – the assumption had been that the government would ride out the crisis . . . 'I only really knew what I read in the newspapers', Clarke would remark.

Prime Ministers have resources which derive from an internally and externally structured context. The use of these resources depends on the available tactics:

- they can use there authority to make unilateral decisions (as Thatcher did in vetoing membership of the ERM);
- they can rely on a more or less permanent alliance of senior ministers (as Major tended to do with Clarke, Heseltine and to an extent Howard);
- they can ensure they have the support of the majority of the cabinet (as Callaghan did in the IMF crisis);
- they can build bilateral alliances of differing degrees of permanence (Major and Lamont over economic policy).

The tactics a Prime Minister adopts will depend on her or his degree of dependence and how he or she perceive the situation. Tactics are an expression of agency and therefore, as we will see below when we examine leadership contests, Prime Ministers can make the wrong decisions.

CONTEXT AND DEPENDENCY: TWO LEADERSHIP CONTESTS

The way dependence and tactics are influenced by context is illustrated by two recent leadership contests. The first was the 1990 contest, which resulted in Thatcher's resignation, and the second was John Major's second contest in 1995, when he succeeded in defeating John Redwood's challenge.

The removal of Margaret Thatcher

Most explanations of Thatcher's fall (see for example, Alderman and Carter 1991, Anderson 1991, Norton 1992, Geelhoed 1991, Ranleagh 1991, Watkins 1991) are highly individualistic and short-term narratives, which fail to place the resignation within the context of core executive power. Rather than seeing the resignation as a result of a number of discrete events – the poll tax, backbench insecurity, or the European issue – the model outlined suggests that Thatcher was forced to resign because she failed to recognise her dependency on colleagues within the core executive. In effect, she made tactical errors in the deployment of her resources. At the time of a growing economic recession and unpopularity in the polls, rather than building alliances with her colleagues she chose to ignore them (for a full account see Smith 1994).

Increasingly, from 1985 Thatcher tended to tell ministers what to do rather than to listen and consult. According to James (1992: 98), 'She told ministers what she thought they ought to be doing. If they disagreed, she berated them. If they persisted, they argued it out in cabinet or committee. If a minister argued too often, he was sacked.' Increasingly, decisions were made without reference to cabinet (Walker 1991). The impact of her actions was to frustrate cabinet ministers and to leave a number of disgruntled ex-ministers on the backbenches.

Through her strategy, Thatcher not only undermined the support not only of potential enemies but also of close colleagues. Lawson

(1992: 937) suggests that the Prime Minister frequently made policy statements that departmental ministers, often her supporters, later had to deny. She even developed rifts with colleagues who had been her close allies, like Norman Tebbit and John Biffen (Lawson 1992, Watkins 1991). She shifted her dependency from her cabinet colleagues to her advisers, but only the cabinet could confer sufficient authority for her to operate effectively.

This situation was exacerbated by a number of specific issues including the Westland affair, the poll tax, relations with Europe and the ERM, and the events which led to the resignations of Howe and Lawson. The Westland affair (for details see Linklater and Leigh 1986, Dunleavy 1990, Box 5.4 p. 138) is important because it demonstrated that: Thatcher was vulnerable; she often misjudged her dependence; and her relationship with the cabinet was problematic.

Westland highlighted Thatcher's vulnerability, because she made errors in both handling the affair and handling her cabinet – as a result she lost two cabinet ministers and was nearly forced to resign. According to Howe (1994: 471), Thatcher said before the Westland debate in the Commons: 'I may not be Prime Minister by six o'clock tonight.' Secondly, in forcing Heseltine from office, she did not realise how dependent she was on key cabinet figures. Finally, while in the short term Westland did rein Thatcher in and force her to compromise in cabinet (Young 1989; 459–6), in the longer term it led to her not trusting the cabinet.

At the heart of the Westland affair were competing visions of Britain's relationship with the European Community, which proved to be a second issue that undermined Thatcher's relationship with the cabinet. The importance of the conflict was again raised in relation to whether Britain should join the ERM and the fact that Thatcher and Lawson took very different positions (see pp. 94–5).

As we have seen, the machinations over the ERM led to the alienation of both Howe and Lawson. Eventually Lawson resigned after a conflict over the role of Thatcher's economic adviser, Alan Walters. Lawson believed that Thatcher was receiving more of her economic advice from Walters than from her Chancellor. The resignation of Lawson weakened Thatcher. She had forced the resignation of a senior minister who had a lot of support on the backbenches. Jenkins (1989) suggests she lost the confidence of a growing portion of the Conservative party and Kenneth Baker warned Thatcher that her position was in danger. He reveals that: 'The backbenchers let it be known that they had told Margaret to get her act together' (Baker 1993: 316).

With the Prime Minister in a weaker position, the new Chancellor, John Major, was able to force Thatcher to finally accept ERM membership. However, her position was undermined further when Geoffrey Howe resigned. He believed his position as foreign secretary was being compromised because Thatcher repeatedly undermined the government's position on relations with Europe. This resignation had an important impact on Thatcher's position. As the *Sunday Times* (4 November 1990) highlighted:

> It is the symbolism of Sir Geoffrey's resignation that makes it significant. The fact that Mrs Thatcher could not keep someone as inoffensive and as accommodating as the Deputy Prime Minister in her cabinet only fuels public discontent with her highhanded ways. When things are going well Mrs Thatcher can get away dragooning her cabinet into whatever causes she chooses. When things are going badly . . . her imperious style only increases her unpopularity.

To make the context more problematic, these events were occurring during the unfolding drama of the poll tax. Butler *et al.* (1994) emphasise that the poll tax was introduced with cabinet support and through the proper procedures of cabinet government. However, in pushing through the poll tax and refusing to abandon the policy, Thatcher ignored the advice of senior ministers like Lawson, much backbench opinion and the views of the public.

The events surrounding Thatcher's resignation are well known and have been reported fully elsewhere. What is important is to demonstrate that Thatcher's resignation was not a result of Michael Heseltine, the weaknesses of her campaign or even the loss of backbench or electoral support. These events were important secondary factors. Ultimately, Thatcher undermined her own position by not realising that the exercise of power depended, not on destroying colleagues, but on maintaining their support. Even a normally cautious former cabinet secretary was prepared to say that there was a 'steadily widening gulf' between Thatcher and her cabinet, that 'she was getting more out of touch', that 'my impression was that after I had gone the gulf went on widening, and that by the last year of her time she was really not in sufficient contact with her cabinet colleagues' (Armstrong 1994: 447).

She made the wrong tactical decisions in relation to her use of resources. Undoubtedly, the poll tax was important in her fall, but it was part of the context of resignation rather than the direct cause. If Lawson and Howe had remained in the cabinet and continued to support Thatcher, it is unlikely that she would have been removed. In Howe's view (1994):

> We could have avoided clashes over ERM entry in 1989 which ruptured irretrievably the once solid troika which Nigel Lawson and I had formed with Mrs Thatcher. One cannot help feeling that her own reputation might be the greater today – indeed she might even still be in power – if she had not tested it to destruction in pursuit of an ideological obsession.

Douglas Hurd made a similar point when he argued:

> The main reason for Margaret Thatcher's loss of leadership was, I believe, her failure over the years to make the best of the cabinet system . . . She did not understand that colleagues too had knowledge and views, and she relied on individual powers excessively (quoted in Butler *et al.* 1994: 190).

It was this failure to recognise dependence which ultimately led to Thatcher's fall. Without cabinet support she could not stay in office. In the early 1980s when the economy was in recession and the party low in the polls, Thatcher was careful to build alliances to ensure that she had the crucial support for her policies. In the mid-eighties, with economic and electoral success, Thatcher relied less and less on her cabinet. Her success increased her freedom to deploy her resources and made her less dependent on the cabinet. However, in the late 1980s with economic and electoral problems gathering, Thatcher did not realise the need to change her strategy and again ensure that the crucial alliances existed. Consequently, she was forced out of office.

Major Asserts His Authority? The leadership contest of 1995

Most of the literature on the Prime Minister in the 1980s and 1990s portrays Thatcher as a strong and Major as weak. The argument of this chapter is that Prime Ministers cannot be characterised as weak or strong – they have a set of institutional resources that can be used in a variety of ways depending on the context. Therefore, Thatcher sometimes had greater freedom to use those resources while at other times she was more dependent (even if she did not realise it). The context for John Major was always such that he was highly dependent on cabinet support first, because he lacked the electoral authority and later because the of economic, political and electoral problems his government faced. After the débâcle of Black Wednesday, when Britain was forced from the ERM, the government appeared uncertain about its economic direction (Thompson 1996b) and was extremely unpopular in the polls. As Stephens remarked:

> Many Tory MPs believe a stronger Prime Minister – and one with a clearer ideological vision – would have been able to restore the party's self-discipline. But for all his personal frustration Mr Major is powerless to take on his critics while his own personal and political standing is so low (Stephens 1994).

It was the combination of these factors that led to Major resigning the leadership in 1995.

The key problem underlying Major's political position was the depth of the recession that was well underway when he took office, and the apparent difficulty in bringing it to an end (Thompson 1996a). The economic problems resulted in both a loss of support in the polls and increasing concern within the Conservative Party. Pattie and Johnson (1996: 61) give some idea of the electoral problems that the Conservatives faced:

> After the collapse of sterling on 'Black Wednesday', Conservative popularity fell alarmingly. Opinion polls consistently gave the party around 25 per cent of the vote. The party also performed disastrously in actual elections. The Liberal Democrats scored dramatic by-election victories in previously rock-solid Conservative seats . . . and Labour's victory at Dudley in 1994 produced the biggest Conservative to Labour by-election swing for 60 years. In the 1993 county council elections, the Conservatives won the equivalent of only 31 per cent of the national vote (Crewe 1994: 110) and lost control of the previously safe shire counties like Surrey, Kent and Norfolk.

The electoral crisis exacerbated the existing problems within the Conservative Party. There was increasing dissatisfaction among right-wing backbenchers over Major's approach to Europe, and there were a large number of former ministers who were now backbench MPs and critical of Major's leadership (Seldon 1997: 547). Reportedly, right-wing Conservatives were trying to gather enough signatures to challenge Major for the leadership in November 1994 (*Financial Times*, 26 and 27 November 1995). The discontent continued throughout the winter of 1994–5. However, the situation was made worse by the poor showing of the Conservatives in the May 1995 local elections. Within this context Major's position was precarious:

> Around Major stands a party shattered and divided, a government mesmerised by its defeats. Since the failure of Black Wednesday on September 16 1992, when sterling's departure from the exchange rate mechanism tore the heart from its economic strategy, the government has been the most unpopular in post-war history. The engagingly frank Mr Clarke once admitted that the government was in a 'dreadful hole'. The hole has become a crater (Stephens 1995).

The faction fighting within the party increased even further. A large number of MPs were dissatisfied with Major's performance and feared the loss of their seats. In June 1995, fuelled by Thatcher, the dissatisfaction with Major was focused around the issues of Britain's relationship with Europe. A number of MPs were concerned that Major would not rule out participation in a single currency (*Financial Times*, 15 June 1995). This dissatisfaction was fired further by Thatcher launching a week of criticisms of the Major government to coincide with publication of her memoirs (*Financial Times*, 15 June 1995). Increasingly, a number of senior Cabinet ministers appeared to be thinking about challenging Major (see Seldon 1997: 564), and, consequently, the right was prepared to launch a leadership contest in November 1995. Major's position was made more precarious when the Chancellor, Kenneth Clarke, who himself had a high degree of political authority, let it be known that he would leave the government if it adopted a more Eurosceptical position.

Major's tactic, in such a weak position, was to resign and offer himself for re-election. Before he did so he ensured that he had the support of the cabinet, but nevertheless John Redwood, the Welsh Secretary, resigned and announced that he would challenge Major for the leadership.

Major succeeded in winning two-thirds of the vote, and placed himself in a position where he could assert his authority. That a cabinet minister stood and Major still won secured the Prime Minister's position further. Despite similarly difficult external situations, Major succeeded where Thatcher failed: he was very careful to steer a line on policy – particularly in relation to Europe – that aimed to keep on board all positions within the Party. He continued to recognise his dependence on cabinet support and in view of Major's ability to keep the right and left together, MPs were unwilling to vote for Redwood, who was likely to split the party. Major, unlike Thatcher, was very careful to cultivate backbench MPs during the leadership campaign.

However, despite the victory, Major remained in a very dependent position because a substantial minority of MPs, 89, voted for Redwood. Moreover, apparent policy failures, poor economic performance and a weak showing in the polls reinforced the political difficulties. This weakness is most clearly demonstrated by Major's shift on European policy. Although never a Euro-enthusiast, Major was a Euro-realist who recognised the need for Britain to achieve the best possible position in the EU. In his view Britain's interests could not be furthered by obstructionism (George and Sowemimo 1996). However, as Major's majority declined he adopted an increasingly Eurosceptical position. Initially wanting Britain 'at the heart of Europe', he became sceptical in his language, strongly supporting the veto of EU business introduced during the fight over the BSE issue, and he conceded the demand for a referendum on Britain's membership of EMU despite the opposition of Kenneth Clarke. Major was continually having to ameliorate conflicting interests within the cabinet and he was never in a strong enough position to force his own line. (Of course, Thatcher was also unable to unite her Cabinet around Europe, and it was also a key issue in her fall. Major's failure to impose a line on the EU was not necessarily the result of a weak character but of the way the European issue has affected the party (Baker *et al.* 1993)).

Although it was consistently denied that Heseltine was offered anything for his loyalty during the leadership contest, he emerged after the ballot as Deputy Prime Minister with very specific responsibilities (Parker 1995). Heseltine effectively established a Deputy Prime Minister's department that had 'real clout in the Whitehall machine'. The new office included the Office of Public Services and Science with a staff of 70 officials and responsibility for efficiency and competitiveness, which provided Heseltine with the remit to intervene across Whitehall. In addition, he was given the chair of four cabinet committees, including the EDC, which was responsible for competitiveness. The creation of this powerful economic committee involved the swallowing of eight other committees (Blitz and Adonis 1995). He was also given control of a new EDCP committee which was responsible for coordinating government policy and met daily. Nevertheless, for Seldon (1997: 602), Heseltine 'proved himself utterly loyal . . . Neither in public nor in private did he undermine Major.' Major's new dependence on Heseltine possibly strengthened Major's position because the 'leader-in-waiting' supported the prime minister.

Major finished his period in office in a very dependent situation. Heseltine had become established as Deputy Prime Minister with an institutional base and was effectively irremovable. Kenneth Clarke was strongly supported on the left of the party and was seen as a successful Chancellor. Therefore, despite policy differences, he was fairly secure. Meanwhile Portillo, as the most senior representative of the Eurosceptical wing of the party, was also in a strong position despite making a number of speeches that were not completely in line with government policy. After the contest, Major effectively maintained his position as leader by working closely with Heseltine and Clarke, and with their support he was relatively secure. However, the small size of his parliamentary majority in 1996 forced Major to make a number of concessions to those on the Eurosceptical wing of the party, who were prepared to use their pivotal power when it came to voting (see Chapter 8).

Major appeared weaker than Thatcher because he was less prepared to stamp his own vision on government policy. However, it is difficult to blame Major's failures on his personality. His style and personality may have affected the choices that he made. However, those choices were structured within a particular political and economic context. Major's context was very different from Thatcher's; the economy was weak, the party more divided and public support low. However, Major survived where Thatcher did not because he was aware of his dependence, and he was prepared to make concessions and deals.

CONCLUSION: POWER AND THE PRIME MINISTER

The media, with their emphasis on personality, and the prime-ministerial government debate, with its focus on who has power, have distorted the understanding of the Prime Minister. It is clear that the Prime Minister does have more resources than other actors within the core executive and that the Prime Minister can make a number of crucial decisions. This does not mean that the Prime Minister is all-powerful or that the style of the Prime Minister changes the nature of government. Like other actors, the Prime Minister operates within a structured arena that constrains actions. Indeed, on his or her own the Prime Minister can achieve little and so is dependent on colleagues and the cabinet. Thus, the cabinet is not about dominance and control but about building alliances. A good Prime Minister is aware of the dependencies that exist within the core and what tactics to use in order to exchange resources in the most advantageous way.

It is difficult to conceptualise the role of the Prime Minister because it is both institutional and individual. The Prime Minister is constrained by what the office can do, and by the resources available, but Prime Ministers choose how to deploy these resources, and they have some leeway in changing the available resources. Moreover, the actions of one Prime Minister can become the institutional constraints of a succeeding Prime Minister. Prime Ministers, by being able to affect the shape of the office to some degree, affect how it is perceived when they are replaced. In this sense Thatcher was important, because she redefined what a Prime Minister could do and she highlighted the limits of prime-ministerial action. This is not to say that Thatcher was an example of prime-ministerial government, but that she used the resources in a particular way.

The office of Prime Minister provides a clear example of the relationship between structure and agency. By its very nature the agent is obvious and his or her actions are relatively easy to discern. There are also various levels of structures, which limit the actions of the Prime Minister from the resources available to the office, to the dependence on the cabinet, to the limits of the state's capabilities, and to the constraints of the national and global economy. Prime Ministers are more reflexive – more aware of their social situation and how it is constructed – than we are normally in our everyday life. Prime Ministers face constraints in every action and they need the strategic capability to evaluate the options that are available within this structured context. Strategic capability explains why some Prime Ministers are better than others. Consequently, the notion of prime-ministerial government makes very little sense. The Prime Minister can neither govern – as governing occurs through a myriad of institutions – nor actually make decisions without dependence on a whole range of other actors and institutions, and without taking account of the structural context. What the Prime Minister does is play a tactical game that creates the necessary alliances for achieving goals.

5 Ministers, Civil Servants and Departments: The Core Executive and Policy-Making

It is within departments that most policy-making occurs. As Tony Crosland acknowledged: 'The individual department must surely be the mainspring of executive activity. They should put up policies, and cabinet should accept or reject them according to whether they are consistent with general government objectives' (quoted in Kogan 1971: 163). Departments control the policy-making resources of time, administrative capability, expertise and knowledge. The role of the cabinet is largely to resolve disputes. Even hyperactive prime ministers like Margaret Thatcher, who desire involvement in a range of policy areas, are limited by time to a few high-profile areas. Therefore, to reach a comprehensive understanding of the operation of the core executive it is necessary to examine the relationships between ministers and civil servants, the operations of departments and the relationships between departments. The analysis of ministerial–civil service relations has been framed in terms of who has power. In this chapter I will demonstrate that such a criterion oversimplifies these relationships, which are based on dependency. For either to achieve their goals they need each other. The aim of this chapter is to look at the policy process at the departmental level. It will begin by examining the traditional approaches to minister–civil service relations.

TRADITIONAL APPROACHES TO THE CIVIL SERVICE

As just noted, the relationship between ministers and civil servants has been framed in terms of 'who has power?' From this agenda, three main approaches have developed in popular and academic discourse: the constitutional, the conspiratorial and the New Right. Each of these perspectives ascribes to either officials or ministers dominance in the policy process but, as I will demonstrate here, they are all a simplification of the policy process.

The constitutional position

Although generally abandoned by textbooks, the constitutional position is still supported, publicly at least, by senior civil servants and politicians. Harold Wilson argued that if a minister could not control the civil service, he was not up to the job (Wilson 1976). More recently, Norman Fowler (1991: 112) defended the constitutional position:

> Civil servants can tell you the case that will be put against your department and they give you their own views. It is important that they do, for they have more experience of working in the particular policy area than any minister. But in the end it is the minister who decides.

According to Sir Brian Hayes, a former Permanent Secretary at the Ministry of Agriculture:

> Civil servants ought not to have power because we are not elected. Power stems from the people and flows through Parliament to the minister who is responsible to Parliament. The civil servant has no power of his own. He is there to help the minister and to be a minister's agent . . . the job of the civil servant is to make sure that his minister is informed . . . that he is made aware of all the options. It is then for the minister to take the decision (quoted in Young and Sloman 1982: 20–1).

The constitutional position is that officials advise and ministers decide. There are, of course, a number of areas where the minister cannot, or does not, decide because she or he has limited time or interest. More importantly, it is false to separate the world of policy-making into discrete categories of advising and deciding, because the policy process is interactive, the notion of policy is nebulous, and the lines of advice and decision are often blurred. Many civil servants admit that they influence the outcome of policy, for example, by initiating policy ideas. Moreover, if a minister never demurs from official advice, is she or he making a decision?

Despite the problems, the constitutional position is important because it defines the way policy-makers, both politicians and officials, see their roles, and consequently it influences their behaviour. The public utterances of politicians and civil servants, continue to reaffirm the constitutional model. The model effectively protects the interests of both parties. Ministers are presented as decisive and accountable policy-makers, and officials can be seen as neutral policy advisers whose only role is to support the minister. Other interpretations raise constitutional questions concerning responsibility and accountability for policy, and therefore they may lead to closer public examination of the role of ministers and officials.

The conspiratorial view

The conspiratorial view, although supported by politicians on the left and the right, has its intellectual roots in Marxist analysis of the British state. Miliband (1969) maintained that the shared class backgrounds of senior civil servants, politicians and business leaders led to common interpretations of the world and its problems. Since officials came from the same milieu, they were sympathetic to the interests of the dominant class and consequently provided a check on the more radical policies of a Labour government.

Radical politicians on the left have frequently subscribed to a view of civil servants as committed, political actors whose goal is to force ministers back to the middle ground. In the 1970s it became common to blame civil service power for the failure of government to deliver and for Britain's economic decline (see Theakston 1995: 186–95). Joe Haines, reflecting on his period as press secretary to Harold Wilson, wrote: 'I believe that the civil service today is at the peak of its power' (Haines 1977: 25). In 1977 a minority report of the Expenditure Select Committee looking at the power of the civil service claimed that departments have very strong policy goals: 'When they are changed, the department will often try and reinstate its own policies through the passage of time and the erosion of the minister's political will' (Sedgemore 1980: 29; see also Benn 1981, Meacher 1982).

In the 1980s the conspiratorial view was also held by some of the more ideologically committed on the right. A number in the Conservative Party, consciously wishing to break with the post-war consensus, were suspicious of a civil service they regarded as imbued with the importance of big government and the welfare state. Margaret Thatcher was distrustful of the civil service, believing, like Benn, that it was a force for compromise and consensus. Despite her liking for individual civil servants, she thought that the majority lived in a rarefied and élitist world, immune from the pressures of the market and believing they knew what was best for Britain (Fry 1995, Hennessy 1990: 632).

The accuracy of the conspiratorial view has been undermined by the success of the Conservative government in overturning the post-war consensus. Few Conservative ministers indicate in their memoirs that they were constrained by their officials (see Richards 1997). Moreover, both politicians and officials maintain that Benn felt thwarted by his civil servants not because they were against him but because he did not have the support of the cabinet or the prime minister. Again, the importance of this approach is what it says in regard to how officials and politicians view each other. It would be unreasonable to assume that officials were without policy (if not party political) commitments which may flavour the advice they proffer ministers (see, for example, the way Treasury advice favoured particular solutions at the time of the IMF crisis (Dell 1997)). Officials believe they present ministers with 'the facts', and they see ministers as undermining civil service professionalism if these facts are ignored. Consequently, problems can arise between officials and ministers if they do not trust each other. Mistrust can occur when a minister with clear policy goals feels she or he is being thwarted by the officials presentation of 'the facts'. In such a situation there is not so much a conflict over policy but a misunderstanding. The official believes that his or her advice is being ignored (thus undermining the official's role), while the minister believes that he or she is being impeded by officials (thus undermining his constitutional position).

The New Right perspective

Thatcher's view of the civil service was also influenced by public choice accounts of bureaucratic behaviour. As was shown in Chapter 2, public choice theory sees officials as budget maximisers, whose interests are served by maximising the size and the budget of their agency. Officials are not concerned with the interests and goals of politicians, but aim to maximise their own interests. In so doing, they provide goods at a higher price than the private sector.

This perspective was given empirical support by the experience of a former civil servant, Leslie Chapman. In his view, once officials are relieved of market discipline, they continually overman and overspend without any real control from the political masters or the taxpayer. Confirming the expectations of public choice, Chapman (1979: 52) maintained:

Almost every pressure on management in the civil service, and probably within the rest of the public sector, is a pressure to spend more and more money. The reason for this is that positive pressure to save can come only from those who benefit from such savings, that is, the taxpayers, who have no organized voice. The pressures to spend or to avoid economies, on the other hand, fall directly and heavily on management.

Although there is much intuitive attraction in the public choice explanations of public bureaucracy, as Dunleavy (1991) points out, it is an oversimplified account of the civil service and overestimates the desire for budget maximising. Consequently, it cannot explain policies of retrenchment and privatisation that challenged notions of budget maximising after 1979. More importantly, public choice theory ascribes too much power to officials and therefore ignores the resources of politicians in controlling the bureaucracy. Again, this approach is important because it has influenced the Conservative government's views and policy towards the civil service (see Chapter 7), but it has little to offer in terms of understanding the nature of official–minister-ial relationships.

ANALYSING OFFICIAL–MINISTERIAL RELATIONS

As I argued in previous chapters, zero-sum conceptions of power are difficult to sustain. This argument is supported by an analysis of the role of officials and departments. What is crucial in understanding departmental policy-making and the relationship between ministers and civil servants is not who is dominant and who has influence, because this assumes that one set of actors dominates another. Rather, the focus of analysis should be on the nature of the interaction between ministers and civil servants and the impact these relationships have on policy.

The ministerial–civil service relationship is built on certain institu-tional foundations, but it is also interactive, dynamic and organic. The institutional elements are: the cultures, structures and interests of departments (and divisions within departments); the roles and re-sources of the civil service; and the roles and resources of ministers. Nevertheless, these institutional elements have a certain flexibility and are open to reinterpretation. External events and ministers can change the interests and cultures of departments and officials, and ministers can reinterpret their roles (Richards and Smith 1997). This process of reinterpretation is continual and evolving, reflecting changing personalities and circumstances.

It is not the constitution, as Hennessy (1995) maintains, that is the hidden wiring of the British political system, but the civil service. Officials effectively maintain the system by reproducing the rules of government. The constitution largely exists in the heads of officials, and it is their interpretation of the constitution that structures the behaviour of officials and ministers. Officials live by, and reproduce, the rules of the constitution. Often officials determine how the constitution is to be interpreted, whether officials or minister have broken it and when it changes. To a large degree, the constitution is what officials do. Central in the constitutional framework is ministerial accountability, and this convention allows ministers to structure the behaviour of officials because on the basis of this conventions officials profess, and believe in, loyalty to ministers. Officials reproduce the rule of loyalty to ministers and therefore sustain the nature of the ministerial–official relationship. As a result, the relationship is complex because its structures – the constitution and rules of the game – are humanly conditioned and continually remoulded.

Underpinning the ministerial–civil service relationship, and indeed the whole operation of Whitehall, is secrecy:

> Secrecy is the bonding material which holds the rambling structure of central government together. Secrecy is built into the calcium of a British policy-maker's bones. Of all the values incorporated into the culture that moulded Bancroft and Armstrong, secrecy is *primus inter pares*. It is the very essence of the Establishment view of good government . . . (Hennessy 1990: 346).

Secrecy suits both ministers and officials – it means no one can be directly burdened with responsibility for decisions. Ministers only have to account for the *final* decision and not for how they came to that decision. The role of officials in decisions is largely hidden, and even the new freedom of information act will not reveal official advice to ministers, effectively hiding the policy process. In the view of the former Cabinet Secretary, Sir Robin Butler, secrecy is 'in the interest of good government' (*Guardian*, 5 January 1998).

One of the most striking revelations to emerge from the Scott report on arms sales to Iraq (see Box 5.1) is the strong reluctance of officials to reveal in any detail the policy-making process. In one instance, when preparing for the committal proceedings for the Matrix Churchill case, Mr Beston, a DTI official, sent a second official, Mr Medway, a memo stating that he had discussed the Interdepartmental Committee (IDC) machinery for considering export licences, and revealed that recommendations for licences were always submitted by Foreign and Commonwealth Office (FCO) and Ministry of Defence (MOD) officials for the approval of their ministers. He continues:

> I think it important to indicate the sort of interdepartmental scrutiny to which such applications were subject. We cannot suggest that the DTI merely acquiesced in whatever recommendations the IDC, or other Ministers, made but I have avoided explaining what happened in the event of disagreements. I shall probably have to do so if cross-examined and would try to say little more than that the matter was resolved by the Ministers of the various departments (Scott 1996: 1195).

Scott asks: 'Why should Mr Beston not have set out the true *de facto* relationship between the DTI and the other licensing departments?' Why should officials be so concerned to hide the way policy is made? One reason may be that it undermines the constitutional notion that officials advise and ministers decide.

When discussing the reasons for issuing public immunity certificates, an official both gives a useful account of the policy-making process and indicates the degree of paranoia concerning secrecy that pervades the upper echelons of the core executive:

> All the listed documents fall into a class of documents which relate to the formulation of Government policy and the internal dealings of Government departments. Such policy was decided at the highest level, and the listed documents include documents preparatory to advice given for the benefit of Ministers in office during the relevant period. Decisions made by Ministers are frequently preceded by detailed discussion within and between Government departments and by consideration of the various possibilities open to Ministers. It is out of such discussions and considerations that the advice to be tendered to Ministers is often formulated . . . It would in my view be against the public interest that documents of oral evidence revealing the process of providing for Ministers honest and candid advice on matters of high level policy should be subject to discussion or disclosure (Scott 1996: 1275).

BOX 5.1
The Scott Inquiry into the sale of arms to Iraq

The Arms to Iraq inquiry was triggered when the trial of three directors of the company Matrix Churchill, who were accused of selling arms (or dual-purpose goods) to Iraq was abandoned because it had become clear that the Thatcher government had relaxed the guidelines covering arms sales to Iraq and Iran without informing the public or Parliament. Shortly before the start of the Gulf War in 1990, the government knew that machine tools were to be supplied to Iraq that were intended for the manufacture of armaments, even though the stated policy was not to sell arms, or anything that could be used for making arms, to Iran or Iraq. The government had secretly changed policy. The government's argument was that the guidelines governing arms sales had been relaxed, but that this did not constitute a change of policy. The problems had come to light because firms, including Matrix Churchill and Sheffield Forgemasters, were making weapons or munitions machinery for Iraq. MI6 knew of the exports, but Customs and Excise did not. Customs and Excise therefore arrested and charged a number of people with offences related to the export of arms. During the trial, government ministers used public interest immunity (PII) to prevent the defendants from obtaining government documents that would prove their innocence. What the defence wished to demonstrate was that the security services had full knowledge of the exports and that the firms had been encouraged by the Trade Minister, Alan Clark, to export arms. After the evidence of Alan Clark and the judges' review of the PII material, the trial collapsed, revealing the extent to which government had misled the public.

Largely to deflect the heat from the opposition, John Major set up the Scott inquiry to analyse what had occurred. The resulting report provides the most detailed account of the internal workings of government outside the public records office. It revealed, although this fact did not become clear until 1992, that the government had relaxed the guidelines on arm sales in 1988. The report demonstrated that:

The conduct of policy regarding defence sales to Iran and Iraq during the period under review was accompanied by consistent endeavours on the part of officials and Ministers to prevent being made public information that might lead to critical public debate about export licensing decisions (Scott 1996: 226).

It therefore confirmed the degree of secrecy within British government – and to some extent the government's dismissiveness of the public; the way both ministers and officials interpret their own rules of behaviour; the difficulty for Parliament in holding the government to account; and the extent to which the constitution provides very little constraint on either politicians or civil servants. Scott also believed, despite government denials, that there was a change of policy and not merely a relaxation of the guidelines. (See Tomkins 1996, Norton Taylor 1995, Scott 1996.)

The draft memo highlights clearly and concisely the complexity of the policy process within the key institutions of the core executive. The development of policy involves a series of discussions and negotiations first within and then between departments at official level. All departments within Whitehall have authority, and it breaks the rules of the Whitehall game to make a policy that may affect the remit of another department without discussing the policy with the department concerned. The importance of this rule was demonstrated when the Home Secretary, Jack Straw, and the Secretary for International Development, Clare Short, reacted angrily to the announcement by Robin Cook, the Foreign Secretary, of a change in state of Britain's overseas dependencies without consulting the other departments (*Guardian*, 5 February 1998).

Much of the work of an official involves assessing who should be consulted over a policy. Such assessments may then lead to informal and formal interdepartmental meetings. In most instances, the role of officials is to carry out the preparatory work in terms of both finding information and developing a feel for what other departments will accept. On the basis of drafts and negotiating positions, ministers make decisions, but in close consultation with officials and with other ministers. Crossman saw this in a more conspiratorial way: 'Whitehall likes to reach an official compromise at official level first, so that Ministers are all briefed the same way' (Crossman 1972: 73). Much of Whitehall works on knowing who to talk to and when. It is in this sense a set of overlapping and informal networks. Nicholas Henderson points to the 'network of Private Offices' as 'one of the means by which the policies of different Departments of State are coordinated', and emphasises the importance of knowing who really does the appropriate job (Henderson 1993: 113).

Who talks to whom, and when and how, depends on the policy area, but as a broad outline of the process the quote from the Scott report provides a useful account of the policy-making. Of course, central to this process is the belief that the public should not know the details of policy-making. The subtleties of the process are held to be too difficult for voters to understand, while any revelations would undermine the certainties of the Westminster model and ministerial accountability. The civil service and ministers like to retain the secrets of their magic circle, even though most people know that the idea that civil servants advise and ministers decide is an illusion. However, in the rest of the chapter I will attempt, with the help of interviews, the Scott report, ministerial memoirs and the work of other scholars, to show how officials and ministers interact in the policy process. I will highlight how policy is a process and not a rigid hierarchy where orders are given and taken.

STRUCTURE, AGENCY, DEPENDENCY AND POWER IN MINISTERIAL–OFFICIAL RELATIONSHIPS

The traditional accounts of the civil service clearly indicate who has power. In the case of the constitutional model it is the minister, and in the New Right and conspiracy models it is the civil service. Undoubtedly there are examples of officials frustrating ministers' policy goals. Perhaps the best-documented case is the Fulton proposals for the reform of the civil service in the late 1960s (see Fry 1993 and Kellner and Crowther Hunt 1980). On a more mundane level, Norman Tebbit confesses that the DTI could not disengage from the film industry until after the retirement of the Permanent Secretary, Sir Leo Pliatsky, who was a keen film buff (Tebbit 1988: 165–6). Nevertheless, to see the civil service as all-powerful is to misunderstand the relationship. However, an important paradox emerges from the conspiratorial and New Right approaches: considering the advantages of officials in terms of their permanence, knowledge and time, why do they *not* dominate all ministers? Ministers are disadvantaged because of their short tenure of departmental briefs, and because they do not have the knowledge necessary to run a department or even to make policy. As one former Permanent Secretary said: 'Now, in eighteen months in charge of a department there is jolly little that you can do on your own; there is precious little you can do even with the full-bloodied support of your officials.' This leads to situations in complex areas like the economy where it is

> extremely difficult for an average Chancellor in his two-and-a-half years to counter the Treasury view in any coherent rational way, bearing in mind the fact that his first year must be largely spent being initiated into the manifold complexities of his new job; bearing in mind, too, the long time-scale required both for the formulation and implementation of most policies and the subsequent period which has to elapse before their impact can properly be assessed. No wonder one Permanent Secretary at the Treasury who served under three post-war Chancellors recently estimated, in an incautious moment, that seventy five per cent of the time, successive Chancellors accepted uncritically the advice he gave them (Kellner and Crowther Hunt 1980: 211).

Kellner and Crowther Hunt highlight how new governments and new ministers allow civil servants to reopen old battles and how, through official committees, they are able to consider issues in detail and present ministers with a particular framework of decisions. The system appears to favour the permanent incumbents over the temporary ones.

The paradox of the imbalance of resources is resolved because the actors – ministers and officials – operate within a structured world into which each brings different resources and, in order to achieve goals, they need each other. The relationship is structured by the institutions within which they operate (that is, the departments, the mechanisms of cabinet government and party); by the different resources, which again are institutional and constitutional; and by different perceptions of each other and their respective roles. But while it is a structured relationship, it is one in which both parties bring their own unique elements and one, because it is based on perceptions and a constitution that exists through the reproduction of rules rather than on paper, that is continually open to reinterpretation. Ministers and civil servants have different resources; they do not occupy the same structural positions and constraints; and their abilities to act and to achieve their goals vary (see Table 5.1). As one former official said of the relationship:

It seems to me that the essence of it (the relationship) is dynamic interaction. It is not that there is one set of values, propositions, positions and needs that the politicians have, and another set that the official system has, and they have to sort of compromise, but rather they interact.

Another official saw the relationship working well when it was one of 'give and take'.

Official and ministers are dependent on each other and so create an evolving and occasionally seamless relationship. Ponting (1986: 14) perceptively states:

The question of where power lies between ministers and civil servants inside Whitehall can never be answered satisfactorily. The dividing line depends on so many things, the political strength and intellect of the individual minister, the type of decisions being taken, the amount of administrative detail involved, the level of political interest in the outcome of the decision and the personal relationship between the individuals. All these factors mean that boundaries of power are fluctuating continuously.

This is an important point and it again highlights the need to see power as fluid and relational, and not as an object. Therefore, it is necessary to specify the conditions within which these relations occur and the various resources that the actors bring to the policy process (see Table 5.1).

Resources

Despite the apparently overwhelming predominance of resources in the hands of officials, they do not dominate the policy process, because ministers also have resources. Officials will rarely achieve anything without the addition of ministerial resources. The resources of officials are fairly obvious, and result from their permanence and control over an organisation with information, experience, and time to make, and ultimately to deliver, policy (although increasingly delivery is now outside of the department). Without this machinery, there is little that a minister could achieve.

While officials have administrative resources, ministers have the political resources essential for policy outcomes. Ministers' political

Table 5.1   Resources and structures of ministers and civil servants

	Civil servants	Ministers
Resources	Time Expertise Experience Knowledge Whitehall network Anonymity	Authority Access to cabinet Political alliances Political support and legitimacy Access to media Alternative sources of advice
Internal structures	Rules of the game Constitutional elements – ministerial responsibility Neutrality	Maintenance of ministerial hierarchy Ministerial responsibility
External structures	Departmental interests Political demands Economic circumstances	Departmental interests Economic and political constraints Time
Agency	Interpretation of rules Official alliances Alliances with ministers Ability to take decisions in discrete policy areas	Ability to make policy Authority over officials Ability to override organisational and departmental imperatives

authority and legitimacy enables them to develop support for policies with their colleagues, the cabinet and the outside world. Without cabinet and Treasury support, departments could achieve nothing, and so officials need ministers to legitimise policy and to gain financial and political support. As one former permanent secretary suggested,

> First of all, the minister has got to be decisive. He must know what he wants to do. He must be prepared to listen to advice, to question advice and then to make up his mind and go ahead taking things to cabinet and winning his battles in cabinet. So you need someone who is strong . . . He's got to be decisive and strong and if he is not, as I said, the fortunes of the department fall. There is a misunderstanding, which is quite common, that civil servants like weak ministers because they can rule them, they don't at all. That's no good because when the minister is on his own in cabinet they are not there to rule or do anything else to influence him. So you want someone who is active, intellectual, quite bright of course, can whip things up . . .

Once ministers have the authority, they work with officials to develop policy, and it is the official machinery for making policy that ministers need. In particular, the officials have knowledge of who to talk to and how to build the necessary Whitehall consensus. Moreover, most officials are intensely loyal to their minister, and they are consequently extremely able at offering political cover both within Whitehall and in the outside world. Officials and ministers are not in conflict, but are symbiotic. Ministers need the expertise and officials need ministers with weight who can gain money, time for legislation and interdepartmental support. With a weak minister a department will achieve little.

Structure

Civil servants are constrained by their structural situation. As indicated in Chapter 2, structures are comprised of two types: external and internal. External structures are imposed on people from outside, and internal structures are reproduced by the behaviour of actors. One of the central roles of officials is to sustain the rules of Whitehall – they maintain the constitution. Elizabeth Symons, former general secretary of the First Division Association, sees the principles that bind the civil service as:

> ministerial responsibility and ministerial accountability; that the Civil Service must give impartial service and is politically neutral; and that appointments to the Civil Service should be made on the basis of fair and open competition . . . we believe that the Civil Service itself still holds these dear (HC 390-II 1992/3: 57).

The importance of the constitutional view is that it structures the day-to-day behaviour of officials. The professional ethic of the civil service is based on: officials remaining separate from ministers; retaining some political neutrality; and their ability to serve any minister. The civil service code is based on the amorality of the official; they will do the minister's bidding (Richards 1996, Richards and Smith 1998). Moreover, civil service behaviour reproduces the structural context; they conceive of themselves as neutral policy advisers. Therefore, ministerial authority is extremely important in Whitehall; officials cannot ignore the will of the minister. If the minister explicitly expresses a wish for a policy then officials have to deliver, or else undermine the official perception of the constitution that is so important for the officials' own political protection. As one former permanent secretary said in an interview:

> My job was to carry out the minister's decisions. Ministers obviously decided policy issues which I disagreed with but if I had had my penny worth in and my views had been overruled, it was my job to accept the final decision and carry it out, which is what I did.

It could be argued that 'He would say that, wouldn't he?', and it raises questions about the nature of the minister's decision, but it is important to realise that official actions are framed by the constitutional imperatives Even implicitly, officials have to be careful to act within both the constitutional framework and the confines of ministerial authority. Any action outside this authority lacks legitimacy. This position has advantages for the officials, because their behaviour is seen as legitimate as long as they act within ministerial authority, even if the minister has not expressed a particular policy preference. The corollary is ministerial accountability. If things go wrong then it is the minister who is held to account.

The work, values and options of officials are also structured to varying degrees by policy networks. Officials are involved in two types of networks – internal – with other parts of Whitehall and external – with outside interest groups. The nature of the networks often depends on the department or division. For example, the Police Division of the Home Office has continual contacts with the Association of Chief Police Officers (ACPO), and it is unlikely that changes in police regulations or criminal law would occur without detailed discussion with ACPO. On the other hand, in the DSS, particularly between 1979 and 1997, there is very little contact with pressure groups. Most policy developments occur in-house. Nevertheless, through the welfare to work programme developed under the Labour government and the Job Seekers Allowance developed by the Conservative government, the Job Seekers division of the department has formalised contact with the Department for Education and Employment. This creates a formal network that effectively covers the responsible divisions within the DSS and the DfEE and the Benefits Agency. This network structures the work of officials and the way policy is made:

> What we have had to do from the centre is set up a joint stewardship board in which everything is split. Every brief we put to ministers on the Job Seekers Allowance is joint. The senior officials have to agree

to the content and 99 per cent of the time we do. In occasional instances we have to get ministers to sit down together and thrash it out (interview with DSS official).

The structural positions of ministers and of officials are very different. Officials are constrained largely by internal structures: the rules of the game they reproduce constrain their activities. Ministers also reproduce internal structures in terms of their relations with other ministers and to some extent with civil servants. Indeed, they are given *Questions of Procedure for Ministers* (Cabinet Office 1992, 1997a), in which the rules are clearly laid out concerning issues of collective responsibility, appeals to cabinet and cabinet committee and trips abroad. The same document also instructs ministers on relations with civil servants: 'Ministers have a duty to give fair consideration and due weight to informed and impartial advice from civil servants, as well as other considerations and advice, in reaching policy decisions' (Cabinet Office 1992: para. 55; 1997a: para. 56). Relations between ministers and prime ministers are also strongly governed by informal rules and codes.

However, the most important constraints on ministers are the external structures: the degree of political support; the economic situation; the adaptability of the civil service. The constraints faced by ministers are enormous. For Rose (1987: 7–8), 'The programmes of big government are not a reflection of the personalities of transient politicians; they are carried out impersonally by officials.' Ministers are constrained by what the outside world will accept; by what their colleagues will accept; by what can be afforded; by existing programmes and legislation; and by the structures and interests of the departments. Ministers cannot assume office and immediately change the direction of the department (Richards and Smith 1997). Crosland (quoted in Kogan 1971: 159–60), speaking of his time as Education Secretary, summarised the constraints on a minister very well:

I would say first the legacy of history – the material legacy of thousands of buildings and institutions of particular types and sizes; this greatly limits your freedom to make rapid changes in policy. Secondly, the high degree of autonomy of much of the educational world – the fact that power and decision-making are not centralized in Whitehall but are dispersed among local authorities, universities, Research Councils. Thirdly the existence of strong pressure groups of all kinds . . . Lastly, and perpetually, not enough money . . .

Ministers have, often, distinct ideologies and personal and political ambitions. They have an ability to act that is not available to officials. Officials are constrained by the rules of the game, but ministers also face important constraints on their actions. They are constrained by the inertia of the institutions and by the size and complexity of the programmes they find once in office. It is extremely difficult for ministers and their officials to control either the delivery of services or the demographic pressures that create demands for services (Rose 1987). Many policies are based on legislation that is often complex and takes many years to revise. However, there is also a role for agents.

Agency

Officials and ministers occupy distinct structural situations with access to an alternative set of resources and, as a consequence, they do not share similar options when faced with the same event. Both civil servants and ministers are agents, but the nature of their agency differs. Officials cannot change the direction, structure or major policies of a department. Some senior official can be extremely influential in terms of advising on new policies; they can make decisions within discrete policy areas and they can reinterpret the rules of the game. Perhaps their greatest role as agents derives from how they present advice to ministers. Officials can affect the advice that ministers receive. Situations are continually changing, and the bureaucracies adapt to new circumstances. Former Conservative Education Secretary Edward Boyle believed that new officials in positions of authority affect the way facts are seen and the issues that are regarded as important (Kogan 1971: 84). Officials cannot literally be continually directed by ministers on what action to take, and therefore a large part of the work of officials is, in the words of Lord Callaghan (HC 390-ii1992/3: 137), to 'pick up the scent'. Officials have to get a feel for what the minister wants. There are few formal mechanisms for relating the minister's views on a whole range of policy areas. One official revealed in an interview, shortly after the election of the Labour government in 1997, the *ad hoc* nature of the process:

> At the moment it is quite difficult for us to pick up ministerial signals. The ministers talk among themselves and share more about themselves than they ever do with us. Traditionally, I will get to know what is going through a minister's mind by a whole series of meetings and discussions. You often get to know your minister best

when you accompany him on a visit or sitting with him on an aeroplane and they begin to talk . . . One of the ways we tune in is through special advisers and this is working quite effectively and I guess that relies on personalities.

The Scott report also indicates how officials are continually trying to get a feel for their minister's goals. Officials are generally astute at adapting their behaviour in the light of ministerial statements. Nevertheless, the important but subtle point is that behaviour is based on *interpretation,* which creates a space for discretion. Officials affect policy because the way civil servants interpret the demands of a minister affects outcomes. Nevertheless, officials are greatly constrained by ministerial authority, and to act contrary to the wishes of a minister would be a serious error. Moreover, if ministers insist on a policy then officials have no choice but to deliver. The structural context within which officials act limits their behaviour, but it does provide room for manoeuvre.

If officials are generally concerned with maintaining the structure of the Whitehall rules, then ministers are agents of change who have the authority to impose new policies if they desire. Again, as Crossman (1972: 77) revealed:

> I am absolutely clear that the chance you have as a Government or as a Minister of changing things in Britain is enormous; provided that the Government is a team; provided the Ministers are capable of keeping their political drive while helping the Department and working eighteen hours a day. Provided that they have these qualities, *they have an instrument which is trained to accept change* (emphasis added).

For the minister, the institutional constraints imposed by a large departmental bureaucracy also provide an opportunity for action. The departmental machine is one of policy professionals who control information and have experience in developing and implementing policy: the civil service provides the capabilities for ministers to achieve their goals. As a former permanent secretary in the DSS admitted:

> The important thing that I always told the Secretary of State is that he needs to be very clear about two or three strategic things he wants to do in his time. If he is clear about those, and tells the civil service, and he impresses it on them, they will help him to achieve those aims,

if they are realisable. But assuming they are sensible aims, *they probably will be after discussion*, then he needs you to deliver that.

The paradox of the civil service is that while it often thinks that ministers are wrong or weak, it is the keeper of the constitution; the constitution really only exists through the actions of politicians and officials, and as officials wish to maintain the constitution they have to accept the authority of the minister. To a great extent, officials are limited by their own belief structure; their constitutional view of the world governs their behaviour. They can push a minister towards sensible aims, but in the end they have to accept his or her goals. For example, civil servants could see the problems in privatising BT because of the cost, the technical difficulties of selling it off, and the loss of their influence, but they could not ultimately ignore the demands of ministers. Moreover, Lord Tebbit, Secretary of State in the DTI at the time of privatisation, revealed in an interview that officials initially argued that privatisation was impractical, but once the decision was made they urgently went about implementing the policy. Officials cannot override ministers. However, they will be much more amenable to 'sensible' aims than to aims that ignore their advice
The power of officials is strong, because of their importance in the policy process and their control over knowledge and implementation. But it is limited to discrete policy areas within departments, and by the desires of ministers. Ministers and civil servants have to be able to trust each other because if the relationship breaks down little can be achieved. As one former official said: 'You've got them [Ministers] and use them, and try and get into a constructive relationship with them. The civil servants equally want to have a constructive relationship.' The nature of the relationship is captured well by Kogan (1971: 42):

The making of policy is continuously in the hands of civil servants who create, as it were, low-frequency policy waves. Ministers bring with them high-frequency activity which can initiate, change, strengthen or condemn a whole policy.

Ministers who have a clear agenda and cabinet support are in a strong position to achieve their policy goals. They are agents in a structured situation of institutionalised departmental interests and policy issues, but they are able to stand slightly outside and impose change on policy. Dudley and Richardson (1996) highlight how certain ministers are innovative policy actors, and they demonstrate how Brian Mawhinny, the former Secretary of State for Transport, was able to shift a department that had long been seen as a supporter of road building to a policy that was much more in tune with the environment.

Ministers are in departments in order to make choices, and they are less aware of the rules of the Whitehall game than civil servants. In addition, they are able, unlike officials, to build political support for their policy goals that can place them in a strong position. As Kogan noted, when discussing Education ministers: 'Ministers are listened to by the education service because they have authority to make decisions which affect organizational behaviour' (Kogan 1971: 33). The differences in their ability to act, and the different resources that they bring to the situation, create interdependence between ministers and civil servants.

The interdependence of the civil service–minister relationship

Ministers and officials need each other because of their different resources and different structural positions. Ministers need officials to reproduce the Whitehall game and its constitutional foundations. Officials need ministers to act and to provide legitimacy, political support and finance for the work of the department. The different structural positions produce different advantages. Officials do have control over the bureaucratic machinery and have the time to control most of what goes on in a department. Ministers can only pay attention to a limited number of issues. Therefore, officials have the discretion to act where the ministerial light does not shine. However, once a minister pays attention to an issue it is extremely difficult for the civil service to thwart him or her, and indeed there is more prestige in achieving the minister's goals. Tebbit (1988: 182) says of his officials in the Department of Employment: 'I found that I had the benefit of officials of the highest integrity and ability. Once I had laid down policy they were tireless in finding ways to deliver what I wanted.'

The distribution of resources and mutual dependence means that to see it in terms of a conspiracy model is too simplistic. As Theakston (1987: 106) highlights:

Life in Whitehall is not lived in a state of permanent conflict between ministers and civil servants. Analyses of policy-making which focus on adversarial confrontations between ministers and the civil service oversimplify and distort. Relations are complex and fluid, and the

lines of division are more often than not to be found not *between* the
political and bureaucratic elements in government but *within* them as
alliances of ministers and officials compete with each other to
advance particular goals or defend common interest (see also Drewry
and Butcher 1991: 82).

Even Crossman (1972: 74), a critic of the civil service, argued:

> The effective Minister is the man who wins the support of his
> department without becoming its cherished mascot. To do so he
> needs to strike a balance. He needs their acquiescence, at least, of
> what he is up to, and for this he needs to be a success in the
> department's eye. So he's got to appease them by winning a number
> of their battles for them in the Whitehall war.

For a minister, the civil service is both a constraint and a facilitator. It
is a constraint because: departments have cultures; it controls the
information ministers receive; and it interprets the facts and defines
what is possible. It has a negative power (see Haines 1977). Benn and
Crowther Hunt talk of civil servants setting the framework of policy
decisions and thereby forcing ministers into a particular agenda, but
these frameworks are a 'negotiated order', not tablets of stone.
Ministers with their own agendas, or with alternative sources of advice,
can establish their policy preferences. Within the rules of the game, civil
servants have little choice but to advise ministers on their policy
preferences. The ministerial imperative explains why some civil servants became so frustrated with the Major government. They were
faced with a set of ministers with their own ideological agenda, who
were not prepared to accept the civil service agenda. In addition, there
was an increasing tendency for ministers to look to outside sources of
advice, and therefore to develop policy without consulting with civil
servants, leaving officials to work out the detail rather than develop the
options. Indeed, one official resource, permanence, was increasingly
being attached to ministers; for example, Peter Lilley was in the DSS
for six years and often had more knowledge than many of his officials.

The impact of ministers depends crucially on how they use the
bureaucratic machine. The relationship between ministers and civil
servants is by necessity symbiotic, but does break down on occasions,
as in the case of Tony Benn (see Smith *et al.* 1998a). Ministers have
leverage, because civil servants need ministers who have: political
authority in relation to officials and the public; the ability to build

coalitions with other ministers and the prime minister; a position to convince the cabinet; the ability to obtain money from the Treasury; and access to Parliament (see Crossman 1972: 70–1). Perhaps most importantly, considering the way the constitution frames the beliefs and actions of officials, they need ministers to make decisions. Officials have discretion once a policy is made; they can try to prevent policy being made; they can try to influence outcomes, but only ministers can make decisions and officials have to await their position. From reading memoirs and talking to officials, it is clear that what they most like is a decisive minister, and they dislike ministers, such as Norman Fowler and Keith Joseph, who agonised over everything. Without ministerial decisions officials cannot act which is why ministers are so important as agents. It is part of the professional ethic of civil servants to develop the policies that governments want. As Butler, Adonis and Travers (1994: 209) point out in their study of the poll tax débâcle: 'it is embedded in the professionalism of the modern civil service, which far from placing a drag on controversial or apparently unworkable policies, places a premium on giving them effect . . .' Officials have little to gain from stopping policy, and it is in their interest to assist their ministers. Tebbit (1988: 183) records that his officials liked the previous minister, Jim Prior, 'but were conscious that he lacked the prime minister's support and was unlikely to win cabinet battles. Like all organisations, departments like to be on the winning side and they saw in me a winner in the Whitehall civil wars.' Normally officials and ministers will be working together because it is only way that both can achieve their personal and organisational goals.

Ministers bring two important, and related, resources – political capital and authority. Their authority, like the prime minister's, is structural and derives from the constitutional position of ministers, their relationship to the department and their position in the hierarchy of cabinet. Political capital derives from their more fluid relationships with Parliament, party and senior colleagues. Greater political capital increases the ability of ministers to use their political authority, and, with high political authority and high political capital, ministers and officials can achieve more.

This symbiotic relationship has costs and benefits. When both parties bring their respective skills and knowledge base to the process, the minister has an effective machine for developing policies, and officials feel they are part of the policy-making process. The costs are more in terms of what this means for outsiders in both the rest of Whitehall and the public – policy-making excludes the outside world.

As Box 5.1 illustrates, officials did not want to reveal either the nature of the policy process or the policy in relation to arms sales. The report believed: 'The closeness of the relationship between ministers and civil servants has a tendency to put Whitehall in a cloistered world detached from the citizens they should be serving.' The danger is that it becomes so closed off that it is removed from reality. Again, the Scott report revealed that when Iran attacked ships in the gulf – including British ships – rather than saying that Britain would no longer sell parts to Iran because they had attacked British ships, policy-makers attempted to justify the change of policy in terms of interpretation of the guidelines (Scott 1996: 230).

Structure and agency

This chapter has demonstrated that the relationship between ministers and civil servants is a complex, structured relationship, which highlights some interesting facets of the relationship between structure and agency and the different forms of social and political structures. Civil servants reproduce the structures of government in their heads and in their behaviour. They have a very clear set of rules concerning how government should operate in terms of official and ministerial relations, and this governs much of their behaviour.

This does not, of course, mean that civil servants are merely reproducing a set of rules. They are in a powerful position, and they can reinterpret the rules in ways that suit their situation. Central to civil servants is ministerial approval for their actions; often, however, this approval is implicit – they are doing what they believe the minister wants and not what he has expressly told them to do, and the difference creates a space in which civil servants can make policy or political choices. An interesting example of the way officials can reinterpret the rules arises in the Scott report (see Box 5.2).

The example in Box 5.2 raises a number of interesting issues. The officials were aware of the rules of the game, but they wanted to increase their autonomy over the decision-making process, partly to expedite the issuing of licences. The interests of officials and ministers were in conflict, and officials interpreted the rules in a way that favoured their interests. They could use the resources of their time, direct control over decision-making and the minister's lack of attention, control the process. However, once the minister clearly stated his position a second time, the officials had no choice but to concur. Their ability to interpret the rules was limited by ministerial authority, which

---

BOX 5.2
Decision-making on export licences

The committee that was involved in reviewing export licenses was an interdepartmental committee made up of officials from the DTI, the Ministry of Defence (MOD) and the Foreign Office (FCO). What was interesting about this committee was the informality of the rules concerning whether matters should be referred up to ministers. Initially, a large number of issues were referred up to ministers (Scott 1996: 197). Usually, referral occurred when there was no agreement by the officials on the issuing of licences, demonstrating the high degree of control they had in this area. However, as time passed, officials made an increasing number of decisions without referral. As one official wrote, 'Once a definitive list of [IDC] decisions prepared by the FCO is available I will ensure that a fuller report is sent to you for Minister's (for Defence Procurement (DP)) information.' Scott recognised: 'It appears that, so far as the MOD was concerned, the IDC would be taking definitive decisions. The report of the decisions would be sent to the Minister for "information"'. (Scott 1996: 261). Officials had managed to reinterpret the rules so they effectively became the decision-makers.

However the minister did not easily delegate such important powers. The minister, Adam Butler, asked to see the list before it was passed to the DTI. Scott reports:

> It was an obvious prerequisite, if the Minister was to be in that position, that he should, as a matter of routine, be informed of the IDC decisions in sufficient time to enable him to intervene if he wished to do so. A practice to that affect was not instituted.

Rather, an official wrote to other senior officials and to the minister referring to the attached lists of export licences that had been endorsed. The note said 'that "these decisions will now be conveyed to the companies concerned". The minister was being presented with a *fait accompli*' (Scott 1996: 198).

What Scott reveals is that despite ministers wishes, officials were attempting to make decisions without referring the matter to ministers. It was believed that ministerial involvement would slow the decision-making procedure. Even after the minister had

insisted he should see the decisions with time to make amend-
ments if necessary, officials continued to send the minister the list
of final decisions. Scott concludes, 'Until the intervention of the
Minister in July, the need for expedition in order to further the
interests of defence sales was treated as of greater importance than
Ministerial approval of IDC licensing decisions.'

illustrates an important distinction between officials and ministers. The
structural locations of ministers and civil servants within Whitehall are
different, and this difference affects the way they influence the policy
process and the relationships that exist within departments.

RELATIONSHIPS WITHIN DEPARTMENTS

If departments are policy-making bodies, then much of the process of
policy-making goes on inside the departments. Central to departments
is the idea that there is a departmental view. On many occasions, both
officials and ministers are captured by the departmental imperative.
Such is the importance of the departmental view that in the creation of
the new super ministries in the 1970s, the establishment of a departmental view was seen as being a high priority (Radcliffe 1991). These
values are central to the department. They can unite or divide a
department, they limit the policy options and access to the policy
agenda, and they may divide departments against each other. The
departmental view is derived from a number of sources. Often,
departments develop close relations with particular interest groups in
policy networks, and there is a tendency then to see their role as
representing those interests in Whitehall. For example, in the Ministry
of Agriculture, the policy network between the officials and the
National Farmers' Union effectively established the departmental line,
with both parties seeing the continuation of agricultural subsidies as in
their interest (Smith 1990) (see Box 5.3).

In addition, both officials and ministers have an interest in their
departments doing well, and so they are concerned with protecting
their own budgets and areas of responsibility. Finally, departments are
often associated with particular policies that can outlast ministers and
governments, and there is a tendency for departments to become

concerned with protecting those interests. Kenneth Baker (1993: 168) found when he moved to the Department of Education that:

> Of all the Whitehall Departments the DES was among those with the strongest in-house ideology. There was a clear 1960s ethos and a very clear agenda which permeated virtually all civil servants . . . It was devoutly anti-excellence, anti-selection, and anti-market. The DES represented perfectly the theory of 'producer capture', whereby the interests of the producer prevail over the interests of the consumer. Not only was the department in league with the teacher unions, University Departments of Education, teacher-training theories, and local authorities, it also acted as their protector against any threats which Ministers might pose.

Nevertheless, in some departments it is not only officials who succumb to a departmental view. There is also a tendency for ministers to be captured by these concerns. Kaufman (1997: 14–15) warns against the dangers of departmentalitis:

> If you contract departmentalitis you will go along to a Cabinet Committee determined to win, regardless of the merits of your colleagues' case. You will carry with you a brief which tells you the department's view, or explains the department's interest if this is not manifest. If you contract departmentalitis you will forget that you are part of a government, that the fortunes of the government are more important than the fortunes of your own department.

There are frequent examples of politicians critical of agricultural policy who become Ministers of Agriculture only to find themselves fighting to protect the interests of the farmers. In this sense, they are inculcated into the pre-existing policy network (see Box 5.3). There is, particularly in European Union fora, a strong institutional imperative to protect the interest of farmers. For the department, the EU means that its budget and role continue to be significant, and for Britain it means that money gained for British farmers is a net gain to Britain from the EU.

Government departments are not blank sheets on which ministers can write their own policy desires. Through their history, institutional biases and cultures departments have long-term policy preferences. As we will see in Chapter 8 (and Box 5.3), the established policy networks in department constrain ministers. For example, in the Trade side of the Department of Trade and Industry there has been a preference for free trade almost throughout its two-hundred-year existence. As one former permanent secretary said in an interview:

> In the Department of Trade there was a strong Cobdenite free trading ethos. And, I think it is fair to say that almost anyone who has served in that department at any respectable level became infected with it up to, and including, the Secretary of State.

Consequently, when ministers pushed for protection of an industry:

> There was resistance, certainly at official level because the officials concerned believed in keeping the channels of trade open and believed that if we started putting protection on one industry there would be, certainly, pressures for restrictions by other industries as well . . . So the officials would be against giving into the pressure and ministers pretty soon came round to much the same view. Both Conservative and Labour ministers.

BOX 5.3
The agricultural policy network

Agriculture probably provides the best example of a closed policy network between a government department and a pressure group. In the post-war years, the National Farmers' Union (NFU) and the Ministry of Agriculture (MAFF) developed a very close relationship and the NFU became involved in all aspects of agricultural policy-making. This relationship developed due to the requirements of war and the immediate post-war food and economic crises (Smith 1990). Through the annual review of agricultural prices the NFU was given institutionalised access to the whole process of setting agricultural subsidies. In addition, the ministry and the union were not usually in conflict, but agreed on the goals of agricultural policy, which were to increase agricultural production and to ensure that prices were set to provide farmers with a reasonable standard of living. From 1945 until well into the 1980s, no minister from either party made any changes of significance to this agenda. Any groups or interests that opposed the policy were effectively excluded from the policy process.

Departments do not always change with new ministers or even new governments. Sometimes ministers do not want to change departments, either because the have little idea how to change or because they believe the political costs are too high. Often it is easier and less risky for the ministers to accept the warm embrace of the department and its briefs than to initiate new policies (Kaufman 1997).

However, even when ministers are committed to significant change it may be difficult, because in certain departments there are severe problems with changing policy in the short-term. For instance, the pensions policy developed by the Major government will have a fifteen-year cycle of development and implementation, and for a new minister to replace that work will take another fifteen years. Therefore, ministers in a department for only a short period can often not grasp the complexity of some of the problems that they face.

When Sir Keith Joseph was appointed Industry Secretary in 1979 he was concerned with shifting the department away from what he saw as its interventionist traditions. He was committed to disengaging from industry and introducing a *laissez-faire* policy. However, Sir Keith Joseph was unable to effect an immediate change in policy. In the words of an official:

> Keith Joseph didn't throw them [interventionist policies] out of the window straightaway, he was willing to examine with us, very carefully, what we were doing, why we were spending this money and what effect it was likely to have.

Despite the clear ideological preferences of Joseph, he was not able or willing to change radically the policy direction of the department. As one former deputy secretary remembered of the Joseph era: 'their policy was incremental. Basically, and in practice, most policies have to be implemented like that, a very radical change over night is too destructive and organisations can't cope.' Another senior ex-official put it even more strongly:

> The Department of Industry was pretty interventionist and didn't become any less so, frankly. In the information technology field we had a minister, Kenneth Baker, who was absolutely 100 per cent interventionist, constantly inventing schemes and things; we used to have a new scheme every fortnight. That culture I think persisted, there was a very close relationship with industry. Although industry

often say there wasn't, there was, particularly with certain sectors of industry.

In the area of high technology, for instance, there was the continuation of substantial financial support despite the free market rhetoric (Cortell 1997).

However, it is clear that the Joseph period heralded the beginning of an important change in the direction and culture of the Department of Industry and the process of disengagement from industry. Following Joseph, Thatcher appointed a succession of ideologically motivated ministers who accepted her *laissez-faire* disposition. These ministers produced an important reorientation in the department's preferences. However, this shift led to something of a crisis of identity for the DTI, with right-wing critics asking why a free market policy needs a Department of Industry – a question that has continued to reoccur (*Daily Telegraph*, 16 October 1995). Lord Young recalls that when taking up his position as Secretary of State, he felt that it was the 'Department of Disasters' and had lost its way (Young 1990: 237).

Young was able to harness the change of direction, informally re-titling the department – the 'Department for Enterprise'. He crystal-lised the change of direction and the department focused on extending the free market. Young consciously reviewed and restructured the department, with the aim of creating a department of wealth creation: 'I wanted to reduce government intervention, to reduce spending and to release enterprise. We had to move away from civil servants and ministers telling industry what to do' (Young 1990: 240). Young established a unit to review the work of the department, curtailed regional aid and ended sponsorship. He replaced the traditional goals of the department with a new set of principles based on advising rather than directing industry:

> The needs and demands of society can only be met by increasing prosperity. The prime objective of the Department is to assist this process throughout the economy and to champion all people who make it happen . . . Our objective will be to produce a climate which promotes enterprise and prosperity (Young 1990: 250).

The main tools to achieve these objectives were the market, deregula-tion and advice to business, not state intervention. For Young, the main role of the department was to influence attitudes. Consequently, the foci of the department became: the Deregulation Unit, which was concerned with eliminating red tape; the implementation of the Single European Act through the single market initiative; and the establishment of the advisory division concerned with providing advice to industry. In essence, despite frequent changes in structure and a major shift in ideological direction since 1979, it was only in 1987 that a significant change in culture occurred.

It is interesting to contrast the fortunes of Joseph and Young. Both joined a department with a bias towards industrial intervention; both were operating under similar ideological and economic pressures for reform and both consciously desired a new direction in industrial policy. Yet, Joseph was frustrated. He became Secretary of State at a time when there was economic pressure to redirect the department and ideological pressure from the prime minister, while he himself desired change. However, partly because of his personality and partly because of the external pressures he faced in terms of rising unemployment, recession and the demands of interest groups, he failed to radically change the department. One former senior Industry official, perhaps unconsciously, gave away the importance of the departmental line to civil servants when he revealed:

Keith Joseph who had very strong views about industry . . . now he would listen to the briefing on a particular issue, which was painful and difficult for him, but he would go through it and have a thorough discussion with officials, and let us say he was persuaded in the end by the official argument.

Joseph was a precursor to the critical change in the department: he attempted to use external pressure to change the direction of the department, yet, despite his well-documented free market beliefs he did not change the preferences of the department. Instead, he initiated a gradual shift in thinking. On the other hand, Young was clear that he was not going to accept the tendency towards intervention in the DTI, and so he forced the department to review its goals, abandon intervention and change its structure in order to pursue the goal of encouraging enterprise. He implanted a significant change in the strategic selectivity of the department. Today, the preferences of the department are oriented towards issues of deregulation and free enterprise, and the Blair government has given little indication that it will change direction again. Young faced a combination of structural pressures, a line of ministers who had changed the direction of department and possessed the vision to implant these changes onto the department. He successfully changed both the organisation and the culture of the department, which eased the process of policy change.

Therefore change does not necessarily result from a new minister or government because of the organisational and historical constraints on departments. Change in departments requires a minister with strategic vision, prime ministerial or cabinet backing, and what Cortell and Peterson (1998) call a window of opportunity. Before significant change in organisational structures occur there is a trigger: 'Every trigger – whether a crisis or non-crisis situation creates the opportunity for structural change if it discredits existing institutions or raises concerns about the adequacy of current policy-making processes'. (Cortell 1997: 9), and this creates a window of opportunity. These windows may be micro or macro windows, which present actors with varying degrees of opportunity for change:

> crises are environmental pressure that highlight wide-spread ineffi-
> ciencies in extant domestic institutions or afford élites wide-ranging
> autonomy from short term political constraints – open macro
> windows. They, therefore, create the possibility for wide-scale struc-
> tural modifications that seek to break with prevailing customs and
> procedures. Change does not occur automatically however. Whether
> policy entrepreneurs seek to exploit open windows depends on their
> preferences (Cortell and Peterson 1998:18).

Britain's economic crisis of the 1970s, combined with a significant electoral victory in 1979, created the window of opportunity for change in industrial policy, but, because of his personality and political opposition, Joseph was unable to make full use of this window. It took Young's strategic vision combined with prime-ministerial support to break the traditional constraints of the department and affect long-term change in the departmental line.

Departmental lines do not determine policy because ministers can impose their will, but the departmental line is the terrain on which a minister lands when he takes up office. In certain cases, as Headey's (1974) research suggested, this can lead to ministers without an agenda adopting departmental policies. Even ministers who have their own policies are reacting to, and reshaping, the existing departmental lines. Combating and changing the departmental line costs more than working with it. Moreover, in large departments where ministerial oversight is limited the departmental line is likely to determine policy in at least some areas.

It is important to realise that departmental lines are often not monolithic, and that often conflict may occur within a department over the direction it is taking. Officials have to consult with their colleagues in other parts of the department and develop a policy that is agreed by a range of sectional interests making the perpetration of a single departmental line difficult (Ponting 1986: 98–9, Smith and Stanyer 1976). These internal conflicts are replicated in conflicts with other departments.

RELATIONSHIPS BETWEEN DEPARTMENTS

Ponting (1986: 102) relates how

> [m]uch of the work of Whitehall is institutionalised conflict between the competing interests of different departments. Each department will defend its own position and resist a line that while it might be beneficial to the government as a whole or in the wider public interest, would work against the interest of the department.

This conflict can take a number of forms. It can be bilateral, whereby departments attempt to sort out a problem that concerns shared territory. Or it can be multilateral and formal, where an issue involves several departments and can be resolved only in a cabinet committee. Frequently, the conflicts occur over issues of expenditure or territory (see Madgwick 1991). Crossman records how in his first meeting with his Permanent Secretary at the Ministry of Housing she told him that he had been responsible for selling the department down the river because of Wilson's decision that Fred Willey should be in charge of planning: 'As soon as she realised this, Dame Evelyn [Sharp] got down to a Whitehall battle to save her department' (Crossman 1975: 25). The Westland affair and the salmonella in eggs affair (Smith 1991) illustrate how interdepartmental conflicts can sometimes get out of control (see Box 5.4).

One of the revelations from the Scott report was the way departmental views and organisational imperatives structured the behaviour of officials in terms of policy decisions such as the issuing of export licences. The three departments involved in the interdepartmental committees had particular interests to protect. The DTI was concerned with encouraging trade and ensuring British companies were not disadvantaged. The FCO aimed to ensure that trade with Iran and

---

BOX 5.4
The Westland Affair, 1985–6

The Westland Affair demonstrated that conflicts frequently concern policy. The Department of Trade and Industry fought an
intense battle, particularly with the Ministry of Defence, over
whether the troubled Westland Helicopter company should be
saved by a European consortium or the US company Sikorsky.
Michael Heseltine, the Secretary of State for Defence, backed the
European option, believing that the Sikorsky bid would lead to
the end of European helicopter production. Leon Brittan effectively believed the market should decide, and that if the Westland
board believed the Sikorsky deal was best then the government
should not intervene.

The intensity of the battle was such that it involved secret
meetings of ministers and various interests, and leaks to the press.
Essentially, the cabinet decided to accept Brittan's position. But
Heseltine was unwilling to submit, and therefore through a series
of leaks and meetings he attempted to rally support for the
European consortium. There was an open split in the cabinet,
which culminated in a letter from the Attorney General being
leaked stating that there were 'material inaccuracies' in Heseltine's
case. When, at a cabinet meeting, Thatcher said all statements on
Westland should be cleared by the Number 10, Heseltine resigned
and left the meeting. This was followed by the resignation of Leon
Brittan after he misled the House of Commons over a letter from
one of the interested parties complaining of the DTI's handling of
the issue and he took responsibility for the leaking of the Attorney
General's letter (Dunleavy 1990, Linklater and Leigh 1986, Cloonan no date).

Iraq would not upset the balance between these two countries or upset
US and Middle Eastern allies, and the MOD did not want British
weapons used against British troops. Consequently, the DTI did not
like the guidelines on arms sales to Iran and Iraq. As a DTI memo
stated:

[t]he DTI's principal objective was to maintain the best possible
opportunities for trade with both countries, both in civil goods and

services and 'acceptable' defence exports, and to ensure that existing contractual obligations are honoured . . . These objectives would best be served by maintaining the maximum possible flexibility in the guidelines (Scott 1996: 171).

Despite the export control being against the interest of the department, it was the DTI that had responsibility for issuing export licences (Scott 1996: 111). In the IDC, if the MOD and FCO did not object to the licences, then the DTI would issue them, but if the MOD and FCO objected then the DTI would refer the matter to a minister, again demonstrating how ministers can be useful resource for officials. One of the causes of the Arms to Iraq Affair was the wish of the DTI to flexibly interpret the guidelines. The FCO on the other hand wanted a stricter interpretation because its main interest was presentation, not to the public, but overseas.

Scott also provides an excellent example of the way structural imperatives and agency can interact in the interdepartmental decision-making process. Alan Clark, Minister for Trade, was concerned with increasing exports, and his view was that the guidelines were a public relations exercise to hold off criticism; as such, they were not really policy. In July 1989 he was shifted from Trade to Defence, and Lord Trefgarne became minister for Trade. In Scott's words: 'Lord Trefgarne, at the MOD, had generally accepted the advice of his officials on matters relating to exports to Iraq and Iran' (1996: 431). In his period at MOD, there was no example when he disagreed with a recommendation for refusal of an ELA:

> When he became Minister of Trade at the DTI his Ministerial brief . . . was to promote exports. It is not surprising, therefore, to find Lord Trefgarne, wearing his DTI hat, became much more determined in support of ELAs (export licence agreements) for Iran and Iraq than he had been in his previous office wearing his MOD hat.

With the shift in posts, there was an 'important shift in the balance between the junior ministers'. Clark at the DTI could not defeat combined forces of the MOD and the FCO – when he referred matters up to minister, he lost (p. 431):

> Once, however, Mr Clark had become Minister [Defence Procurement], the balance appears to shift. In most of the disputes that, after July 1989, reached Ministerial level, the MOD and the DTI were

ranged against the FCO. The change was not in attitude of the Minister for Trade. The change was in attitude of the Minister (DP).

Clark was much more prepared to question the advice of MOD experts. On this occasion, one minister (Lord Trefgarne) was consistent with his institutional position when he was minister in Defence and the DTI, while Clark had a particular view that he carried with him from the DTI to the MOD. Thus, Clarke exercised agency; in so doing, he shifted the balance within the IDC, which created a possibility of a more relaxed interpretation of the guidelines.

THE THATCHERISATION OF WHITEHALL

A number of commentators have suggested that the period of Conservative governments, from 1979 to 1997, led to the politicisation of the civil service and an increasing tendency for ministers to dominate officials. There has been much discussion concerning how eighteen years of Conservative government changed the relationships between officials and ministers and, indeed, between the prime minister and departments. Lord Callaghan believes there were 'revolutionary changes' in the civil service, which affected the impartiality, integrity and incorruptibility of the civil service (HC 390–II 1992/93: 139). Several authors have identified a decline in the influence of the civil service during the long period of Conservative government (Foster and Plowden 1997; Campbell and Wilson 1995). Eighteen years of a Conservative government with a clear ideological agenda appears to have reduced the ability of officials either to influence the framework of policy or to delay implementation until a new government is in office. According to Campbell and Wilson (1995: 60):

> Civil servants were increasingly defining their role as being implementors rather than policy analysts, people who gave ministers what they said they wanted rather than functioning as what they disparagingly called 'quasi-academics' who tried to show politicians the full consequences, adverse as well as positive, of their policy proposals.

As we saw at the beginning of the chapter, Thatcher was always distrustful of the civil service and its consensual approach, and sought more commitment from her officials. This view led to the accusation of the politicisation of the civil service, or, at the least, following events such as Norman Lamont's legal expenses being paid by the Treasury and the Matrix Churchill Affair, some unease about the changing relationship between ministers and officials. For Callaghan, 'the Government has been in power so long, I fear the Civil Service is no longer the buffer it was between the public and Ministers. I fear that we are getting to the state where the Government has been there so long that they regard the Civil Service as part of their private fiefdom' (HC 390-II 1992/3: 138).

Richards's (1997) study of the impact of Conservatism on officials demonstrates the absence of overt politicisation of the civil service, but suggests instead a 'personalisation' of Whitehall. For Richards (1997: 172), 'a more plausible assessment of the Thatcher approach to top appointments suggests that she appointed people with management experience or can-do reputations'. Thatcher attempted to move away from the traditional élitist mandarin to more managerially orientated types who would, whatever their personal political beliefs, be effective and efficient in implementing government policies. Richards further suggests that the appointments were, on occasions, more personal, with Thatcher having a greater input into the appointment procedure than previous Prime Ministers, and having very distinct personal likes and dislikes.

A second way that Thatcher affected the running of Whitehall was her relationship with departments. Both Callaghan and Wilson generally left ministers to run departments. Wilson, particularly in his second term, acted much more as a team manager, and Major was rarely in a strong enough position to impose policies on the likes of Kenneth Clarke, Michael Howard and Peter Lilley. Thatcher, on the other hand, as we saw in the last chapter, seems to have been much more involved in the detail of policy-making. She had a very direct impact on education and health policy reform, and she often operated bilaterally with ministers in the development of policy.

Another important point is the way the context affects relationships. The context of the Blair Labour government is very different from the Major or Thatcher governments. When the Conservatives came to power in 1979 they took a considerable time to overcome the constraints of organisational cultures. Officials did not attempt to thwart ministers, but they did have mindsets developed during the post-war consensus, and the options they offered tended to come from that agenda. By the 1990s, ministers had a long experience of government and the framework in which officials operated had changed greatly. Labour ministers face a situation where they have no experience of government and where the civil service are operating within a particular framework, and until the new ministers are able to change this framework, it will provide the agenda for their policy options.

CONCLUSION

The central argument of this chapter is that the relationship between officials and ministers is highly structured. The structure derives from the rules of the game and the institutional context. In principle, officials are advantaged in terms of resources, but their use of resources is constrained by two factors. First, it is difficult for officials to use their resources without ministerial authority. Second, the rules of the game are such that officials accept ministerial authority. While this limits what civil servants do, it has certain advantages, because it means they are not responsible for the decisions of departments. Therefore, the relationships between officials and ministers are not based on conflict, because the basis of their power is different. Officials operate in the interstices between ministerial decisions and the rules of the game. Their power is in interpretation, whereas ministers operate at the apex of the department in a broader political context and their power is in making decisions.

Consequently, ministers and officials are dependent on each other. For ministers to achieve their policy goals, and for civil servants to have a successful department, they need each other. Each brings different resources to the policy process, and for each to succeed these resources need to be exchanged. Although the civil service controls tremendous resources, it is difficult for it to use them because of the need for ministerial authority. The relationship between ministers and officials is a structured relationship, with civil servants reproducing the rules of the Whitehall game and each minister acting as an external agent, using the department to achieve his or her policy goals. Because ministers are in very different structural positions with different resources, their impact on the policy process varies. They influence outcomes in different ways, and therefore it cannot be said that ministers or officials dominate.

6 Coordinating the Core Executive: The Cabinet Office, the Prime Minister's Office and the Treasury

This chapter will examine the processes of coordination in the relatively fragmented core executive. The previous chapter highlighted the strength of resource-rich departments in the policy process. Their autonomy raises the question of how the core executive is coordinated if departments are responsible for most policies. Indeed, notions of governance suggest that problems of coordination will only become greater as the central state fragments further.

Formally, the core executive is coordinated by the cabinet, sustained by the convention of collective cabinet responsibility: the cabinet makes decisions and all ministers within the government are collectively responsible for those decisions. Yet, like much else in British government, this view of government reflects constitutional myth rather than reality. Collective responsibility suggests that cabinet is a forum for open discussion where all contribute and, therefore, are prepared to abide by decisions (Dell 1994; Hennessy 1995). Cabinet is the apex of the executive, bringing together the departmental chiefs to inform, decide and to coordinate. However, cabinet is rarely a forum for decision-making; its role is usually to ratify particular decisions. The idea of collective cabinet responsibility has resulted in politicians and analysts perceiving the cabinet as the key coordinator (see Wakeham 1994), but in reality the cabinet is becoming like monarchy – in Bagehot's words, a dignified element of the constitution (see Hennessy 1995: 96–7). In Lawson's (1992: 125) view:

> The least important aspect of Cabinet membership, certainly in Margaret Thatcher's time, were the Cabinet meetings themselves. The imprimatur of Cabinet was taken seriously, and there were

occasional Cabinet meetings that really mattered, such as those that concluded the annual expenditure round. But in general, and for good reason, key decisions were taken in smaller groups – either the formal Cabinet Committees, of which the most important were like the Cabinet itself, chaired by the Prime Minister; or still informal meetings of Ministers which she would usually hold in her study upstairs. The Cabinet's customary role was to rubber stamp decisions that had already been taken, to keep all colleagues reasonably informed about what was going on, and to provide a forum for general political discussion if time permitted.

Decision-making rarely occurs in cabinet but in departments, Number 10 and cabinet committees. In the words of one permanent secretary, policy-making occurs in 'chimneys', with departments having an interest in maintaining control over *their* policies. Consequently, the core executive has a tendency to fragment. Within a system that is institutionally biased towards fragmentation the crucial question arises, who or what coordinates if it is not the cabinet? Lawson implies that the site of coordination is within the cabinet system through cabinet committees and the Cabinet Office. This may partially be true, but the Cabinet Office is more a formal administrative machine than a coordinator and, until recently with the creation of the Office of Public Service (the OPS was originally the Office of Public Service and Science, OPSS), it lacked the political authority for coordination. The cabinet committee system is concerned more with discrete issues than the overall operation of government.

This chapter suggests there are three potential coordinators: the Prime Minister's Office; the Cabinet Office and the Office of Public Service (OPS); and the Treasury. This raises the questions of whether three separate bodies can coordinate, and how relations are managed between the various coordinating elements. The chapter suggests that coordination is structurally weak because of competition between different coordination bodies and because no single institution controls sufficient resources to dominate departments. Because of this structural weakness, the whim of the Prime Minister can have an impact on the coordination process and, as we will see, Thatcher, Major and Blair have all changed the processes of coordination. The structural location of the Prime Minister means she or he is able to change the institutions of coordination. This chapter demonstrates how, during the 1980s, the influence of the Cabinet Office declined as the Treasury and the Prime Minister became increasingly important in the process of coordination.

The 1990s have witnessed a further shift of coordination functions to the Prime Minister, with an increasing role for the OPS and a loss of influence for the Treasury. We begin by examining the role of the Treasury.

The Treasury

Formally, the Treasury is an economic, and not a coordinating, department. However, the importance of its functions, the status of its ministers and the impact it has on all other departments uniquely places it to affect the operation of the core executive as a whole. The Treasury controls and plans the expenditure of all departments; before recent reforms it also controlled and planned the manpower, pay and gradings of all civil servants. Consequently, it is networked to all elements of the core executive. It also has responsibility for macro-economic policy and taxation (Pliatzky 1989). Indeed, the British system is unusual in having economic and financial responsibilities within one department (Healey 1990: 385). As Lawson (1992: 273) reveals,

> the Chancellor has his finger in pretty well every pie in government. This follows partly from his responsibility for Government spending and partly from tradition. As a result, he can exert a significant influence on policies which are announced by other ministers and which the public does not associate with the Treasury at all.

Cabinet ministers at the receiving end of Treasury fingers have also confirmed their impact. The former energy minister David Howell told Peter Hennessy (1986: 96) that 'the nexus between Number 10 and the Treasury is decisive, it overrules, it is everything. The Treasury also knows that it can win.' Lord Carrington confirmed in an interview: 'The Treasury always wins,' and a number of former cabinet ministers said in interviews that the Treasury was the key coordinating department. This section examines the nature of the Treasury's resources and how it affects the running of government as a whole. However, as the chapter will demonstrate, the Treasury does not control as much as it thinks, and to some degree its influence has declined recently. Crucially, the Treasury and the Chancellor have a number of resources unavailable to other departments.

Colonisation

The Treasury, as Lawson indicates, manages to have a finger in nearly
every pie by both colonising departments and policies. Most policy
issues involve the Treasury in order to review the financial and
economic implications. The supervisory role manifests itself in a
number of ways. At the political level, a Treasury minister is on every
cabinet committee involved in taking a decision that may conceivably
result in extra expenditure (Healey 1990: 376), and official committees
always include a Treasury official. Lawson suggests that he spent much
of his time as Chancellor 'on a cabinet committee on any one of a vast
range of subjects, from defence procurement to social security reform
. . .' (Lawson 1992: 273). Within the department, there is an expenditure division headed by a grade 3 with what are now called standing
teams of the public expenditure division effectively shadowing each
area of government. The function of these teams is to advise the
Chancellor 'on the allocation and control of financial and human
resources throughout the public sector' (Thain and Wright 1995: 95).
Subsequently, they continually monitor the flow of expenditure
through departments. The Treasury has 124 expenditure controllers
with responsibility for maintaining and controlling expenditure within
departments, and they spend much of their time examining departmental expenditure, checking the accuracy of their claims, and negotiating increases and reductions in spending (Thain and Wright 1995).
These tentacles place the Treasury in a commanding position, as Thain
and Wright (1995: 104) discovered:

> An advantage which the Treasury possesses over other departments
> is that of perspective. From its central position, and the centrality of
> the expenditure function, the Treasury is uniquely placed to see the
> 'bigger picture'. A skilled expenditure controller can perceive and
> make connections between policy issues and expenditure items which
> have arisen separately in different programmes . . . The Chief
> Secretary and the Chancellor have a unique view of the totality of
> public expenditure, and through cabinet and its committees, the
> opportunity to help shape and transmit down through the Treasury
> the general priorities in government spending.

Nevertheless, like other areas of the core executive, the relationship
between the Treasury and departments is one of interdependence.
Heclo and Wildavsky (1981) revealed in their study of the Treasury

how the relationship between the Treasury and spending departments is largely based on trust. In order to allocate resources the Treasury needs the cooperation of departments:

> Above all, neither the Treasury nor departments can perform their respective functions satisfactorily, achieve their policy aims, and try to optimise their values, without exchanging the resources of authority, finance, information, and expertise which each possesses in different amounts and combination (Thain and Wright 1995: 200).

Heclo and Wildavsky believe that the importance of gaining trust means the Principal Finance Officers (PFO) – who have to account (with the Permanent Secretary) for the expenditure of their department and to deal with the respective expenditure controller in the Treasury – have a tendency to over-consult with the Treasury. In order to build a good relationship they perhaps give more information to the Treasury than they need to, which actually serves to increase Treasury control over other departments (Heclo and Wildavsky 1981: 17)

Most of the time the rules of the game work satisfactorily, partly because the Treasury has colonised Whitehall. The finance division within a department is run by the PFO, who many see as the Treasury's representative in the department (Heclo and Wildavsky 1981). Partly because the relationship is built on trust, the PFO and the Expenditure Controller tend to be open with each other, and the PFO sees it as her or his role to inform the Treasury when 'limits have been reached' (Thain and Wright 1995: 203).

The Treasury also colonises by getting its people into other departments, and in particular many permanent secretaries are former Treasury officials, and they have a tendency to be sympathetic to the Treasury's ways of working. Despite some resentment in the departments about its control, most departmental officials accept the Treasury's right to intervene (see Heclo and Wildavsky 1981). Many non-Treasury officials, however, also believe that the Treasury officials' lack of management experience means they are not very effective permanent secretaries or departmental managers. One official in the Cabinet Office spoke of the Treasury in the 1990s in very negative terms:

> the Treasury were at the same time running the most incompetent internal management system I have ever seen and were also trying to

impose on other departments systematic management as conceived out of an academic book. Begging your pardon, I mean it wasn't real.

The status of the Chancellor

The Chancellor is a crucial position in any government. The post is one usually given to someone of high seniority in the party who carries his or her own authority. At other times, when the Chancellor is a less imposing figure, as in the case of Lamont or Major, it is usually because they are very close to the Prime Minister. In either situation, they have considerable authority with the rest of the cabinet. In addition, the Chancellor is at the apex of a department that is widely perceived as exceptionally able, and which has control over large elements of the behaviour of other departments and the macroeconomy. Indeed, as we will see below, many of the decisions made by the Chancellor are made singularly or at the most in consultation with the Prime Minister. Consider, for example, Gordon Brown's decision in May 1997 to give the Bank of England independence. Although the independence had to be formalised with legislation, Brown effectively made one of the most significant changes in macroeconomic policy in the post-war era without consulting the cabinet or Parliament.

Such is the strength of the Chancellor's position that Prime Ministers often feel they cannot survive their resignation. As we saw in Chapter 4, Thatcher believed she would have difficulty after Lawson's resignation in 1988. Similarly, during the 1976 IMF crises, Callaghan (1988: 435) felt that '[a]t a pinch we could afford to lose the Secretary for Energy, or *in extremis* even the Foreign Secretary, but the Government would not have survived the resignation of the Chancellor'. As a result of this importance, the Chancellor sits on more committees than any other minister (except Heseltine when he was Deputy Prime Minister) and is chair of many of the most important ones (Healey 1990: 383). Such is his or her position that other cabinet ministers have little choice but to succumb to the desires of the Chancellor, especially if he has the support of the Prime Minister.

Prime Minister–Chancellor relations

The relationship between the Prime Minister and the Chancellor is crucial to the operation of the whole of the executive. They are the two most resource-laden individuals within government, each with a high level of authority. They are, however, highly dependent on each other. The Prime Minister is dependent on a Chancellor to deliver economic success, and the Chancellor frequently needs the Prime Minister's support for economic policy and to force the cabinet to accept limits on public expenditure. In Healey's (1990: 388) view, the job of Chancellor is impossible without the support of the Prime Minister. Working together, the Prime Minister and Chancellor are extremely strong and it would be rare that any coalition of ministers could defeat a combined Chancellor/prime-ministerial alliance (see Table 6.1). A strong alliance characterised the early years of the Howe–Thatcher relationship. Thatcher's domination of economic policy in her first parliament is often taken for granted, but she was only able to determine the policy direction because of the support of Howe (see Dell 1996). Howe and Thatcher effectively agreed the main precepts of economic policy, and Howe implemented much of it without cabinet consultation; when there was consultation it often resulted in strong cabinet opposition. Despite problems in their relationship, they were relatively close ideologically in terms of economic policy, and were able to implement a radical economic and public spending policy with little coherent opposition (Gilmour 1992, Howe 1994). Again, Blair and Brown provide the crucial nexus of the 1997 Labour government, consulting together many times a day (*Observer,* 19 October 1997). Blair provides the overall direction of government, and Brown and the Treasury scrutinise expenditure plans in great detail. Indeed, it is suggested that Brown has considerable independence in economic policy and control over key aspects of social policy through the welfare to work policy. According to Johnson (1998), 'It is a rule of thumb that in every important department of state, there is a minister loyal to Gordon Brown.' Routledge (1998: 296) confirms that Brown's political influence spreads 'far and wide beyond the Treasury, and not simply through the control of spending'.

Chancellors are often in a strong enough position to operate with some degree of independence from the Prime Minister. If economic policy is working well, and the Chancellor has the support of the parliamentary party and the cabinet, the Prime Minister would rarely have the authority to overrule the Chancellor or to sack him and survive. Both Kenneth Clarke and Gordon Brown were given considerable discretion over economic policy. In 1988 Lawson managed to shadow the DM, despite the express disapproval of the Prime Minister. Because of his economic success and the fact that he was seen as the architect of the 1987 election victory, he was more or less, in Thatcher's word, invincible and gained almost complete autonomy over economic policy (Keegan 1989; Lawson 1992). Thatcher wonders in her memoirs whether she should have sacked Lawson at the time and concludes:

> I would have been fully justified in doing so. He had pursued a policy without my knowledge or consent and he continued to adopt a different approach from that which he knew I wanted. On the other hand he was widely – and rightly – credited with helping us win the 1987 election. He had complete mastery of his brief. He had strong support of Conservative back-benchers and much of the Conservative press had convinced themselves that I was in the wrong . . . Whatever happened, I felt that if Nigel and I – supported by the rest of the Cabinet – pulled together we could avert or at least overcome the consequence of past mistakes and get the economy back on course for the next general election (Thatcher 1993: 703).

Table 6.1   Relationships between Prime Ministers and Chancellors 1976–98

Prime Minister/ government	Chancellor	Main themes of economic policy	Relationships
Labour Callaghan 1976–9	Healey	Wage restraint and control of inflation	Cooperative and mutually supportive
Conservative Thatcher 1979–83	Howe	Control of inflation through monetarism	Cooperative and mutually supportive
Thatcher 1983–9	Lawson	Control of inflation through controlling borrowing and interest rate and exchange rate policy	Broke down over exchange rate policy and ERM membership
Thatcher 1989–90	Major	Joining ERM	Thatcher dependent on Major
Major 1990–3	Lamont	ERM to control inflation Later tight fiscal policy to control inflation	Broke down after Black Wednesday Conflict over policy direction
Major 1993–7	Clarke	Tight fiscal policy to control inflation	Cooperative Major dependent on Clarke Some conflict over monetary union
Labour Blair 1997–	Brown	Tight fiscal policy Welfare to work	Cooperative and interdependent

Kenneth Clarke was also seen as a successful Chancellor in relation to a weak Prime Minister, and had a high degree of independence in economic policy. Such was his strength, that the Prime Minister, Major, was unable to abandon the 'wait and see' policy on Britain's membership of a single currency, despite strong party and cabinet opposition to the policy (see Seldon 1997).

Changing contexts can result in the Prime Minister limiting the autonomy of the Chancellor. As Bernard Donoughue suggests, 'Crises . . . require the active involvement of the cabinet (in economic policy-making) and provide the Prime Minister with the opportunity to intervene.' He maintains that during the IMF crisis, the

> Chancellor wanted the approval of his Prime Minister and colleagues in order to spread the responsibility collectively. He also needed the Prime Minister to lead and deliver the support of other Ministers . . . Therefore, in these crises, the Chancellor needed the Prime Minister to rally such colleagues behind him and this in turn gave the Prime Minister an enhanced opportunity to intervene (Donoughue 1987: 8).

At times of economic crisis, the Prime Minister has the authority to take over much of the direction of economic policy. It is so important to the success of the government that no Prime Minister is likely to abstain from intervention in such a situation. Thus policy-making during the ERM crisis in September 1992 revolved almost solely around an axis of Lamont and Major (Thompson 1996b).

Finally, there are situations where breaks in dependency occur between the Prime Minister and the Chancellor, and this can result in disaster for the Prime Minister, the Chancellor, the government, or all three. The most notable, discussed in Chapter 4, is the breakdown in the relationship between Thatcher and Lawson, which resulted in Lawson's resignation and was an important factor in Thatcher's eventual demise. A more recent example is the relationship between Lamont and Major. Although in the earlier period of the Major government Lamont and the Prime Minister worked closely together, after the forced exit from the ERM in 1992 there was mutual recrimination, as each attempted to blame the other for the policy failure. Lamont was prevented from returning to monetarism (Thompson 1996b), and there were significant disagreements between Major and Lamont over economic policy (Seldon 1997: 336). Nevertheless, despite disagreements, there was mutual dependency. Major did not want Lamont to resign after Britain's exit from the ERM, because he feared he too would have to go. Eventually, after prolonged disagreements, Lamont was forced to resign. The policy failure and a poor prime-ministerial–Chancellor relationship contributed significantly to the 1997 election defeat.

Superiority

The Treasury has incorporated a sense of its own superiority, in relation both to other departments and to ministers, into its culture. According to Edward Boyle (Kogan 1971: 112), the Treasury has the propensity 'to think of itself not only as the best department, but as the department which really knows other departments' work better than they do themselves'. It is the Treasury that employs 'the brightest chaps'. Michael Posner, a former Treasury Official, told Young and Sloman (1984: 24):

> The Treasury has always been the powerhouse. Harold Lever once said that moving to the Treasury from another department was like coming to the Savoy from a two-star hotel out of the provinces . . . The Treasury has always contained very clever people, at least as clever as one meets at High Table in an average Oxbridge college. They're well read, they're accomplished, they're intelligent, they're knowledgeable, they're powerful.

This sense of their own brilliance and importance is to some extent shared by the rest of Whitehall, and so when the Treasury says something it is seen as right or good. Haines (1977: 40) portrays this perception negatively:

> The belief in their own infallibility is one of the Treasury's greatest mistakes. It is a belief, however, that dies hard in Whitehall and Westminster and especially among politicians who regard the Treasury knights with something of the reverence with which Red Indians approached totem poles.

More importantly, there is widespread acquiescence to the Treasury's intervention in other departments. For Haines, 'they *are* sovereign in Whitehall'. Although the brilliance of Treasury 'chaps' may not be as great as they themselves assume, the Treasury does possess a framework for analysing departmental expenditure and one which is exercised without departmental preferment. One of the strongest rules of the game in Whitehall is loyalty to the department, and therefore the scepticism of Treasury officials provides a useful perspective, which can raise important questions concerning the viability of programmes. Treasury officials are taught to be suspicious of unexpected increases in spending, open-ended commitments and disguised expenditures. To achieve goals of financial stringency, Treasury officials are prepared to probe and question. The interference may annoy departmental colleagues, but one of Whitehall's norms is that it is the Treasury's 'reputation for toughness which inhibits would-be spenders' (Heclo and Wildavsky 1981: 49–50).

Monopoly of information

The Treasury has almost a complete monopoly of economic and public expenditure information. This makes it extremely difficult for ministers or departments to challenge its arguments. As we have seen, ministers are highly preoccupied with departmental matters, and if they do have the energy to challenge Treasury prognostications, they then have to try to find an alternative sources of information. As the former Permanent Secretary at the Treasury, Douglas Wass (1984: 11–12), has argued on economic issues:

> No other minister has at his command the back-up of analytical support that the Chancellor receives from his Treasury and Revenue Department officials and the Bank of England. How can his colleagues be assured that they are getting the whole story and not just the one which the Chancellor wishes them to hear? They have indeed no direct access to the official advice which the Treasury provides. Yet they are obliged to come to a view on the basis of what one of their colleagues, a committed party, is telling them.

Hence, the Treasury has the institutional bases, the authority and the information to intervene in other departments in a way that would be foreign to any other department and not acceptable from any other department. Consequently, the role of the Treasury is extended from its economic and public expenditure remit to a wider policy role.

The Treasury's policy role

Much of the Treasury's dominance is predicated on its responsibility for three interrelated and crucial policy areas: the economy; the budget and public spending. It is worth paying particular attention to the public expenditure policy round, because it demonstrates clearly the complexity and context of the operation of the core executive. The public expenditure round is conducted in a political arena in the context of structured set of resources. As we saw above, the Treasury has a particular set of resources, which are greatly strengthened by prime-ministerial support. At the same time, the Prime Minister and the Chancellor are constrained by the general economic situation and longer-term political goals. They are also confronted by the departments, with their own resources in terms of direct control over policy and expenditure, who present a number of pressures, often short-term, for increased expenditure. These resources or constraints include the following:

Political status   Ministers, may profess a commitment to reduction in government spending, but they rarely want to see *their* departmental expenditure reduced. A minister is judged by both colleagues and officials in terms of how well they do for the department, and a crucial measure of this success is the ability to increase the departmental budget. With more money, a minister can have a greater impact, and this increases his or her political weight. Jordan and Richardson (1986: 222) provide the example of Sir Keith Joseph, who 'talked fundamental monetarism in the Cabinet [but] he left the Department of Trade and Industry with a reputation as a big spender'. The failure of John Moore at the DHSS in 1987–8 was also blamed partly on his failure to sufficiently increase departmental expenditure. The department expects the minister to succeed in the expenditure round.

Departments' expectations   In addition to ministers having an interest in greater expenditure, departments also place pressure on ministers to squeeze a drop more out of the Treasury. Lord Parkinson (1992: 240–2) gives an illustration of the institutional pressures that departments exert on increased expenditure. He recalls his opposition to the game of overbidding to the Treasury in order to achieve what the department wanted.

> I felt the whole process was an exhausting waste of time, and that if the spenders put in meaningful bids in the first place, and the Treasury behaved reasonably, the whole process would be a good deal shorter, much less acrimonious and would leave ministers free to concentrate on getting value out of their current programmes rather than spending so much time arguing about next year's. When

I put this case at a meeting of ministers and senior officials, it was regarded as heresy.

Programmatic demands Many programmes such as education, health and social security, are demand-led, and if there is a statutory obligation to provide a service then there is little the department or the Treasury can do to control expenditure. The NHS expenditure is affected by how many people are ill or, for example, a cold winter. In addition, it also suffers from higher than average inflation. The costs of many programmes are uncontrollable.

Public and interest group pressure Pressure groups and the public also create tremendous pressure for more expenditure. Through policy networks, some pressure groups are in constant contact with departments and are in a position to demand more spending on their service. Often official and ministers will see this as the pleading of special interests, but if groups are able to harness public concern then the department can use the pressure as a lever for extra expenditure. Each winter produces scare stories from the NHS as part of the pressure to gain extra money. There are numerous examples where pressure has resulted in extra governmental pressure – compensation for haemophiliac victims of AIDS; farmers and BSE; extra health expenditure.

Elections The public pressure for increased expenditure is particularly great at election time. Ministers do not want complaints about public services in the run-up to an election, and the pleadings of spending ministers will have more weight in an election year. Moreover, Chancellors are also tempted to pump money into the economy in the run-up to an election, especially as they are increasingly convinced by the importance of the 'feel-good' factor.

These pressures make the public expenditure round, despite its technical nature, extremely interesting politically (see Box 6.1). The battles over spending demonstrate in an acute way the workings of the core executive and the impact of the conjuncture of structure, institutions, agents and tactics. As well as the internal institutional pressures described above, many of the constraints on the public expenditure round are determined by economic circumstances beyond the control of government. Economic recession reduces government revenue and increases the cost of social security programmes. As a result, governments have either to cut public expenditure or to raise taxes. During the period of the Keynesian ascendancy, governments tended to increase public expenditure at time of recession in order to encourage economic growth. From the 1960s onwards, governments found it increasingly difficult to take account of economic events in the outside world, and by the 1970s it was no longer clear how much demand the government should inject into the economy to produce increased employment (Healey 1990: 379). Since the early 1980s, increased spending and public borrowing has been viewed as bad for the economy, producing higher inflation and creating levels of taxation that large numbers of voters are no longer prepared to accept. Consequently, public spending policy has revolved around reducing or at least controlling the level of public expenditure. This commitment to expenditure control continued with the election of a Labour government in 1997. The latter formally tied to the Conservatives' spending plans and to increasing expenditure only when economic growth makes extra money available.

We can identify three sets of pressures on the public expenditure process. The departmental pressure for more expenditure, the economic pressure on the amount of money available and Treasury and prime-ministerial pressure to control or even reduce the level of public expenditure. It is within this structured context that the various actors attempt to resolve the public expenditure battle. Thain and Wright (1995: 227) highlight how public expenditure is

> not determined residually after calculation of prospective revenue . . . but partly as a result of 'top-down' considerations concerned with broad macro-economic strategy, and partly 'bottom-up' as a result of the pressures from spending ministers for additional resources during the Survey.

The public expenditure round is more or less a continuous process (Box 6.1). Once the spending round is finished in November, with the public expenditure White Paper, departments are already considering their spending bids for the following year. Departments are in a continuous process of reviewing their expenditure, relating it to outcomes and evaluating the requirements for the future. This has become formalised through the MINIS systems, which are formal and complex management procedures for assessing departmental expenditure.

The main body of work, as far as the Treasury is concerned, starts in July. From 1992 onwards, the government has set a New Control Target; this is the absolute limit of public expenditure, and if ministers believe they have a case for extra spending then the money has to come

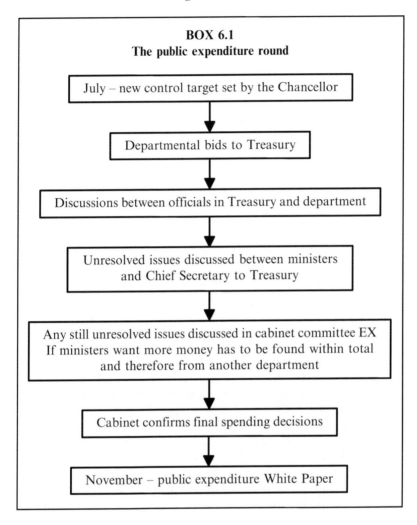

BOX 6.1
The public expenditure round

July – new control target set by the Chancellor

Departmental bids to Treasury

Discussions between officials in Treasury and department

Unresolved issues discussed between ministers
and Chief Secretary to Treasury

Any still unresolved issues discussed in cabinet committee EX
If ministers want more money has to be found within total
and therefore from another department

Cabinet confirms final spending decisions

November – public expenditure White Paper

from another department. Consequently, the cabinet is involved in discussing priorities and a new public expenditure cabinet committee, EDX (EX under the Labour government), has been established, with the Chancellor in the chair, to oversee allocations within departments (Burns 1995). This change has effectively strengthened the Treasury in relation to the departments. No longer are departments pleading in a neutral committee, the star chamber, for extra money; they now have to make the case to a committee which the Chancellor chairs and which has to allocate spending within an absolute limit. In July the cabinet sets priorities, then the Public Expenditure Survey committees are established that represent the PFO of the department concerned and Treasury officials.

Departments put bids into the Treasury, and these are discussed between officials. If agreement can be reached then there is no need for issues to go up to ministerial level, but often official discussions revolve around easily resolvable issues. In the past, ministers would have been involved in long and detailed discussions concerning spending. With the new system, disputes are resolved in the EX because spending has to be considered as a whole and not on a department-by-department basis. Departments have a strong incentive to resolve as much as possible at official level and not to allow wider debate because, of course, they could lose money. The role for ministers in this operation is to convince their cabinet colleagues, and to some extent outside observers, that their case should be a priority. The increasing news of education or health spending crises are often a part of ministerial tactics in influencing expenditure outcomes. Stories will be leaked in order to convince colleagues that their case is the most pressing.

Despite continual efforts to reform the techniques of the public expenditure programme, and despite their explicit goals of reducing public expenditure, consecutive Conservative governments failed to reduce the level of public expenditure. Even with the new system, departmental haggling continues, as Seldon (1997: 344) reveals of the 1992 round:

> The conclusions of EDX were brought to a special cabinet meeting on Monday evening, 2 November, where Portillo outlined his recommendations, and ministers haggled for four hours . . . The cabinet continued deliberating on Tuesday and again at the regular Thursday meeting. Eight hours were spent reaching agreement.

While the Conservative governments reduced the rate of public expenditure increases and reduced spending as a proportion of GDP, they failed to achieve their ultimate goal. Much of public expenditure is beyond the control of governments, because of pre-existing policies, demographic changes and economic conditions. Moreover, as rational choice theorists suggest, politicians have departmental and electoral reasons for wishing to protect their expenditure. Consequently, we are left with the question of whether the Treasury can control expenditure, let alone the core executive, effectively, particularly when departments are so strong (see Jackson 1992, Hogwood 1992, Rose and Davies 1994, Thain and Wright 1995).

The concern with purely financial issues means that the Treasury's commitment to coordination is largely negative. It can stop plans that conflict with the government's overall economic or expenditure goals, but its has little input into strategic thinking. However, there are some exceptions to this negative role. Deakin and Parry (1996) illustrate how the Treasury does have a social policy, as it attempts to link priorities in social policy to wider economic pressures. Peter Lilley's reforms to social security policy from 1990 onwards owe something to Treasury concerns with the rising cost of welfare and the need to fundamentally review the system (Richards and Smith 1997). A leaked Treasury document, which was dismissed as 'blue sky thinking', indicated that the Treasury is concerned with relating economic trends to wider policy issues. The document emphasised a radical rethink of welfare policy in the light of economic constraints that Britain is likely to face in future years (*The Times*, 18 July 1996). Undoubtedly, much of Labour's policy on the reform of welfare policy has come from the Treasury. There is strong interdependence with the DSS requiring finance and the Treasury in return demanding reform. This dependence was reinforced by personal links between the former secretary of state, Harriet Harman, and the Chancellor.

Reforms to the Treasury and a loss of power

As Chapter 7 demonstrates, the core executive has undergone fundamental reform since 1979. These changes have affected the Treasury perhaps more than any other department. In response to the creation of agencies, greater delegation of financial responsibility and new information technology, the Treasury was the first department to undertake a Fundamental Expenditure Review (FER) in order to identify its objectives and to consider how work might be better organised to achieve its goals. The result was the reduction of certain tasks, the consideration of other tasks for privatisation and

> given the more strategic – and delegated – approach in future to control departmental running costs it is no longer necessary, or in our view sensible, for the Treasury to control the personnel management or pension entitlements of civil servants in other departments. We therefore believe that the Treasury's current work in this area should be passed to the OPSS (HM Treasury 1994).

These changes are significant because they demonstrate that Treasury functions are shifting to the OPS and individual departments. The Treasury has reduced its control over the detail of departmental spending and is concerning itself with totals. This has resulted in a dramatic decrease in the number of Treasury employees. In 1990 it had 3000 staff and by April 1995 it was below 1200 (Burns 1995). The number of senior staff (grade 5 and upwards) has been cut from 100 to 75.

While these reforms may be seen as sensible in the context of new circumstances and changing relations with departments, it is hard not to see them as resulting in a loss of Treasury influence. Healey believes the Treasury's 'central role is to control the existing apparatus of government rather than to initiate change' (Healey 1990: 376). Its powers of coordination are largely negative – it can stop departments doing things in order to protect macroeconomic goals. However, with the loss of detailed control, any policy coordination will more or less disappear, undermining the central role of one of the key coordinating institutions. Deakin and Parry (1996: 7) see the Fundamental Expenditure Review creating a role for the Treasury as sorting out government objectives and linking them to economic trends, 'leaving it as the central intelligence function of British government on the relations between the economy and public policy'. Hence its role is still one of reviewing the work of government as a whole, but it now lacks the capabilities to provide detailed checks on the work of departments and agencies (see Parry *et al.* 1997).

At the same time as the Treasury's coordinating role has weakened, the role of the Prime Minister's Office seems to have increased. Nevertheless, despite some structural changes in the position of the Treasury, Gordon Brown intends to reassert its central role. Brown has a high degree of control over economic policy and the role of the other economic department, the DTI, seems to have been minimised. Moreover, Brown has imposed strict spending limits on departments, and all new policies have to be reviewed by the Treasury for spending implications. All spending departments report to the Chancellor on their expenditure reviews (Routledge 1998), giving Brown considerable strategic overview of the general direction of policy. Blair depends greatly on Brown, and Brown is aware of the importance of prime-ministerial support. The closeness of their relationship means that Brown's influence extends beyond the Treasury's economic remit. However, one of the most interesting developments in recent years is the growth not only of the Prime Ministers's Office but also of the Office of Public Service

(OPS). Potentially, a combination of the Prime Minister's Office, the Cabinet Office and the OPS could replace the Treasury as the key coordinating department. In the following sections the chapter will review the coordinating role of these elements of the core executive.

THE NEW CENTRAL NEXUS: CABINET OFFICE, OPS AND NUMBER 10

The period since the late 1980s has seen a shift in the location of the centre of the core executive. Under Thatcher, resources were shifted to the Prime Minister's Office and the Treasury. The Treasury was given control of the civil service with the abolition of the Civil Service Department; it controlled economic policy and had detailed control of public expenditure. Thatcher strengthened the role of the Number 10 office and increased the involvement of the Prime Minister in departments. She also saw herself as a key player in economic policy. For Thatcher, Treasury weakness in the 1960s and 1970s was one of the key causes of Britain's economic decline, and therefore she was intent on reasserting Treasury control. Consequently, with the backing of the Prime Minister, the Treasury was in a very strong position. For much of the 1980s, the Prime Minister–Treasury nexus was the coordinating centre of the core executive. As Hennessy (1994: 487) concluded, following a participants seminar on cabinet government:

All (commentators) agreed on the Prime Minister–Chancellor of the Exchequer nexus as the special relationship within modern British government. It was so central and powerful that even such an arch prime-ministerialist as Edmund Dell felt that there was no need for a PM's Department as the Treasury and Number 10 'combined form a good basis for the sort of strong centre of government which I would like to see'.

Since the creation of the OPS, however, and, in particular, with the role of two individuals, Michael Heseltine and Peter Mandelson, resources have shifted away from the Treasury to a new nexus. Once again this centre is focused around Number 10, but it includes the Cabinet Office and the OPS, which have been given greater responsibility for the civil service and for coordination of the work of government. The changing relations between them has shifted the centre of government away from the Treasury.

The Cabinet Office

The Cabinet Office is the formal centre of government; its role is to coordinate the work of government departments and to ensure that the cabinet's will is implemented (Seldon 1995) (see Figure 6.1). Hennessy (1990: 390) claims:

> The Cabinet Office is *the* crucial junction box of central government system . . . when it comes to formulating policy at the critical stage just before it goes to ministers collectively, all wires lead to No. 70 Whitehall.

Yet as Dynes and Walker point out, there is a hole at the centre of British government, with the Cabinet Office unable to impose central coordination on the federation of resource-rich and constitutionally independent departments: 'The Cabinet Office is a peculiar department, simultaneously weak and strong . . . the cabinet sometimes appears to be less of a nerve centre in Whitehall than a post office' (Dynes and Walker 1995: 21). This hole is being made larger by the apparent differentiation of the state (see Rhodes 1995b, 1997a, and this volume Chapter 7). With the execution of policy-making and implementation being delegated to agencies, regions and the EU, it is increasingly difficult for the centre to control the policy process.

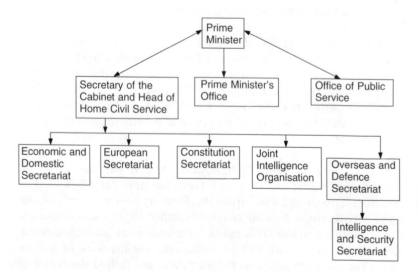

Figure 6.1   The Cabinet Office

The problems for the Cabinet Office are several-fold. It lacks resources, whether in terms of finance, policy-making capability, or independent authority. If the Cabinet Office is to achieve anything it relies on the backing of the Prime Minister. On its own it relies on the cooperation of departments, but while there is strong dependency between the Treasury and the departments, departments rarely need the Cabinet Office in the same way. Much of what the Cabinet Office does is pure administration: it circulates papers, organises cabinet committees, and distributes agendas. The important work in terms of discussions between departments or work within departments will go on without the Cabinet Office. The Cabinet Office does not have the staff or the capability to oversee what goes on in departments, and while it may believe that it is controlling the work of Whitehall, it sees very little of the day-to-day business, even when it is interdepartmental. While in the Cabinet Secretary the Cabinet Office clearly has a key Whitehall player, his impact depends to some extent on his relationship with the Prime Minister.

According to the Cabinet Office's departmental report: 'The sole objective of the Cabinet Office Secretariat is to provide an effective, efficient and impartial service to the Cabinet and its committees and coordinating departmental contributions to the Government's work' (Cabinet Office 1997: 5). A former Cabinet Secretary, the permanent secretary of the Cabinet Office, described his work in an interview:

The Secretary of the Cabinet is answerable to the cabinet, and to the Prime Minister, for the proper running of the machinery for inter-ministerial collective discussion and decision. A considerable part of the job really consists in making sure that the flow of business is properly managed, that the issues are focused so that the chairman of the committee, or the Prime Minister as the case may be, has a clear view of what issues are to be decided, what positions are likely to be of the people taking part in the discussion. And also, when there is some problem, as it were to be resolved, or worked at inter-departmentally, the Secretary to the cabinet may be able to do a certain amount, is able to do a certain amount, at official level to try and reconcile conflicting or diverging department views.

From this perspective, the role of the Cabinet Office is very much concerned with coordinating departments and resolving conflicts that arise in interdepartmental policies (see Box 6.2).

BOX 6.2
The work of the Cabinet Office

The work of the Cabinet Office is organised around six secretariats. The key tasks of the secretariat are:

- To ensure that the collective responsibility of ministers in
  respect of key policy matters is supported effectively at all
  times. The work is to a great extent demand-led and covers a
  wider range of policy issues.
- To ensure collective decision-making is conducted in a timely
  and efficient way. Where appropriate, collective considerations
  take place before policy decision are taken, to identify and
  coordinate effectively issues affecting the interests of several
  departments. The office ensures that decisions are consistent
  with overall government policy and, where appropriate, coordinates effective follow-up of policy decisions.
- To ensure that papers are properly prepared and correspondence dealt with promptly; that ministerial chairmen are
  properly briefed; that decisions are recorded clearly; and that
  agendas and minutes of meetings are circulated promptly
  (Cabinet Office 1997: 15).

The six secretariats function as follows:

- *Overseas and Defence* has responsibility for staffing the Cabinet
  Office briefing room during defence exercises and leads relations with NATO during crisis management exercises.
- *Economic and Domestic* coordinates domestic issues that require
  collective and ministerial discussion and provides information
  on cabinet committee business. It also coordinates collective
  exercises such as the government's legislative programme, and it
  has responsibility for civil emergencies.
- *European* has a crucial role in coordinating Britain's approach
  to the European Union. The secretariat ensures that European
  policy developed by one department does not contradict either
  the government's policy as a whole or the work of another
  department. For example, it would be very easy for European
  environmental legislation to contradict policies related to the
  single market. This secretariat has very close links with Brussels

through the UK permanent representative to the European Union, which reports regularly to the Cabinet Office and is therefore an important source of intelligence for domestic departments. The European secretariat also has a central role in informing departments on how to negotiate in the Union (see Chapter 8).

- *Constitutional* was created by the Blair government to oversee the constitutional reform process, and in particular the issues of devolution and freedom of information that have an impact throughout Whitehall.
- *Joint Intelligence Organisation* is concerned with sifting intelligence material for ministers.
- *Intelligence and Security Committee Secretariat* serves the Intelligence and Security Committee, which was established in 1994 to examine the 'expenditure, administration and policy' of the security services.

The Cabinet Office has two crucial roles. One is ensuring the operation of collective responsibility. This role invests the Cabinet Office with a degree of authority and some control of resources, because it is responsible for establishing the need for cabinet committees and controlling the flow of papers to them. According to an official, the Cabinet Office has a large say in determining what goes to cabinet committee 'and the Secretary would say "I think this should go to this committee and that should go to that committee"'. It also has responsibility for ensuring that departments respond to decisions. However, it is the Prime Minister who is ultimately responsible for the creation and membership of cabinet committees. In addition, departments will often attempt to resolve issues bilaterally without going to formal committees, and so bypass the Cabinet Office.

The second role is to control the information flow through Whitehall, and to ensure that ministers receive the necessary papers for cabinet and cabinet committee. Again, this function provides the potential for significant influence, but there is little that the Cabinet Office can do with the information. At most, it is in a position to inform the Prime Minister of what is going on in Whitehall. The Cabinet Secretary needs to have some idea about what information to send to the Prime Minister and about which issues to make ministers aware. But despite his close relationship with the Prime Minister, the

Cabinet Secretary does not have complete control over what the Prime Minister sees, as a former Secretary stated:

> You were not taking that decision on your own because a lot of the papers that were copied to you as Cabinet Secretary were also copied to Number 10. So the decisions you were taking were not whether the PM saw or didn't see these papers but whether it should be resolved below that level if it could be.

The potential impact of the Cabinet Office is very great, but how it uses resources depends to a large extent on the authority of the Prime Minister. Hennessy (1986) points out that during the years when John Hunt was Cabinet Secretary, 1973–9, 'Power flowed into the Cabinet Office.' Hunt used the Central Policy Review Staff – which was set up by Edward Heath in 1971 as central strategic policy capability – to develop non-departmental policy (Blackstone and Plowden 1988) – as a source of economic information, and thus was able to add a policy element to the bureaucratic nature of the Office. According to one official:

> If there are things that the department which is leading on a particular subject has got into a bit of a muddle or has got too close to things, you need a sharp eye and a good nose for discovering just the right moment to ring up and say 'Why not have a meeting?' Very often this generates an almost spontaneous desire to pull the thing together even though the department concerned may have sweated blood in getting this far (quoted in Hennessy 1986: 21).

In practice, while the Cabinet Office can sometimes pull things together, it is rarely a powerful institution. Its impact depends almost exclusively on how the Prime Minister decides to use it. Under Thatcher, it lost out to the Treasury and her use of personal advisers, and under Blair coordination is generally the concern of the Prime Minister's Office (see below). A more crucial forum for resolving conflict is the cabinet committee system.

Cabinet committees

A large part of the coordinating role is fulfilled through the operation of cabinet committees, which are a crucial mechanism for analysing

Table 6.2   Cabinet committees under the Labour government, 1997

Chair	Committee	Number of Members
Prime Minister	Defence and Overseas Policy (DOP)	6
	Constitutional Reform Policy (CRP)	13
	Intelligence Service (IS)	6
	Northern Ireland (NI)	6
Deputy Prime Minister	Home and Social Affairs (HS)	20
	Environment (ENV)	18
	Local Government (GL)	19
	Subcommittee on London (GLL)	21
President of the Council and Leader of the House	Legislation (Leg)	14
	Subcommittee on Drugs Misuse (HS(D))	12
	Subcommittee on Health Strategy (HS(H))	15
Lord Chancellor	Queen's Speeches and Future Legislation (QFL)	11
	Devolution (DSWR)	19
	Subcommittee on the incorporation of the European Convention on Human Rights (HSH)	17
Secretary of State for Social Security	Subcommittee on Woman's Issues (HS(W))	14
Foreign Secretary	Subcommittee on European Issues ((E) DOP)	19
Chancellor of the Exchequer	Economic Affairs (EA)	18
	Public Expenditure (EX)	9
	Subcommittee on welfare to work (EA WW)	13

Source: Adapted from Hood and James (1997).

policy and resolving disputes. During the Thatcher era, the four principal standing cabinet committees provided 'the critical nexus through which the major decisions of government were taken' (Seldon 1995: 139). With the growth of cabinet business much detailed work has been shifted to cabinet committees, with only the major strategic policy developments or disputes being discussed in cabinet. Most issues that involve more than one department, more money or a significant new policy development will be discussed in cabinet committee. Committees allow issues to be discussed in more detail than in cabinet and they facilitate the resolution of interdepartmental conflicts.

Cabinet committees are the institutional mechanisms for melding departmental autonomy with collective government. Nigel Lawson commented in an interview: 'I had complete autonomy to work out proposals. I then obviously had to have them approved by cabinet.' The forum for cabinet approval is cabinet committee, except when ministers need parliamentary time. In this instance they have to make their case before the full cabinet. But cabinet committees are fraught with difficulties for ministers because, in a sense, they are almost pure politics; they involve building alliances, sorting out interdepartmental rivalries and winning arguments in order to achieve policy goals. First, it is important, if possible, to get the Prime Minister on side or, at least, not opposed – if the Prime Minister is opposed then very few other cabinet ministers are likely to support a case. Therefore, most ministers will check either with Number 10 or the Prime Minister directly what the leader's reaction is likely to be to a new proposal. Second, the minister has to reassure the Treasury over any financial concerns, and so it will often involve the PFO, and maybe a minister, talking to the Treasury about the likely financial implications of a new policy. Third, it is important to win the support of some of the senior ministers on the committee possibly by sounding them out before papers formally go to the committee. A former senior minister gives a good account of what can go wrong:

> The first Education Bill that John Patten produced, he had a ten minute talk, not forty, with the Prime Minister and thought he had him on side and came to the committee to pursue these proposals and, to put it bluntly, the big beasts duffed him up. Michael Heseltine and Ken Clarke in a very polite way just duffed him up. I summed up the meeting saying, 'Secretary of State I think a lot of colleagues are sympathetic to the proposal you have put before us today but it is quite clear that there have been a number of interesting points made and perhaps you would like to reflect on these points and may be we could come back to it once these points have been digested.' In other words, take this bloody thing home and do your homework. And then I got William Waldegrave, the Oxbridge man, and told him to see John Patten and tell him to shape up. He had come to cabinet committee thinking it was routine with a slightly high handed approach. They detected this at once and

became totally opposed to what he wanted to do and duffed him up. Now the mistake there was not building a consensus.

Ministers have to play a complex game in cabinet committee, and it is an arena where ministers from other departments can affect policy.

These committees are also an important source of influence for the Prime Minister, who will often establish the membership of committees in order to produce the outcome he or she favours. Callaghan fixed cabinet committees to ensure the thwarting of the Bullock report on industrial democracy, and Thatcher used cabinet committees to maintain a dry coalition on economic policy. The Prime Minister also furthers his or her influence by chairing most of the key cabinet committees, with the result, according to Nigel Lawson, that he or she has the ability to veto policy developments of which she does not approve.

Whether a coalition of two ministers can defeat the Prime Minister in cabinet committee will depend very much on the situation. On most occasions, if the Prime Minister opposes a position in committee then it will strongly influence the discussion and an anti-Prime Minister coalition is unlikely to develop. In the early 1980s, Thatcher vetoed membership of ERM despite being in the minority. By 1992, when she was in a much weaker position, she was unable to resist the pressure of Hurd and Major for ERM entry.

Cabinet committees are central to the coordination process. A crucial rule in the Whitehall system is cooperation and consultation, and interdepartmental issues have to progress through a process of agreement. When issues of great importance, key strategic changes or policies that affect a number of departments arise they are worked out through cabinet committees. This procedure gives ministers, and officials, in the shadowing official committees, the opportunity to pay a degree of attention to a particular problem and to thrash out any conflicts of departmental interest. It is also a means of ensuring coordination of government policy through the committees being chaired by the Prime Minister, the Deputy Prime Minister, the Chancellor or a non-departmental minister. Cabinet committees are now the focal point for collective decision-making. But even here there are important weaknesses in the system. Many issues do not get to cabinet committee. The bypassing of committees was greater under Thatcher when decisions were made either bilaterally or in *ad hoc* and informal meetings (Hennessy 1986, Lawson 1992). Moreover, as Lawson (1994: 442–3) informs us:

when an issue comes to be collectively discussed, in a cabinet committee where real decisions are taken, in a cabinet committee, say, chaired by the Prime Minister of the day (as a number of them are), then a minister who is involved in some running battle with the Prime Minister over a matter where he has departmental responsibility may well feel reluctant to spend too much of his political capital, arguing a case against the Prime Minister in a field which is totally outside his departmental responsibility. It is some other Minister's baby and some other Minister's responsibility.

These problems again emphasise the centrifugal forces of departments and the tensions that exist between the Prime Minister and the departments, rather than between the cabinet and departments. Foster (1997) argues that the whole cabinet system lost influence during the 1980s, and that Thatcher effectively moved away from a system of formal cabinet committees: 'Since 1979, every step of [the] previously standard procedure has been broken. Departmental ministers generally still initiated policies, but on occasions so did other ministers, even the Prime Minister. Announcement of policy . . . may have preceded cabinet approval'. In Foster's view, ministers still needed Treasury and cabinet approval, and papers were written and sent to a cabinet committees but:

Lady Thatcher developed a practice, which she carried through by force of personality, by which *ad hoc* groupings of ministers were frequently used instead, often because they were known to be favourable to the outcome she wanted. In more recent years departmental ministers had a choice: they might ask the Prime Minister to put it on the cabinet agenda or for him or for the Deputy Prime Minister to set up such a grouping or himself set up such a grouping; or he might believe it enough to persuade the Prime Minister with minimal consultation with other ministers affected (Foster 1997: 5).

The Cabinet Office has become little more than an official machine, and the cabinet committee system has been replaced by *ad hoc* bilateral and multilateral meetings. For example, the crucial decision to adopt the poll tax was not taken in a formal cabinet committee (see Butler *et al.* 1994). Preferring to make decisions at *ad hoc* meetings with the ministers she believed most relevant, 'Thatcher largely emasculated the system in its old form' (Foster and Plowden 1997: 235). For Foster and Plowden, Thatcher's interventionist style undermined the capabilities of the institutional coordinating machinery because it was increasingly bypassed. The new system could work with an interventionist and hyperactive Prime Minister, but it was too personalised to operate with a more hands-off approach (Foster 1997). Thatcher undermined the formal machinery operating through a series of *ad hoc* committees. She then relied on Whitelaw and then Wakeham to sort out any problems that arose. This system created a hole in the centre of government when the Prime Minister played a less interventionist role and didn't have a fixer to act as a broker of cabinet agreement.

Draper (1997) infers that despite the existence of cabinet committees under the Labour government (see Table 6.2), they are, as to some extent under Thatcher, little used. Hennessy (1998: 3–4) goes further, suggesting that the Blair government has abandoned cabinet government, replacing it with a '"Napoleonic" style of government'. Instead of Cabinet, Blair seems to be relying on task forces to deal with interdepartmental issues and problems (see Table 6.3). The key difference with cabinet committees is that these bodies have been set up to deal with specific issues and they include a large number of outsiders (Daniel 1997). It is interesting that of the 23 task forces, only 4 are chaired by ministers. These bodies indicate a more pluralistic approach to policy-making and less reliance on civil servants for advice. For traditional mandarins, like the former Cabinet Secretary, Sir Robin Butler, the use of so many outsiders is leading to poor advice, policy errors and lack of accountability (*Guardian,* 5 January 1997). Indeed, the absence of ministers does raise the question of the weight the final reports will carry within government. Unlike cabinet committees their decisions will not carry cabinet authority, and may lack the necessary departmental support to be implemented. This weakening of cabinet office machinery and the cabinet committees perhaps explains why recent years have seen the growth of the Prime Minister's Office.

The Prime Minister's Office

The post-war period has seen a significant increase in the Prime Minister's administrative capability, with the development of what is the embryo of a Prime Minister's department (Burnham and Jones 1993; Pryce 1997). The most significant elements in this area are the

Table 6.3   Task forces set up by Labour government, 1997

Task force	Chair
Youth Justice	Norman Warner
Welfare to Work	Sir Peter Davis
School Standards	David Blunket
Literacy	Michael Barber
Numeracy	David Reynolds
Creative Industries	NA
Tax and Benefits	Martin Taylor
Private Finance	Adrian Montague
NHS Efficiency	Alan Milburn
Better Regulation	Chris Haskins
Football	David Mellor
Advisory Group on Competitiveness	Margaret Beckett
Export Forum	Tom Harris
Special Educational Needs Group	Estelle Morris
Advisery Group on Continuing Education	Bob Fryer
Review of the CPS	Iain Glidewell
Review of Film Policy	Tom Clarke and Stewart Till
Review of Pensions	Tom Ross
Review of Health Inequalities	Donald Acheson
Review of London Health Service	Leslie Turnberg
Review of Surrogacy Law	Margaret Brazier
Civil Litigation and Legal Aid Plans Review	Peter Middelton
Working Group on Teacher Bureaucracy	Peter Owen

Source: Daniel (1997).

growth of the Policy Unit, the increased use of personal advisers and the greater power of the Press Office, all of which emphasise the way in which the behaviour of a Prime Minister creates the new structures for his or her successors. The Policy Unit was only created in 1974 by Harold Wilson, and until then Prime Ministers relied on personal advisers and the Central Policy Review Staff (CPRS) created by Edward Heath. However, the CPRS, or 'Think-tank', existed in principle for the whole cabinet. The importance of the Policy Unit, according to Donoughue (1987: 20), is that 'it was systematic, it was separate from the Whitehall machine and it was solely working to the Prime Minister'. Its initial remit was to ensure 'the Prime Minister is aware of what is coming up from departments to cabinet. It must scrutinise papers, contact departments, know the background to policy decisions, disputes and compromises, and act as an early warning system.' It was also to play a role in coordinating policy and ensuring the manifesto commitments were maintained (Donoughue: 1987 21–2). Thatcher extended the role of the Policy Unit and personal advisers using both as alternative sources of advice and as means of policy-making initiatives. Under Major, the Policy Unit was responsible for key policy developments such as the Citizen's Charter and Back to Basics. For Blair, the Policy Unit has a crucial role in both reacting to departments and undertaking important policy initiatives. The Policy Unit has developed alongside increasingly proactive Prime Ministers. What Thatcher established, and what seems to have become entrenched, is that the Prime Minister is to have a policy role and that that role is to be increasingly institutionalised. The development of the Prime Minister's Office and the Policy Unit has shifted the structures of dependency within the core executive. Whereas in the past the Prime Minister was dependent on colleagues and departments for advice and information, he or she is now increasingly relies on advisers within the PM's office. As Pryce (1997: 196) confirms, 'By 1979 the Prime Minister was at the centre of an advisory network in which the cabinet was only one among many sources of advice the Prime Minister could call upon.'

It was also under Thatcher that the role of the press secretary increased, with Bernard Ingham being very much heard as his mistress's voice. He frequently briefed the media against cabinet ministers of whom she disapproved. Under Major the role of the press secretary was normalised again, but there are signs under the media-conscious Blair that it will again develop a central role.

The Prime Minister's Office has also been affected by the growth in the number and influence of think-tanks. Think-tanks have had greater influence because of distrust of the conservatism of the civil service and the links which exist between the think-tanks and between policy advisers and the Policy Unit. Often there is an exchange of people, which gives the think-tanks a source of influence. It also means that the Prime Minister can obtain policy advice that comes from neither the official machine nor departmental ministers. The role of think-tanks was crucial in the development of the poll tax (Butler *et al.* 1994), and in Thatcher's review of the Health Service, in 1989, she specifically included advisers from think-tanks rather than the Department of Health or the traditional medical interest groups (Smith 1993). This was a tremendous shock to the department and to the idea that departments are the source of policy development. Under Blair's Labour government, one of the roles of David Miliband in the Policy

---

BOX 6.3
The Prime Minister's Office

- *The Private Office* This consists of six civil servants. The key civil servant is the Principal Private Secretary, who coordinates all papers and information for the Prime Minister. The Private Office never stops and the telephone is manned twenty-four hours a day. George Jones (1995) points out that: 'The Private Office is the operation room of Number 10. Everything going into and out of Number 10 goes through it.' It connects the Prime Minister to Parliament and Whitehall, handles all his correspondence and notes all his conversations and meetings. The Private Office is the centre of the Prime Minister's Whitehall network, ensuring he is in touch with all the key actors and institutions within the core executive.
- *The Policy Unit* This is a political unit, set up by Harold Wilson to watch over departments and to provide the Prime Minister with policy advice. Consequently, it is crucial in supporting the Prime Minister in his or her increased policy role. Its role is both reactive and proactive. It advises the Prime Minister how to respond to policy from departments and it offers the Prime Minister advice, criticisms and alternatives. In a number of areas, for example, social policy under Thatcher and the Citizen's Charter under Major, it was proactive and developed new initiatives (see Hogg and Hill 1995). Blair has increased the numbers in the Policy Unit from eight to ten.
- *Personal advisers* With the development of the Policy Unit, there has also been increased use of policy advisers. Both Wilson and Callaghan had their own personal advisers, but their importance increased under Thatcher because of her distrust of the civil service and of some of her colleagues. For Thatcher, Sir Alan Walters and Sir Charles Powell (who was a career civil servant) played important roles advising on economic and foreign policy respectively, often briefing her against her Chancellor and Foreign Secretary. Blair sees his personal advisers as having a crucial role in the Labour administration. Jonathan Powell as chief of staff has a critical role in advising Blair and has executive authority over officials.

- *The Press Office* The Prime Minister has an office which deals with the media and provides briefings for the lobby. Bernard Ingham turned this into a powerful position, by being seen as speaking directly the words of the Prime Minister. Thatcher was more aware of the power of television than any other Prime Minister and, consequently, she and her advisers attempted to manipulate how she was presented on television and to put pressure on the media to present the government in a certain way (Cockerell 1988). Blair has made the position of press secretary an explicitly political appointment by placing Alistair Campbell in the role. He has a crucial role in coordinating the presentation of government policy and ensuring that the government is seen in the best possible light.
- *The Political Office* Under Thatcher and Major this was the Prime Minister's link to the parliamentary and national party. The head of the political office under Blair, Sally Morgan, is someone who is seen as having good contacts throughout the party and who knows the union leaders who retain some influence in the party.

Unit is to provide a link between Number 10 and the think-tanks, so that the Prime Minister is aware of new ideas and has alternative sources of advice (*Guardian*, 3 June 1997).

The growth of the Prime Minister's Office has given the Prime Minister the ability to intervene in certain areas of policy by providing independent policy advice. It has enabled him or her to attempt to fill the coordination gap that has developed as a result of the weaknesses of the cabinet and the Cabinet Office. Hogg and Hill (1995: 97) see the Policy Unit as crucial in attempts at coordination:

Whitehall is not like a centrally-driven business – or even the Roman army: when Number 10 says go, it is not always the case that the system goeth. Of course if the Prime Minister pushes a minister into a corner he or she will normally concede. But wise Prime Ministers do not do that too often, particularly on matters of detail. And with the (Citizen's) Charter, the devil was all in the detail. It was the Policy Unit's job to keep the number of fights the Prime Minister had to have to a minimum.

Burch and Holliday (1996: 31) believe:

> Interviews and public sources reveal that there has been an increas-
> ing tendency for business to flow to the Prime Minister's Office, and
> for ministers to feel the need to consult Number 10 before launching
> significant departmental initiative. These developments have en-
> hanced the position of the Prime Minister's Office at the hub of
> the system, and expanded the potential of the Prime Minister and his
> or her staff to oversee government strategy, to monitor departmental
> work and to initiate policy from the centre.

The Health Service review provides a good example of how a Prime
Minister, frustrated by policy problems in a department, used her own
advisers and external think-tanks to develop and force through policies, thereby bypassing the department and its traditional networks
(Klein 1989, Day and Klein 1992).

Under Tony Blair the importance of the Prime Minister's Office
continues to grow, because Blair sees himself as having a continued
role in the development of policy. This is indicated by Blair's attempt
to replace the official appointment of principal private secretary with a
political appointment as Chief of Staff. In the end the official civil
service post was retained, with Jonathan Powell being given an
explicitly separate political post. For Blair, political appointees and a
strengthened Policy Unit are crucial elements in imposing coordination
on government. The number of political appointees has nearly
doubled, and there are clear lines of communication between political
appointees in Number 10 and the departments (*Guardian*, 3 June 1997).
There are now 19 special advisers in Number 10 costing £1.1m in
1998/9 (*The Independent* 16 June 1998).

However, as Burch and Holliday recognise, this ability to control
policy-making is still limited. The influence of the Prime Minister
operates largely as a veto on development. Departmental ministers
are relatively autonomous in the development of policy; while the
Prime Minister can veto a policy in cabinet committee, it is very
difficult for him or her either to force a minister to adopt a policy or
to prevent the development of departmental policy initiatives. Again,
the Prime Minister is limited by time and by the small size of the
bureaucratic machinery at his or her disposal. Without a common
operating code, the Prime Minister cannot impose order on his or her
colleagues, because there cannot be a continual process of sackings. In

recent years the Prime Minister has been assisted by the establishment of the Office of Public Service (OPS).

The Office of Public Service

The position of the Office of Public Service is unusual in that it is part of the Cabinet Office, and in that sense partly under the control of the Cabinet Office and the Prime Minister, but it has its own permanent secretary and minister. The formal role of the OPS is

> to promote and support government and the provision of effective and efficient public services; and policies which improve United Kingdom competitiveness. The OPS is part of the Cabinet Office. It advises and supports the Chancellor of the Duchy of Lancaster, in his responsibilities for public service reform and Civil Service policy and management functions; the Prime Minister, as Minister of the Civil Service; and the Head of the Home Civil Service (Cabinet Office 1997: 3).

Central to its role is the organisation and improvement of the civil service. It also supplies common services to departments. Despite the apparent limited nature of its formal functions, it has become an increasingly important department.

John Major created the department partly to oversee the implementation of the reform of government and the Citizen's Charter. These were two policy initiatives that were close to Major's heart and were particularly important because they were policies that distinguished him from Thatcher (although in fact the reforms were initiated by Thatcher; see Chapter 7) (Ludlam and Smith 1996). Therefore, the OPS was partly an another administrative department but also a policy department for the Prime Minister.

More importantly, the role of the OPS has become greater than was perhaps intended, for a number of reasons. First, Michael Heseltine made it his department when he became Deputy Prime Minister in 1994, and he expanded its role by bringing with it the deregulation unit and competitiveness from the Department of Trade and Industry. At the same time, he was prepared to use the department as a base from which to speak on any issue in government which attracted his attention. He managed to place himself in a position of chairing more important cabinet committees than the Prime Minister, and a central role was to chair the new committee on coordination and presentation of government policy (EDCP). He also had the right to attend any cabinet committee he wished (Seldon 1997: 601). Effectively, Heseltine created a strong Deputy Prime Minister's Office, which could develop its own coordinating role. His EDCP met every morning, in order to consider 'day-to-day responses to media interests, and coordination of policy in both the short and longer terms'. This was, however, in the context of a Prime Minister who seemed increasingly weak and unable to impose any overarching strategy on the government as a whole. Consequently, Heseltine was attempting to fill a vacuum.

Blair also realised the danger of having competing centres of coordination in government in the Prime Minister and the Deputy Prime Minister. Therefore his deputy was given a large policy department, where he has little time for overall coordination of government. Instead, Blair has sought to retain the coordination role of the OPS by placing a loyal ally and more junior minister in the OPS with the specific charge of coordinating the role of the Prime Minister and effectively being the Prime Minister's eyes in Whitehall. Peter Mandelson's job as Minister without Portfolio was 'to assist in the strategic implementation of government policies and their effective presentation' (*Guardian*, 3 May 1997). His role was to fill the coordinating position that Heseltine never quite succeeded in creating, and he has a seat on all key cabinet committees. In 1998 this role was filled by Jack Cunningham but with the status of a Cabinet Minister.

It is also an aim of Blair's to break down the functional separation of Whitehall by creating task forces of civil servants to pull departments together and to ensure that initiatives maintain their momentum when they are extra-departmental. Mandelson said, 'I think that what he [Blair] will want to do is to create a strong centre in government, so that all its various arms and departments have a very clear sense of direction' (*Guardian*, 3 May 1997) Thus, the OPS has become key to Blair's network for prime-ministerial coordination. There is now a daily strategy briefing, where Mandelson, press officer Alistair Campbell, chief of staff Jonathan Powell, David Miliband (Blair's policy adviser) and Brown's adviser, Charlie Wheelan, decide on the day's message and through the minister's adviser inform the ministers of the theme they have to stick to (*Evening Standard*, 3 June 1997) (see Figure 6.2). The Lord Chancellor, Lord Irvine, has also proposed a shift away from departmental turf wars, with departments working for the collective, rather than individual, interest. He is supporting the 'cabinet enforcer' in the role of the Prime Minister's eyes and ears in Whitehall, with the intention of ensuring that departments are working towards the government's collective goals and not stuck in their policy chimneys.

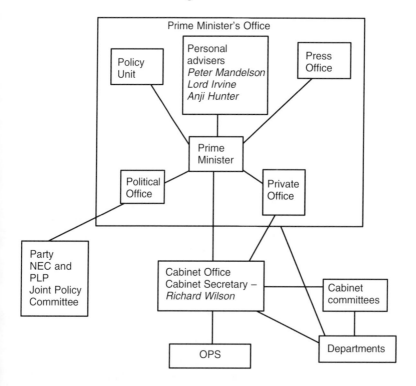

Figure 6.2   Blair's institutional coordination

Third, the OPS has become crucial in terms of operating the reformed British state (see Chapter 7). Thatcher returned responsibility for the civil service to the Treasury and the Treasury strictly controlled staffing and pay. Now responsibility for pay is delegated to departments, but the OPS has responsibility for procedures and rules concerning delegation, for the operation of the relationship between departments and agencies and assisting with the setting up of agencies. The combination of a stronger Prime Minister's Office and a proactive OPS with responsibility for coordination and the structure of government has shifted the coordinating centre from the PM and Treasury to the PM and the OPS/Cabinet Office.

The irony of the Thatcher years is that while she attempted to strengthen the Treasury in order to control expenditure, the reforms she initiated, both in strengthening Number 10 and in creating the new agencies, weakened the Treasury. As Foster and Plowden (1996: 236–7) confirm:

> The demise of the old official cabinet committee system meant that issues, for example, involving trade, competition or employment policy, were less likely to be concerted across government. Unsupported by similar arrangements enabling other departments to reflect their views authoritatively, the Treasury's permanence above the rest was unstable and bound sooner or later to lead to collision between them, as it did. It involved giving one member of the cabinet the effective role and power of Deputy Prime Minister without any debate of this development . . . Subsequently, under less able or vigorous Chancellors, the Treasury became less active and successful in policy coordination, while the irritation remained. Thus the downsizing of the Treasury . . . can also be seen as the last stage of a rebellion among other ministers to cut its influence.

Nevertheless, as we saw above, under Brown the Treasury has not yet given up the fight for a central role.

Hennessy sees the Blair government as bypassing the cabinet as a coordinating mechanism and instead relying on direct control from Number 10. All major speeches, interviews and policy developments have to be cleared by the Prime Minister's Office. Moreover, 'Number 10 is omnipresent in the serious policy reviews. A member of the ten strong Downing Street Policy Unit sits on all comprehensive review teams as does a member of the Prime Minister's Efficiency Unit' (Hennessy 1998: 15). Yet, it is clear that Ministers such as Brown, Prescott and Cook retain considerable autonomy and departments continue to be the site of much policy-making. Blair may have continued the limited role of Cabinet, but, through task forces and the Social Exclusion Unit, the Labour government has attempted new forms of coordination. Nevertheless, a range of centrifugal forces continue to exert pressure and to undermine attempts at coordination.

CONCLUSION

The core executive has been weakly coordinated because of the power of departments and their control of the policy process, and because of the lack of any formal institutionalised coordinating body. The cabinet has the formal powers of coordination, but lacks the mechanisms for any real coordinating role. The coordination vacuum has to some extent in the past been filled by the Treasury, which, in conjunction with Number 10, could provide a relatively strong centre. The problem with Treasury coordination is that it focuses largely on financial issues, and it produces an institutionally determined and long-term battle between and with departments. Moreover, in terms of public expenditure control the Treasury has not been particularly successful.

Therefore, despite attempts in the 1980s to strengthen the Treasury, its role in the coordination process has declined. It has been rapidly reduced in size and has become less concerned with the details of departmental expenditure. Consequently, the coordination of the core executive has increasingly shifted to the nexus of Number 10, the Cabinet Office and the OPS. Under John Major this provided a relatively weak system of coordination, partly because the political difficulties of the government overwhelmed any attempts at coordination and partly because, under Michael Heseltine, a second coordination centre was established by the OPS. Moreover, the basis of this coordination was not really institutional but depended on the whims of Heseltine.

Blair has attempted to reassert prime-ministerial control by formalising the role of the OPS and tying it closely to Number 10, through the appointment of Peter Mandelson, and subsequently Jack Cunningham, as a coordinator. It is too early to estimate the success of this project, but with the weakening of the Treasury, and the isolation of the Deputy Prime Minister, it seems that there is at least only one centre. Whether this centre has the strength to coordinate the federation of departments is an open question, especially when devolution and greater European integration is likely to fragment the core executive further. Moreover, it is clear that the Chancellor has significant policy responsibility, which again has created competing centres of coordination. There is considerable tension between the private offices of Blair and Brown.

Analysis of coordination again highlights some important issues of structure and agency. First, structurally Prime Ministers are in the position to affect the coordinating process in the core executive, and consequently individual decisions by Prime Ministers have increased the resources of Number 10. Second, relations between the Prime Minister and the Chancellor are crucial, but changes in the structure of government and the impact of new public management have structurally weakened the Treasury. Third, the changing role of the OPS has largely been the result of individual decisions, which again have been institutionalised. Major set it up to pursue his civil service policy, Heseltine increased its coordination role and Blair has maintained its coordination role but subsumed it to some extent into the Number 10 network.

Nevertheless, it is the departments that are high in resources and this makes coordinating centres structurally weak. Indeed, the problems of coordination are becoming greater, not less. As we will see in Chapter 7, one of the most crucial legacies of Thatcherism is the fragmentation of the state with privatisation, Next Steps agencies, the increased used of quangos and the delegation of managerial decisions. The Labour government is fragmenting the state further, with the granting of independence to the Bank of England, proposals for new regulatory bodies, devolution and further integration into the European Union. There is a very real question mark over whether the British core executive has the capabilities to coordinate such diverse organisations. The fundamental problem remains that the core executive is institutionally strong in departments and institutionally weak at the centre. In other words, the centre is more dependent on departments than departments are on the centre. The only exception here is the Prime Minister where prime-ministerial authority or support can help a department in Whitehall, and even Treasury, battles.

7 Reforming the Core Executive

The modernisation of the state has long been a theme of parties in government. Sclerosis of the institutions of central government has been identified as a cause of Britain's economic and political failure by both the left and the right (Anderson 1964, Barnett 1986). Consequently, governments of both main parties have attempted to deal with these problems either through piecemeal reforms or by attempts at introducing more fundamental change of the core executive and the wider state. Piecemeal change has often taken the form of the abolition, merging and creation of new departments. Sometimes these changes represented the priorities of the Prime Minister such as Labour's establishment of a Ministry of Technology, and sometimes changing realities, as with the amalgamation of the ministries of Admiralty, War and Air into Defence (see Clarke 1975).

Before Margaret Thatcher's premiership, reform efforts were undertaken by Winston Churchill, Harold Wilson, and Edward Heath. Churchill attempted to streamline the lines of management and improve central coordination by creating 'overlords' with responsibility for a cluster of departments (Hennessy 1986). Problems of accountability and coordination ended the experiment after two years.

Wilson attempted to reform both the structure of government and the civil service. He established new ministries such as the Department of Economic Affairs with the aim of challenging Treasury dominance and of modernising the British economy. He initiated the most fundamental review of the role of the civil service since Northcote–Trevelyan in 1854 with the establishment of the Fulton Committee. The report made important recommendations concerning the staffing, management, structure and professionalism of the civil service (Cmnd 3638 1968). Much of the report was not implemented, but a Civil Service Department was established, a unified structure created, and there was a gradual increase in the number of technical experts used (Hennessy 1990).

Heath was concerned with continuing the modernisation process initiated by Wilson. Heath's White Paper, *The Reorganisation of Central Government* (Cmnd 4506 1970), introduced major changes aimed at improving the management and efficiency of central government through the creation of super departments such as the Department of Trade and Industry and the Department of the Environment (Radcliffe 1991). The giant departments were intended to improve coordination and provide clearer objectives. In addition, the reforms aimed at providing better management systems and expenditure controls (Hogwood 1992, Hennessy 1986). All these attempts were a pragmatic response to the political and economic crises seen as weakening the post-war state.

Both Wilson and Heath sought to modernise the core executive and the state, but it was the period following the election of the Conservatives in 1979 that saw the most sustained process of state reform this century. Although the changes can be seen as a 'dynamic evolution' (Richards 1997) rather than a revolution, the combination of measures produced fundamental changes in both the size of the state and the organisation of the core executive. For Michael Portillo (1994: 1), 'A revolution [was] taking place in public management.' A fundamental and probably permanent change in the nature and role of the core executive occurred in the years after 1979. There has been a shift away from state-provided and delivered services to the use of a wide array of bodies in public provision such as privatised industries, agencies and quangos. Consequently, the state has become further fragmented, suggesting a shift to governance rather than government. This chapter examines the nature of the reforms and asks why they occurred and what impact they have had on relations within the core executive. It begins by discussing Conservative theories of the state.

CONSERVATIVE THEORIES OF THE STATE

Conservatives frequently deny that they have a theory or ideology of the state. 'Other parties may be wedded to fixed and unalterable theories of the state. For better or worse the Conservative Party is not' (Hogg 1947: 14). Despite such disclaimers, there are a number of conceptions concerning the role and boundaries of the state within Conservatism. The roots of reform derive to some extent from the these conceptions and critique of the state.

Most commentators on Conservative ideology identify libertarian and collectivist traditions within Conservative thought (see Gamble 1974, Greenleaf 1973, Eccleshall 1984, Willetts 1992). For libertarianism, the most important goal is liberty, and the state must not 'tell individuals how to run their lives but maintain the framework of public order within which individuals may pursue their own ends and interests' (Greenleaf 1973: 181). For collectivists, the primary goal is order and social harmony. The state intervenes in order to achieve social rather than individual goals. For collectivists, organic Conservatives, society is not made up of sovereign individuals, but is 'an interconnected whole bound by a network of reciprocal rights and obligations'. Those with wealth and privilege have a duty to make collective provision for the disadvantaged (Eccleshall 1984: 86). In reality, most strands of Conservatism contain elements of both traditions (Greenleaf 1973).

Within these traditions there are differing conceptions of what the state should do. Some Conservatives are pre-modernists, rejecting the notion that the state should attempt to achieve grand plans or large social goals. For Oakeshott, politics should be driven by political experience and an understanding of the traditions of the nation. Rationalism in politics is rejected, because of the imperfectability of human behaviour and the likelihood of plans leading to new problems, not solutions (Oakeshott 1962).

However, in the post-war period the dominant Conservative conception of the state has been modernist: the belief that the state can achieve specified goals and improve the lives of ordinary people. Despite different views on what the state should achieve, Macmillan, Heath and Thatcher had ideologically derived goals, and accepted the necessity for a rationalist approach to political problems. They saw the state as an organisation for achieving political, economic and social ends. Even Thatcher, who rhetorically rejected the idea that the state could be used for positive ends, had specific aims – for example, trade union reform – which could only be resolved through state action.

Within Conservative thought there is a range of views of the state. Nevertheless, there are certain conceptions concerning the role and nature of the state that are shared by most Conservatives. First, all Conservatives, even libertarians, are concerned with the maintenance of state authority and social order. Second, central to maintaining order is belief in the rule of law. For Conservatives, if a law is legitimately passed then it must be obeyed by all people, or society will descend into anarchy. No one is above the law, and it must be applied equally to all. For,

the rule of law to which Conservatives pay such respect is as real and solid as the table in the House of Commons. It is no metaphysical conception of natural law, no philosophers' abstraction like the laws of Plato's Republic. It is a body of actual law, imperfect as all actual things must be, but none the less sufficiently embodying the eternal principles to command and exact respect as such (Hogg 1947: 76).

Third, the fundamental goal of maintaining order and the rule of law is to protect private property. All Conservatives, even the most collectivist, who might accept some nationalisation, maintain the absolute priority of private property. Fourth, the notion of private property is tied in with the idea that there is an autonomous civil society that is clearly distinct from the state. This pluralist conception of the state sees autonomous institutions within civil society as mechanisms for limiting state power (see Gray 1993, Hogg 1947). Fifth, an important source of constraining the state is constitutionalism. This is not constitutionalism in the sense of developing written and codified rules of government; rather, it means government working within the boundaries of tradition. The English constitution is 'the accumulated and sifted experience of our predecessors as embodied in traditional institutions, laws and customs' (quoted in Honderich 1990: 136). For Conservatives, it is better to regulate government through these traditions than through sets of formalised rules.

Within the confines of these general perceptions of what the state should do, Conservatism encompasses very different state theories, which are influenced by both libertarian and collectivist thought. At one extreme are the Conservatives who see the fundamental role of the state as maintaining order and the integrity of the nation-state. Ideally, this would be achieved by aristocratic government, which has the wealth, breeding and education to know how to rule in the national, rather than sectional, interest. Hence, 'in politics, the conservative seeks above all for government, and regards no citizen as possessed of a natural right that transcends his obligation to be ruled.' (Scruton 1984: 16). However, Conservatives realised that with the growth of working class organisations some democracy is necessary to prevent revolution. Consequently, Conservatives of this disposition can countenance corporatism, economic intervention and the collective provision of welfare as a means of maintaining order (see Honderich 1990).

At the other extreme is the libertarian position, which sees the state's role as maintaining the conditions for the maintenance of a free market. The state should be limited to an absolute minimum of maintaining negative rights – the right to pursue one's goals without interference. However, as Gray has pointed out, this view of the state is not, in reality, Conservative. It takes no account of the historical context and traditions of the British state, which has never been minimalist, and for Conservatives the role of the state could never be solely protecting liberty (Gray 1993: 5–7). For Gray, there should be limited, rather than *laissez-faire*, government: 'Government activity should be confined to the production of public goods' (Gray 1993: 13). The main public good is peace, but peace cannot just rely on law and order; it requires some sort of social provision for the poorest in society. The market is essential for maintaining a just society, but sometimes people need to be provided with resources to participate in the market (Gray 1993).

The conceptions of the state that have guided the actions of post-war Conservative politicians have come within these two extremes, and to an extent have combined elements of both the liberal and collective, with one dominant (Gamble 1988: 154). Until 1975 the 'progressive right' dominated post-war Conservative theory of the state (Gamble: 1974). They explicitly rejected *laissez-faire* notions (Eccleshall 1984: 105), and reconciled themselves to it having an enlarged and interventionist role (Gamble 1988: 124). The progressive right theory of the state maintains the importance of pluralism by recognising the necessity of intermediate institutions (Hogg 1947), but it is also rationalist and modernist, seeing the state as a means of achieving social goals. From 1951, most Conservatives accepted that 'the state sector was to be administered not dismantled' (Gamble 1974: 63).

For the progressive right, which reached its apex under Edward Heath, the key role of the state was to maintain order by preventing conflict between labour and capital. They accepted that the state should provide welfare and even maintain full employment as a means of ensuring the unity of the nation (Gilmour 1978). They increasingly saw the need to modernise the British state, economy and society in order to provide the wealth to prevent class conflict. At times of economic crisis, progressive Conservatives were prepared both to intervene substantially in the economy and to incorporate key class actors into corporatist policy mechanisms such as the National Economic Development Council and incomes policies. They were prepared to accept some limited public ownership, recognising that the market is not the best means to provide all goods (Hogg 1947: 108–14). For the progressives, 'a state kept within bounds is not an enemy' (Gilmour 1978: 151).

In contrast, the dominant Conservative theory of the state since the late 1970s has been the Thatcherite view, which grew partly as a

critique of Heath's modernism. For Thatcherism, the ultimate goal of
the state was still order, but the welfare state was a cause of disorder
and the declining authority of the state (Gamble 1988). The state
should disengage from certain policy areas. The Thatcherite theory of
the state is a complex synthesis of New Right theory, authoritarianism
and mainstream Conservatism. The rhetoric of Thatcherism focused on
limiting the role of government, especially in the economy, but also in
areas such as welfare. However, despite this rhetoric of disengagement,
Thatcherism contained a high degree of authoritarianism, as Gamble
makes clear:

> the New Right wanted a new approach to the nation, based on the
> fundamental principles of the one nation strategy – strong national
> leadership, a new national consensus, and avoiding the rift between
> politics being seen in class or interest groups terms (Gamble 1974:
> 103).

Thatcherism had a clear agenda, which required direct state action.
While some state intervention was deemed necessary to dismantle the
social-democratic state, much was positive and concerned with reasserting authority (Gamble 1988). Moreover, Thatcherism rejected the
pluralism of traditional Conservatism, taking from Enoch Powell the
idea of the supreme importance of Parliament as the sovereign decision-maker, with the elected executive at its pinnacle. Institutions that
challenged Parliament, even an executive-dominated one, threatened
the rule of law and the will of the nation. Within Thatcherism there was
a deep distrust of intermediate institutions such as local government,
pressure groups, trade unions and even the media, and so it was
legitimate to weaken these. For Thatcherism, the contract of governance is between the parliamentary state and the individual.

This emphasis on parliamentarianism made Thatcherism very open
to the New Right critique of bureaucracy, because the civil service is
another obstacle to the will of Parliament. The New Right regarded
civil servants as self-interested budget maximisers, concerned not with
serving the voters but with ensuring that the budgets of their agencies
were as large as possible. They were a major source of high public
expenditure and increased government programmes. They were likely
to establish close relationships with interest groups whom they could
use to press for larger government programmes (Dunleavy and
O'Leary 1987). For Thatcher, bureaucrats were imbued with the social

democratic consensus, open to sectional interests and interested only in increasing public expenditure.

Despite the *laissez-faire* rhetoric, there was very little sign of limited government under Thatcher. She believed in the authority of Parliament to pursue its goals unrestrained by groups within civil society. As John Gray points out, from a Conservative perspective, the Conservative government, 'contrary to its professed intentions', abandoned the limited-state project, and arrogated itself 'evermore discretionary powers' (Gray 1993: 13, Jenkins 1996).

The Thatcherite theory of the state, with its concern for authority, order and the rule of law, retained much from traditional Conservatism. However, with its anti-pluralism, its emphasis on markets as an unquestionable solution to problems, anti-collectivism and critique of the civil service, it diverged from the progressive Conservative state theory. Major seemed to draw on elements of traditional, progressive and Thatcherite Conservatism in his understanding of the state. He identified the need to cut the size of the state: 'At all levels my ambition is smaller government, efficient government, responsive government.' However, he confirmed the traditional Conservative view 'that government has a vital indispensable role to play' and that it should 'provide high quality education and health and security for the old, sick and others who depend on our welfare'. (Major 1994: 2–3). Major emphasised the traditional Conservative concerns in order and nation, progressive Conservatism's commitment to a role for the state in welfare, and the Thatcherite concern with limiting the role of the state.

It is clear that within Conservatism there are competing conceptions of the state. Thatcher challenged the dominant Conservative theory of the state, distrusted state organisation outside the executive, and embarked on a major reform of government. It is this theory of the state that underpinned the reforms of the 1980s and 1990s. Labour, even after modernisation, has done little to develop an alternative conception of the state. Indeed, Hay (1996) sees Blair's Labour government as accommodating the reformed Thatcherite state. This view appears to be supported by Mandelson and Liddle (1996: 27):

New Labour emphatically does not seek to provide centralised 'statist' solutions to every social and economic problem. Rather its aim is to enable people to work together to achieve things for themselves and their fellow citizens. This may well be brought about through voluntary and community participation in local services.

Labour does envisage a greater role for the state than did Thatcherism, but there is little indication of any significant changes being made to the structures of the state it inherited. The next section will assess the changes that have occurred and the degree to which they were influenced by Conservative state theory. It will also analyse the degree to which these reforms have affected the balance of resources within the core executive.

THE REFORM OF CENTRAL GOVERNMENT

Thatcher and the reform of central government

The reforms in Whitehall gathered momentum under successive Conservative administrations. Despite Thatcher's alternative theory of the state, for a long period she appeared uninterested in the machinery of government (Gray and Jenkins 1991). While Thatcher introduced a number of reforms before 1988, there was little indication that the state would be significantly reformed. The Prime Minister amalgamated the departments of Industry and Trade, abolished the Central Policy Review Staff and the Civil Service Department, and in 1988 split the Department of Health and Social Security into its health and its social security components. Such changes often resulted from prejudice or political expediency, rather than strategic thinking, and were seen as cosmetic rather than substantive (Painter 1989).

Perhaps her most significant changes were in the Prime Minister's Office, with an increased staff, greater use of external advisers, and greater intervention by the Prime Minister in departmental policy (Gray and Jenkins 1987, Hennessy 1986). Under Major, the size of the Number 10 Policy Unit continued to grow. The staff working directly for the Prime Minister increased from 66 in 1983 to 107 in 1993 (HC 390–i 1992/3: 8). Partly to bypass the civil service and overcome departmental inertia, Thatcher also increased the role of thinks tanks, but Major was less willing to give privileged access to these groups.

Central to the government's goals was reducing the size of the state, and crucial in achieving this goal was reducing the number of civil servants to under 500 000 workers. The civil service has been reduced from 748 000 in 1976 to 470 800 on 1 September 1997 (Cabinet Office/ OPS 1997) (see Figure 7.1). However, much of this reduction was not the result of tasks disappearing but of privatisation and contracting out (Drewry and Butcher 1991). In addition, the fall in non-industrial civil

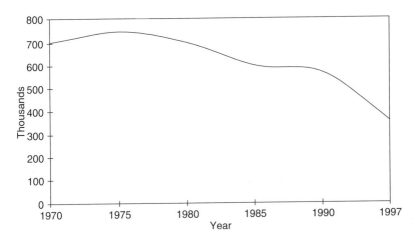

Figure 7.1   Permanent civil servants, 1970–97

servants was only from 565 815 in 1979 to 436 400 in 1997 and at the same time there was an increase in casual staff employed from 6862 in 1979 to 19 600 in 1997.

Thatcher also saw it as her goal to 'deprivilege' the civil service. Civil service pay increases were limited. More recently, there has been a dramatic shift away from centralised pay and grading systems and the introduction of performance-related pay and individual contracts of employment. Today, about 60 per cent of civil servants are covered by 'delegated pay bargaining arrangements' (Cm 2627 1994: 26). Public competition was introduced for certain high-level civil service jobs, and recruitment has shifted to the privatised Recruitment and Assessment Service, which acts on behalf of departments. There has been a significant increase in the number of civil servants on fixed-term contracts, and greater movement between the public and private sector (Barberis 1997).

The key reforms that have occurred are not in the size and functions of the civil service but in the structure of government and in the introduction of management techniques that were central to Thatcher's initial reforms of the state. Early on in her administration, Thatcher was concerned with government efficiency and value for money. She believed, in the words of one official closely involved in the reform process, that 'These guys aren't delivering.' In 1979 she appointed Derek Rayner to introduce efficiency audits into departments, leading to the creation of the Efficiency Unit. The aims of the unit were to scrutinise departmental policies and activities and to find ways of saving public money. Between 1979 and 1985 there were about 300 reviews, saving an estimated £300 million a year. There were problems with departments carrying out reviews and setting up the required performance indicators, but the Unit did introduce better management techniques into departments and forced departments to think about how they operated (Collins 1987, Warner 1984).

The work carried out by Rayner and the Efficiency Unit was systematised through the Financial Management Initiative (Richards 1987). The FMI was intended to promote better information and management in government; to achieve this they were to provide departmental managers with:

1. a clear view of their objectives; and assess and wherever possible measure outputs or performance in relation to those objectives;
2. well defined responsibility for making the best use of their resources including critical scrutiny of output and value for money, and;
3. the information (including particularly about costs) training and access to expert advice which they need to exercise their responsibilities effectively (Cmnd 8616 1982, cited in Zifcak 1994: 28).

As a result, each department was obliged to implement a management system that would ensure that they had the information to assess the mechanisms for achieving their objectives. This change produced some savings, but results were variable and it introduced confusion into the roles of ministers and permanent secretaries (Zifcak 1994). However, departments were given a clearer idea about their costs, and the initiatives contributed to a change in culture with the introduction of managerialism into Whitehall (Richards 1987). According to a former head of the civil service:

> It was a kind of turning point: at once a crystallization of the changes in the management culture of the civil service which had been evolving since at least 1969 (and indeed well before that), and as the starting point of many of the reforms that were to come later (Armstrong 1988).

The deprivileging of the civil service and the greater efficiency increased the managerial role of the civil service, and to an extent changed the relationship between Ministers and officials. As was suggested in Chapter 5, they indicated that officials were to manage the policy process rather than develop policy. Perhaps equally importantly, the FMI was to lay the foundation of the greatest changes to occur in central government this century – the creation of Next Steps agencies.

The Next Steps

Although Raynerism and the FMI clearly pointed to a major change in the culture of Whitehall, their impact was limited by the traditional departmental structure of central government. Consequently, in 1987 the head of the Efficiency Unit, Sir Robin Ibbs, produced the Next Steps report in order to allow for a real delegation of financial and management authority (Hennessy 1990).

The Ibbs report, *The Next Steps*, proposed a division in departments between the policy advisers and policy-makers at the core of a department, and those concerned with service delivery – in other words the implementation of policy – whether providing motor vehicle tax discs, printing government publications, or social security payments. The parts of departments responsible for service delivery were to be hived-off into management agencies, which would have much greater freedom to determine how services were to be delivered, to control budgets, and to hire and fire staff. The intention was to 'clarify the divide between operational responsibility and policy responsibility' (BBC 1994). This proposal would effectively dismantle the apparently monolithic and unified civil service established in the nineteenth century and develop a model where a 'loose federation of many smaller agencies, units and cores predominates' (Kemp 1993: 8, and see Fry 1997).

However, when Thatcher first announced the Next Steps initiative, it appeared that the changes would be relatively minor. According to Hennessy,

> constitutional changes in ministerial responsibility were out as were any attempts to end Treasury control over budgets, manpower and national pay bargaining. Furthermore, the initial list of candidates for executive agency treatment left the big tax-raising and benefit paying empires intact (Hennessy 1990: 621).

The initial Treasury and Civil Service Committees reports were critical of the slow progress in the establishment of new agencies (HC 481 1989/90: vi). The programme led to interdepartmental conflict, as the Treasury attempted to maintain its control over budgets and manpower (Painter 1989). However, from late 1989 the speed of reform greatly accelerated. In the third year of the programme, 19 new agencies were created, with a further 24 under active consideration. This progress took the total number of agencies to 50, employing over 180 000 civil servants (Kemp 1990, HC 496 1990/1). This was the beginning of the explosion in agencies. By 1996–7 there were 134 executive agencies covering around 400 000 civil servants, with more candidates under consideration (Cm 3579 1996/97).

There are a number of reasons why the initiative progressed so rapidly. First, there was a high degree of prime-ministerial authority behind the policy. Major saw the improvement of public service as an essential part of his programme, and it had broad support within the party. Second, Peter Kemp, a Whitehall outsider, was put in charge of the implementation of the programme. He provided dynamic leadership, and was prepared to spend considerable time highlighting the benefits of the agencies and showing departments how to create them (Greer 1994). Third, although departments were initially cautious, once they saw how successful the first agencies were they were soon prepared to join the bandwagon. The agencies seemed to have two obvious benefits: they improved the delivery of services, and they allowed departments to hive-off certain political problems.

The aim of the Next Steps programmes is to release departments and agencies from uniformity. 'The notion of a service-wide system appropriate to everyone is becoming increasingly a fiction' (HC 496 1990/91: 48). Such a view is a major change in the nature of Whitehall and the modern state. The traditional hierarchical bureaucracy has been replaced by an almost federal system of core and periphery, with the periphery not being directly controlled by the centre. This change raises important questions concerning the role of the agencies and their relationships with departments and the Treasury, which also impact on the structure of dependency within the core executive.

Most agencies are concerned with delivering services or with regulation, or else are trading concerns (Dunleavy and Francis 1990). The agencies are intended to concentrate on service delivery and to a have 'a clear quasi-contractual relationship with the core department' (HC 496 1990/1: vii). By being semi-autonomous, they have the freedom to decide how services can best be delivered. Certain agencies, like the Benefits Agency, which are central to their department's role, also have an input into policy advice (HC 496 1990/1: xv). Consequently, the size and function of agencies varies greatly, the largest having a staff of

72 000 and the smallest employing under 50 (Dunleavy and Francis, 1990).

The specific goals and functions of the agencies are set out in framework agreements, which are negotiated between each agency and the responsible department:

> All new executive agencies have a framework document with five main ingredients: the aims and objectives of the agency; the nature of its relations with Parliament, ministers and the parent department, other departments and other agencies; the agency's financial responsibilities, how performance is to be measured; the agency's delegated personnel responsibilities and the agency's role and flexibilities for pay, training and industrial relations arrangements (Greer 1994: 60).

Rather than the relationship between the department and agency being one of command, it is one of a bargained contract specifying tasks and targets. Within that framework, considerable freedom is allowed. This suggests a new set of dependencies between the core of the department providing policy and finance and the agencies providing delivery and information on the impact of policies. Consequently, ministers and officials have less direct control over outcomes.

With so much work being hived off, departments should, in theory, be reduced in size by about 25 per cent (Efficiency Unit 1991). The Department of Social Security (DSS) has seen its headquarters staff reduced from about 2500 to 1200 (HC 550–i 1990/1: 1). However, 88 per cent of chief executives 'reported no significance reduction in headquarters financial or personnel staff' (Price Waterhouse 1994: 8). Nevertheless, as we will see below, the Fundamental Expenditure Reviews (FER) and the Senior Management Reviews (SMR) have resulted in cuts in the core budgets and staffing of departments. The key role of departments is now to support ministers by advising them on achieving government goals and coordinating the agencies (Kemp 1993b: HC 390–iv). Supposedly they can now concentrate on 'policy-making, legislation, resource allocation, essential finance and personnel functions, and the procurement of services from agencies or on contract' (Efficiency Unit 1991, Mottram 1994).

The agencies also raise important questions about the relationships between departments and coordinating departments such as the Treasury. The Treasury was initially resistant to the agencies, because it feared a loss of financial control. Delegated management means that the Treasury has much less control over how money is spent, because detailed management of resources has to be left to chief executives. Instead, the role of the Treasury should be to focus on measuring outcomes and concentrating on 'strategic issues, resource allocation and facilitating best practice' (Efficiency Unit 1991). Consequently, the Treasury is even less able to carry out the coordinating role that was discussed in Chapter 6, and the resources of departments have increased *vis-à-vis* the Treasury.

These changes in the structure of government have also created difficulties for departments and agencies. Chief executives of agencies feel that departments are intervening too much in their work (Efficiency Unit 1994), partly because of the difficulty in distinguishing policy-making, implementation and day-to-day operational matters. For example, there is debate within the prison service over whether decisions over security in prisons are policy or operational matters. The overall level of security is a policy matter, but ensuring the measures are is place is operational (BBC 1994). In practice, there is difficulty determining the boundary.

The nature of the relationship also raises issues of accountability. Officially, agencies should improve accountability. Ministerial accountability still exists, and the minister is answerable to Parliament for the activities of the department. In addition, the chief executive is answerable for the delivery of services, and his or her contract can be terminated if targets are not met. The setting of explicit targets is intended to produce genuine accountability and not the accountability of constitutional myth (Painter 1994: 244). Graham Mather argued that Ros Hepplewhite, the former chief executive of the Child Support Agency (CSA), and John Wilby, of the London Ambulance Service, accepted responsibility for the policy of their agencies:

> No Whitehall mandarins with unlimited tenure contract have accepted responsibility for policy disasters. It is now becoming essential, rather than optional, that there should be some attempt to tackle the systematic malfunction of Britain's lawmaking and the shocking lack of definition of who is responsible for what in the implementation of policy, and who and in what circumstances should be held to account (Mather 1994: 1).

The chief executive also has to answer MPs' letters and appear before Select Committees (Greer 1994). The new agencies demolish the fiction that a minister can be responsible for everything that occurs within the department and delineates clear lines of responsibility – the minister for policy and the chief executive for implementation. According to William Waldegrave, 'there is now a clear distinction between "responsibility, which can be delegated, and accountability, which remains firmly with the Minister" ' (see HC 390–I 1992/3: xi, HC 390–i 1992/3: 14).

However, as ministers, chief executives and civil servants admit, the distinction between policy and implementation is not always clear. There is evidence that 'the precise division of responsibilities between ministers and civil servants . . . has become more uncertain in recent years' (HC 390–I 1992/3: xii). In certain departments such as the DSS, agencies are centrally involved in the policy process. The core department will not make policy without detailed consultation with the relevant agency. To some extent, a large number of policy ideas come from within the agencies. As one official in the DSS revealed,

> I have three sections here, and one section is almost entirely devoted to liaising with the agency. That equates to the amount of time I also spend talking to the agency and the people who deliver and two thirds of my time talking to headquarters.

Two clear examples of the ambiguities over policy are the cases of the CSA and the prison service. The CSA was set up to ensure that absent fathers paid maintenance. However, the policy became associated very much with the chief executive, a civil servant, who was consistently criticised for the policy. There were undoubted failures within the CSA. It appeared to be concerned with crude cost-saving, created a range of anomalies, and failed to meet its targets (*Guardian*, 3 September 1994). It was unclear whether these were operational or policy failures, but it was the civil servant, Ros Hepplewhite, who resigned and very little criticism was aimed at the minister in charge, Peter Lilley. The change to executive status seemed to have undermined the anonymity of a civil servant, and the lines of responsibility for a policy shifted away from the minister.

In the case of the Prison Service, there was disagreement over who should take responsibility for the attempted break out by IRA prisoners in Cambridgeshire in September 1994. In 1991, when IRA prisoners escaped from Brixton prison, responsibility had been laid directly at the door of the Home Secretary, Kenneth Baker, but in 1994 the media focused attention on a civil servant, Derek Lewis, to account for the escape. However, when asked who was responsible, Derek Lewis replied that:

It was quite wrong to be speculating on these issues at this stage. The [Woodcock] inquiry only got under way a few days ago. There is a lot of work to be gone through . . . Until all of that has been put together, no one can draw any conclusion as to what action is needed (BBC 1994).

Responsibility for the escape was no longer clear-cut. It was not until an inquiry was completed by the Prison Inspector, Sir John Woodcock, that responsibility could be apportioned. Even then, the report concluded:

There exists some confusion as to the respective roles of the ministers, the agency headquarters and individual prison governors . . . The inquiry identified the difficulty of determining what is an operational matter and what is policy, leading to confusion as to where responsibility lies (*Guardian* 20 December 1994).

The Home Secretary argued that the escape was not the result of policy failure. The Prison Officers' Association felt that, 'Mr Lewis was put there to deflect things from the Home Secretary' (BBC 1994). The Treasury and Civil Service Select Committee points to occasions where ministers have referred questions to chief executives that they should have answered (HC 496 1990/1). While the accountability of certain civil servants may have increased, the accountability of ministers is unclear and further obfuscated by the establishment of agencies (Mather 1994). A central problem that arose in the case of the prison service was that ministers and agency officials did not agree on lines of responsibility. Some of the officials, to an extent wrongly, believed that they were independent, while the ministers believed that they retained control. This problem was exposed when a minister who believed he had control sacked the chief executive and in that sense denied his responsibility. This breakdown in relations emphasised a problem that has resulted from the reform of the core executive: the increasing number of private sector people recruited into the civil service has created a clash of cultures. As we saw in Chapter 5, the civil service are partly constrained by their own reproduction of the rules of the game, and these rules result in them obeying the commands of ministers. Officials from the private sector, however, are not so aware of the rules and the delicate nature of ministerial–civil service relations, and they are used to being in charge of organisations. One agency official who came from the private sector said in an interview that the difference in public and private sector culture was

> Massive, I thought I understood it before I came in as I had been in contact with people here before but I totally underestimated it. The fact is there are totally different values here . . . This is just not a culture about getting things done . . . Its about protecting ministers, maintaining the status quo.

Despite the problems with the new agencies, and the possibility that departments exercise more control than is at first apparent, a radical change has undoubtedly occurred to the structure and culture of Whitehall. A uniform hierarchy has been replaced by a core–periphery model that distinguishes policy-making and policy execution. Governance is a more effective way of conceiving of the process of policy-making, because the state is fragmenting and there is greater delegation of decision-making. In addition, the culture of management has entered Whitehall. The cosy and closed world of the senior mandarin is disappearing. In the 1950s, officials believed they ran departments; as a former Home Office official revealed,

> It was a pretty self-confident department when I first joined in 1959 . . . Ministers were, I don't think it is fair to say manipulated, but the department had their views they would seek to impose on ministers and certainly attempt to persuade the minister to accept . . . The main characteristics of the department were confidence, sometimes bordering on arrogance, *a sense that ministers were not terribly important*, but a sense of professionalism and integrity which was immensely powerful and ministers were not, as it were, in the middle of things (emphasis added).

In the 1990s, the feeling has been much more that officials manage departments, but that they do so for ministers who are the main source of policy. Moreover, although there are problems with agencies, they have made officials more aware of operational issues and created a new set of dependencies in the core executive. Although these changes were initiated by the Thatcher administration, to some extent they contradict Thatcher's parliamentarianism. They establish a new set of intermediate institutions which are not easily controlled by the executive.

John Major and the reform of central government

Major was prepared to build on the reforms initiated by Thatcher and to make reform a distinctive element of his administration. In 1992 he established the Office of Public Service and Science, with direct responsibility for the civil service and further reform. The department has responsibility for the Citizen's Charter, efficiency and a new reform, 'market testing' (HC 390–i 1992/3).

Many elements of the Next Steps programme, such as increased accountability, better service delivery, and greater responsiveness to the consumer, were built into a central aspect of Major's programme – the Citizen's Charter. The aim of the Citizen's Charter was to increase the efficiency of public services and to make them answerable to the consumer by providing information on the cost and running of services, and by setting targets for the delivery of services (Cmnd 1599 1991). Within Whitehall, the Citizen's Charter Unit was established, which

> should be engaged in constant dialogue with the department's responsibility for the delivery of their own services to check that the Charter principles are being carried through in the policy of those departments and to interrogate them as to why they are not if they are not (HC 390–i 1992/3: 9).

Most departments have established their own charters with targets for services and means of public redress. For example, in the Employment Service the Job Seekers Charter specifies the importance of name badges, politeness and consideration, and the provision of information, and there are targets for the numbers of people to be found jobs, how much time can be taken for people to be seen, and time for answering phones (Doern 1993). In the Health Service the Citizen's Charter seems to be having important, even if symbolic, effects on the way nurses relate to patients, and plan and carry out their care.

The impact of the charters appears to be variable. They do not give specific legal rights and are, therefore, more symbolic than real. Moreover, they sometimes focus on the relatively trivial matters, rather than on key questions such as the levels of provision. However, Doern has some evidence that the charters have at least made agencies think about how they deliver services and whether they are taking enough account of the needs of their consumers (Doern 1993). Under the

Citizen's Charter, agencies are made aware of errors in the delivery of services and have targets for reducing those errors.

The Major administration extended the reforms through the concept of market testing. Developing from the Citizen's Charter was the Competing for Quality initiative. The aims of this programme were

> to concentrate activity on those things for which the civil service has to be responsible;
> to introduce more competition and choice into the provision of service;
> to improve the quality of service delivery to the citizen (Oughton 1994).

Where possible, it was thought that tasks still provided by the public sector should be 'market-tested' to see whether the service could be provided more cheaply by the private sector. Over 130 000 civil servants had to compete for their own jobs in areas such as typing and payroll services (Butcher 1993). Initially, the plan was to market-test £1.5 billion of government services. By December 1993 £1.1 billion of government services had been market-tested:

> Of nearly 400 tests completed, 25 resulted in a decision to abolish all or a substantial part of the activity; 3 activities were privatised; 113 were contracted out; 229 were subject to competition between in-house teams and outside suppliers (of which in-house teams won 147 and outsiders 82); 6 activities were restructured without a formal test; and 13 tests were withdrawn and efficiency gains made internally (Oughton 1994: 7).

The problem with market testing is that it appears to be moving even further from a unified civil service, with certain public servants working in very different conditions to others. It has also been argued that the whole process of market testing has placed agencies under great strain in actually preparing their tenders, and that time has been spent on this task rather than delivering services. More importantly, by forcing chief executives of agencies to undergo market testing, the promised autonomy has been undermined.

Market testing is pushing government much closer to 'contract government' (Harden 1992). The state no longer provides services, but is responsible for drawing up contracts for the development of services. The government's role is to decide what services are to be delivered, to award the contract to the most efficient provider, and to draw up a contract that specifies the rights and duties of the producer and the consumer (Harden 1992). Accountability exists through the contract, and not through parliamentary procedures. This may provide better accountability but, again, little thought has been given to its constitutionality.

The consequences of Next Steps and market testing were apparent in a radical report on restructuring the Treasury, published in October 1994. The report recognised that the recent reforms reduced the work of the Treasury, and recommended that a quarter of its senior civil servants should go by April 1995. The Chancellor, Kenneth Clarke, even wanted the Treasury's economic forecasting functions to be market-tested. With greater delegation of management to agencies and departments, the role of the Treasury in public expenditure could be reduced to setting spending parameters rather than detailed scrutiny (*Financial Times*, October 10 1994). Consequently, the Treasury could be reduced to a small core, and other departments would be forced to follow.

The changes in Treasury impacted on all other departments. They were commanded to undertake a Fundamental Expenditure Review, and a Senior Management Review, which led to the creation of the Senior Civil Service. The changes emanated from two White Papers. The first, *Continuity and Change in the Civil Service*, called for

> leaner, flatter management structures with emphasis on working through hierarchies . . . improved career management and succession planning . . . explicit, written employment contracts for senior civil servants and better and more flexible pay arrangements (Cm 2627 1994: para. 4.15).

The second White Paper called for the establishment of the Senior Civil Service to give effect to the aims of greater flexibility and the leaner and flatter structure, and for departments to hold senior management reviews 'to ensure that departments are organised to deliver the services they provide . . .' and to 'match the management structure to the needs of the work with clear lines of responsibility and accountability' (*The Civil Service: Taking Forward Continuity and Change*, Cm 2748 1995: para. 4.7). The aim was to break down the hierarchy in the upper echelons of the senior civil service and where possible eliminate layers of management among the 3000 top civil servants.

The creation of the senior management review has effectively removed grade 3 civil servants in the old structure and pushed responsibility for policy work lower down the hierarchy to what were grade 5 and grade 7. The old grade 2s have become managers of the policy process, and the department, and in the DTI, for instance, they have been renamed director generals. So the senior structure has changed from one of grades 1 to 7, to one of permanent secretary, director generals of divisions (although the title may change from department to department), and policy managers of sections, who are in charge of grade 7s and higher executive officers. It is at the policy manager level and below that the detailed policy work is carried out. The idea of these reforms is to end the old hierarchical structure and to give departments 'considerably more freedom to design jobs and management structures to suit the department's work'. Therefore the old grade 2 cannot be strictly equated with the post of director general. Jobs are not assessed according to their position in the hierarchy, but are given 'job weights' that correspond to the responsibilities of the position. The purpose is to allow more flexibility in developing team working, and to ensure that the best person is chosen for a particular job regardless of their position in the hierarchy.

The purposes of the changes to the top civil service are two-fold. On one side, they represent the extension of the new public management into the mandarinate, which to some extent had previously protected itself from reform. Contrary to the predictions of bureau-shaping, the changes have produced a significant reduction in the number of senior civil servants. On the other hand, the establishment of the Senior Civil Service is about ensuring that as the rest of the state fragments the core retains a common identity. As the permanent secretary at the Office of Public Service said:

> The senior civil service represents a corporate resource for the service as a whole. And that indeed is the first aim of the SCS – to promote a cohesive group of senior civil servants, seen as corporate as well as a departmental resources . . . The Senior Civil Service has the responsibility of sustaining the key Civil Service values of integrity, impartiality and objectivity and maintaining the principles of fair and open competition and selection on the basis of merit (Mountfield 1997: 5).

This is a significant change, because it undermines the traditional hierarchy on which the senior civil service is based, and it gives departments much greater freedom to organise in ways that suit their objectives. The problem is that officials are being asked to do the impossible: to introduce management and private sector criteria into their work and to retain the traditional values of the public service (Richards and Smith 1998). Increasing numbers of appointments are now being made from the private sector: 'In the last three years, 28 per cent of vacancies in the SCS have been openly advertised and $15\frac{1}{2}$ per cent have actually been filled by outsiders' (Mountfield 1997: 8).

The last fifteen years have seen a major change in the organisation and the form of the state. The state is no longer a hierarchical bureaucracy. There is an increasing division between the policy-makers and the suppliers of services, and services are increasingly provided by a range of bodies. More often, the provision of services is governed by contract rather than constitutional convention. There has also been a move to greater openness, with departments providing more information on what they are doing and how they are performing. The key question is whether these reforms have produced a Thatcherite form of limited government, or a 'hollow state'.

THE CHANGING BOUNDARIES OF THE STATE

A crucial and significant feature of the reform process has been the shifting boundaries of the state, as the core executive appears to have contracted out functions to non-state and quasi-state institutions – the so-called 'hollowing out' of the state. These changes have had important implications both for the relationship between the core executive and the rest of the state apparatus, and for the relationship between the state and civil society.

Changes in the boundaries of the state are most clearly seen in privatisation. As Marsh highlights,

> The scale of privatisation is immense. In fact, by 1991: over 50 per cent of the public sector had been transferred to the private sector; 650 000 workers had changed sectors, of whom 90 per cent had become shareholders, which represented 20 per cent of the population as compared with 7 per cent in 1979; the nationalised sector accounted for less than 5 per cent of the UK output compared with 9 per cent in 1979; about 125 000 council houses have been sold, most to sitting tenants under the right to buy provisions; and contracting-

out was well established in the NHS and the local authority sector (Marsh 1991: 463).

Privatisation was one of the flagship policies of the Thatcher period, and it was continued with vigour by the Major administration with the selling of the final BT shares and British Rail. However, while privatisation has changed the boundaries of the state, it has not necessarily reduced the role of the state. The government has continued to regulate the privatised monopolies, there has been little reduction in the level of public expenditure, and it has intervened greatly in its reforms of health and education (Richardson 1993). In other words, the state has been reshaped rather than hollowed out.

Privatisation was only the beginning of the process of changing the boundaries between state and civil society. Clarke and Newman (1997: 25) provide the example of 'a more "mixed economy" of welfare with more expanded roles for the private, voluntary and informal sectors'. The Conservative government shifted functions to: agencies (as we saw above); the market; the voluntary sector; and quangos.

Markets

The market has been introduced into government and the public sector in a number of ways. The most obvious is through privatisation, but other direct methods include market testing, the introduction of quasi-markets in areas like the Health Service and increased market competition in the Post Office (Martinez Lucio *et al.* 1997). More subtle elements of the market have entered Whitehall with open competition for jobs and the use of private sector management criteria for measuring performance. Even agencies are subject to a prior options review before they are established as agencies to evaluate whether their functions need to be carried out or whether they could be best carried out in the private sector.

Market criteria and market language now permeate many areas of the public service, even when private ownership or control has been kept at bay. According to the *Sunday Times*, 'In England alone, 7,610 extra managers and 10,500 support staff were recruited to the NHS between 1989 and 1991: the payroll bill for mangers alone rose 109 per cent between 1989 and 1992' (quoted in Broadbent and Laughlin 1997: 489). These extra managers effectively exist to implement the internal market and the associated mechanisms of pricing and performance indicators. The market and its methods have been seen as the most effective means of delivering public goods and of increasing efficiency within the public sector, even where 'real' markets cannot operate.

The voluntary sector

Increasingly, the voluntary sector is taking on public functions. The Conservative government stressed the importance of the voluntary sector in providing public provision especially in welfare. With the growth of community care, the voluntary sector has taken on an increased role in providing services that were previously supplied directly by the government. In particular, the role of the voluntary sector increased significantly with the NHS and Community Care Act. According to Russell *et al.* (1997: 396):

> The Act stresses the role of the local authority as an enabler of a mixed economy rather than a provider. A quasi-market is now being developed by statutory agencies, making contacts with the private and voluntary sector for the delivery of services to users. This policy was given strong impetus by the requirements imposed on local authorities to spend the greater part of the Special Transitional grant funding for the initial implementation of community care in the 'independent sector'.

Consequently, Russell *et al.* (1997) discovered in their survey of voluntary agencies that between 1989–90 and 1993–4 the income of the sample organisations increased by 74 per cent, and income from statutory sources increased in real terms by 145 per cent. Moreover, an increasing proportion of the income of agencies now comes from statutory sources. In 1989–90, 41.3 per cent of income came from central or local government. By 1993–4 this had increased to 58.2 per cent (Russell *et al.* 1997). In the area of overseas aid, the income to non-governmental organisations from government has increased three times in real terms between 1983 and 1993–4 (Maxwell 1996: 117)

An important illustration of these changes is the way in which private sector organisations are increasingly taking on the provision of public goods. For instance, in the area of aid policy rather than the state providing aid, it has increased funds to NGOs and they implement a significant part of the aid programme on the basis that they have the knowledge concerning the situation on the ground. Another example is the changing status of the Rehabilitation Unit. It was at one stage part of the DSS; it then became an agency and finally it was privatised with a voluntary organisation being given state money to run the unit.

Quangos

There is also an increasing perception that the government is shifting functions of the state to unelected, 'extra-governmental' organisations:

> a third of all public expenditure – some £46.6 billion in 1993 – is now being channelled through the appointed, contracted out, state. There are some 5,521 quangos and over 70,000 quangocrats put there by ministerial appointments (Weir and Hall 1994).

The central state might be doing less, but public bodies are still carrying out many functions. Despite the Conservative government's aim of culling quangos when elected in 1979, the number of quasi non-governmental bodies has increased significantly during the 1980s and 1990s. The Conservative government saw quangos as mechanisms for intervening into society without using formal state structures. They also had the advantage of removing certain political decisions from direct government responsibility. In addition, the government argued that they were more efficient than the traditional bureaucracy because they ensured people with knowledge of the particular issue took decisions. As a consequence, the 1980s saw a whole range of new quangos such as the Training and Enterprise Councils (TECs), Housing Action Trusts, NHS Trusts, and Urban Development Councils to name a few (see Flinders and Smith 1998). Like voluntary associations, these organisations provide public goods while allowing the government to claim the size of the state is being reduced. In particular, the government has used quangos as a means of bypassing what they saw as expensive, inefficient and untrustworthy local government, with a consequence that a large number of quangos have taken over the functions of local authorities (Stoker 1998) (see Table 7.1).

The problem with these changes is that they do not reduce the size of the state, but extend its reach through different forms. The voluntary sector was once largely independent of government, but it is now increasingly dependent on government for funding and the work it does. This development creates a new set of tensions, as voluntary organisations attempt to retain autonomy while government wants them to fulfil specific functions in return for funding. Rather than infrastructural power being extended through state administrative organs, it now operates through a range of organisations that are either funded, contracted to or regulated by the central state. For Clarke and Newman (1997: 26):

> While the rhetoric of diminishing direct public provision may stress the 'independence' of non-state providers, the relationships that are involved in acting as subcontracted or delegated agents of the state produce an expansion of state power.

In fact, the 1980s saw an explosion of regulation, as the government attempted to replace control with regulation. There are now between 50 and 80 internal regulatory units, that is, bodies that regulate the workings of the state (Hood and James 1996) (see Table 7.2). In addition, there are as many as 32 major regulatory bodies such as OFWAT and OFGAS, which are concerned with regulating large non-state organisations (Rhodes 1997a), and bodies regulating health and education authorities such as the school inspectorate. In addition, there are an increasing number of regulatory bodies at the EU level

Table 7.1   The centrally sponsored local quango state – key bodies (expenditure, £bn)

Functional area	Government-appointed bodies	Self-governing bodies
Education	City Technology Colleges (0.05)	Grant Maintained Schools (1.7) Higher Education Corporations (7.56) Further Education Corporations (3.2)
Housing	Housing Action Trusts (0.09)	Housing Associations (1.5)
Urban Development and Training	Urban Development Corporations (0.5)	Training and Enterprise Councils (1.4)
Health	District Health Authorities (12.9) Family Health Services Authorities (6.8) Health Trusts (6.0)	Local Enterprise Companies (0.5)

Source: Stoker (1998).

Table 7.2   Regulators of central government, local government and the mixed public/private sector: number of bodies in 1976 and 1995, percentage increase 1976–95 and factor of growth of expenditure 197–95

	Number of bodies in 1976	Number of bodies in 1995	Percentage increase, 1976–95	Estimated factor of growth in expenditure, 1976–95
Core Public Sector – Central Government	48	53	10	2
Core Public Sector – Local Government	56	67	20	Between 2 and 3
Mixed Public Private Sector	6	14	133	4
Total	120	134	22	between 2 and 3

Source: Hood *et al.* (1998).

(Loughlin and Scott 1997). The irony is that while the government has introduced new public management to undermine bureaucracy, the expansion of audit bodies increases bureaucracy as organisations attempt to meet the rules, create the 'audit trails' and respond to their regulators.

ASSESSMENT OF REFORM

The nature of the state has changed since 1979. Rhodes (1994) refers to the 'hollowing out of the state' as functions shift from the centre to agencies, quangos, the private sector and Europe. Harden talks of the 'contracting state', as state provision has been replaced by contracts. New Right thought can be clearly identified in many changes, such as reducing the size of government and the civil service, managerialism, privatisation and market testing. Nevertheless, to see these reforms purely as a response to the New Right is to oversimplify.

For example, many of the changes introduced by Thatcher and Major can be seen to be the implementation of reforms suggested by the Fulton report on *The Civil Service* (Cmnd 3638) of 1968. Fulton proposed a more managerial civil service, creating organisations for the task at hand and more open recruitment (Kemp 1990). The reforms are part of a lineage of reform that stretches back to Fulton and to Heath's managerialism in the 1970s. Pragmatism remains a strong element in reform, and there is no indication that the Labour government intends to reverse any of the changes.

New Right conceptions of the state were only one of a number of influences on reform. First, economic decline and the unwillingness of people to pay more in taxation forced the government to try to provide better public services with less resources (Butler 1994). Second, trends towards new forms of governance can be identified throughout the world. The government has been influenced strongly by reform programmes in the US, Australia and New Zealand. A book published in the United States, Osborne and Gaebler's *Reinventing Government*, has become a bible to many British reformers (Painter 1994, Butler 1994). Third, the reforms have been particularly effective because they have been in the interest of politicians and officials. For politicians, it has been a way of devolving political problems. In a number of highly publicised cases, politicians have succeeded in avoiding the blame for policy failure. When IRA prisoners were transferred to Northern Ireland hours after the IRA announced a cease fire, the Home Secretary publicly blamed Derek Lewis for the timing of the transfer, even though he had apparently signed the papers. As Alan Travis points out:

> By allowing him to be used as the public whipping boy for all the riots, breakouts and blunders that plague the prison service, Mr Howard can distance himself from the traditional rock on which many other top politicians' careers have founded (*Guardian*, 13 September 1994).

Agencies are also in the interest of officials, because they have greater freedom from political control over their budgets and administration. This also reduces the hitherto rigid control of the Treasury, allowing departments more autonomy. Consequently, because of the level of political will, the degree of reform has been much greater than commentators would have predicted a few years ago. Fourth, the changes reflect what many people might call the introduction of post-Fordist techniques into government. Social, technological and economic change, combined with new ways of handling information, means that the idea of a uniform, hierarchical bureaucracy as the best mechanism for delivering public services is now being rejected. Osborne and Gaebler argue that government bureaucracy developed at a time of mass markets, shared needs and slower rates of change. It could cope at times of crisis and where there were clear goals. In an environment of increasingly free markets, globalisation and information technology, we need flexible and adaptable bureaucracies (Osborne and Gaebler 1992). The watchwords in the 1990s are disaggregation, differentiation, and making the organisation meet the task. The changes in Britain are partly a reaction to these new conditions.

This policy area provides a good measure of the impact of Thatcherism on Conservative politics. The language of managerialism has come to dominate the Conservative attitude to the state. Through the market testing programme and contracting out, many of the principles of Thatcherism have been pursued much further. Moreover, the initial reform was inspired by the New Right critique of bureaucracy, and by Thatcher's parliamentarianism, which did not want bureaucratic constraints on the power of the executive. However, there is some indication that these reforms had unintended consequences (Marsh and Rhodes 1992b). In terms of expenditure and functions, the state is still very large. Contracts and private provision may have increased, but this is still paid for by public money and is formally under public control. Moreover, by creating semi-autonomous agencies and more quangos, the government's ability to control policy may be weakened.

Implications for the core executive

These changes also have important implications for the distribution of resources and the nature of relationships within the core executive. Up to the 1970s, the growth of the state generally operated through hierarchical line bureaucracies. In departments like the DSS, decisions were taken in the centre and implemented uniformly throughout the country according to a set of extremely detailed rules. In other departments, for example, the Department of Education, the process was more complicated. The department relied largely on local authorities and was in close contact with interest groups. But nevertheless, the number of actors and institutions involved in developing and implementing policy was relatively limited. In the last fifteen years, the policy process has fragmented. Ministers are increasingly likely to take advice from think-tanks and other outside bodies, and the decision and implementation process may include the department, agencies, a regulatory body, a privatised industry, local authorities, quangos and voluntary groups. While Thatcher's intention was to limit the role of the state, the impact of the reforms is actually to extend the role of the state and to make its control by the core executive much more difficult. As Rhodes (1997c: 36) illustrates:

> The fragmentation of British government is plain for all to see. Since 1988 British government has created 109 agencies and the number of special-purpose bodies has multiplied to 5,521 involving more than 70,000 government appointments and an estimated £52 billion of public spending. Add in privatization, services contracted to the private and voluntary sector and functions run by the EU and the extent of service fragmentation is still understated. I can best illustrate by sketching the implementation structures for AIDS policy in the York-Selby area of North Yorkshire. 13 organizations plan the service and 39 organizations are involved in delivering services. There are 24 HIV positive individuals in the area and 6 have developed AIDS (Battista 1994).

The reform process has been contradictory in its outcomes. The reforms under Thatcher and Major undermined the traditional inter-mediate institutions, and replaced them by 'new forms of control: particularly non-elected boards and agencies' (Clarke and Newman 1997), which the government hoped it could control more easily. However, the fragmentation of service delivery has produced unpredictable outcomes and may lead to a loss of control by the core executive.

The creation of the Next Steps agencies, privatisation and the use of voluntary agencies seems to be a move away from Thatcher's concept of a parliamentary, limited state. As the agencies become more established, the ability of the executive may decline even further. The central state has long suffered problems of coordination because of the strength of departments, but with the further devolution of power to agencies the problems of coordination may become even greater. There are signs that the Treasury – one of the key coordinators – is losing some of its control. This increased fragmentation may make it more difficult for politicians to control the policy process. This conflict between agencies and Parliament highlights a contradiction within Thatcherism. Thatcher wanted to increase the authority of Parliament, but was committed to ensuring that the reforms could not be easily reversed: changing the form of the state was a mechanism for preventing an incoming Labour government from easily reversing Thatcherite reforms.

The crucial problem is that while much changed in the state, and in parts of the core executive like departments, the central core changed little. The core executive under the Conservatives never really kept up with the changes that occurred in the wider state apparatus. While managerialism, reductions in numbers and the senior management review were an attempt to change the core, the old features remained more or less in place. The core of the core – the political centre – revolving around ministers, cabinet and the Prime Minister did not change. Therefore, the core executive did not shift from management by hierarchy to management by networks, and the hierarchical structures revolving around the principles of parliamentary sovereignty and ministerial accountability remained in place.

There is some indication that the Blair government is beginning to change the way the core is organised. First, task forces have been introduced (see Chapter 6) that cut across both departmental and public private boundaries. Second, the role of the OPS and the Number 10 Office is now to impose coherence on a fragmenting state. Third, the possibility of the introduction of an organisation close to a Prime Minister's Department is again being considered. However, the changes to date are personal and piecemeal, and it is questionable whether they are sufficient to ensure the core executive changes in line with the wider state. Moreover, as we saw above, the core executive, mainly at the departmental level, has become involved in regulation; therefore its control is not direct but through setting the framework for the activities of the 'para-state' – organisations undertaking public functions whilst not directly being part of the state apparatus.

However, there appears to be a shift from professional power to managerial power in the core and extended state. In the past, the key officials in the government were the professional policy advisers, and they managed the departments from the top to the delivery of services. Increasingly, permanent secretaries are now becoming policy managers rather than policy advisers. Simultaneously, it is a distinct set of managers, the chief executives, who are in control of the delivery of services.

A number of commentators suggest that these changes have shifted the balance of resources in favour of politicians rather than officials (Foster and Plowden 1997, Campbell and Wilson 1995, Richards 1997). Increasingly, officials are seen as the providers of services and ministers the purchasers, and as a result the old relationship of dependence has broken down. However, it is difficult to extrapolate the impact of a long period of one-party government from the wider managerial changes. Undoubtedly, the longer the Conservatives remained in office the more they were aware of what they wanted to achieve and their experience of government increased, and this placed them in a strong position in relation to officials. What is apparent, instead, is that as the state and its responsibilities have fragmented it has become increasingly difficult for the core executive to control public activities. Consequently, the notion of government being about building networks and negotiating rather than about command is increasingly attractive as a way of understanding the role of the core executive in the 1990s.

CONCLUSION

The form of the state has changed greatly since 1979. Managerial criteria have been given much more emphasis, the cost of government is clearer than ever, and there is a concerted attempt to reduce spending. The civil service has been reduced in numbers, and has become much more organisationally diversified, with different rates of pay and more open recruitment at higher levels. Most importantly, the structure of government has changed following the division between policy-making and the delivery of service. There is, as a consequence, greater concern with the users of service rather than the producers. Despite the fact that many of these changes may be more rhetorical rather than substantial, it cannot be doubted that there has been a radical change in the organisation and ethos of Whitehall.

Although ideology was the impetus behind the initial reforms, it is difficult to see Conservative conceptions of the state as influencing the reform process greatly. Certainly, New Right thinking has been important in the introduction of management techniques, 'market testing' and the purchaser–provider split. However, the form of the state today hardly meets New Right models. It is still extremely large, and is ultimately responsible for a whole range of functions, including the collective provision of welfare services. In a sense, Major united elements of progressive and New Right Conservatism, maintaining the commitment to public service while subjecting it to a management ethos and competition from the private sector.

These changes have affected the structure of the resource dependency within the core executive. The core is increasingly dependent on a range of institutions within the para-state. Consequently, officials and ministers have less control over the implementation process. It is also increasingly difficult for the coordinating elements of the core executive to impose coherence on an ever-expanding range of organisations. Nevertheless, these changes suggest, as will be discussed further in the next chapter, that the state has been reconstituted rather than hollowed out.

8 Domestic and International Constraints on the Core Executive

The aim of this book has been to demonstrate that traditional conceptions of power and the constitution are inadequate for understanding the operation of the core executive. Constitutional notions of power are a myth, and approaches that rely on zero-sum conceptions of power are an oversimplification of the policy process. Consequently, the book has examined the mutual dependencies that exist within the core. However, despite the tendency of traditional approaches to see the core executive as a hermetically sealed, self-governing unit, these dependencies exist, not only within the core, but also between the core and the outside world. In this chapter I examine how the core executive is constrained both domestically and internationally by external actors, events and institutions. The very wide and prolific debate over globalisation has focused greater attention on the limits of government. For the so-called 'hard' globalisation school, liberal-democratic states are losing control over their own territory and 'political boundaries are increasingly permeable' (see McGrew 1997: 12). Therefore, I will assess the extent to which the constraints on the state have developed, and how they may have affected the core executive.

The dominance of the notion of parliamentary sovereignty has tended to imply that the constraints on the executive come from within the system and traditionally Parliament. In this chapter I will demonstrate that parliamentary limits on government action are largely a myth, and that constraints on the core executive now come from a range of different actors. Consequently, I will demonstrate how power has moved from the parliamentary arena and increasingly resides within other bodies. In particular, the chapter will examine the impact that the European Union (EU) has had on the organisation of the core executive. I begin by examining the nature of the constraints on the core executive.

CONSTRAINTS ON THE CORE EXECUTIVE

Rhodes (1997a) points out that the debate concerning globalisation and the hollowing out of the state has led to suggestions that the core executive is losing capabilities to societal actors, to other state actors and to supra-state actors. These ideas provide an important challenge to the notion of parliamentary sovereignty and the constitutional view that the executive, with the support of Parliament, is free to make whatever decisions it chooses. With internal and external changes, Parliament has lost power to new social and political actors at the domestic and international level. As Table 8.1 highlights, there are a large number of constraints on the core executive. The question is, therefore: to what extent have these constraints led to a loss of capability in the core executive?

The constraints on the core executive can be broadly conceived as domestic and international. They are also: social, deriving from non-state actors; institutional, deriving from state and extra-state rules and institutions; and economic, imposed by economic structures. In addition, there are what might be called internal constraints, which derive from the lack of capabilities of the state. But a question that arises, in view of the reforms outlined in Chapter 7 and the globalisation of the world economy, is whether the core executive is more constrained now than in the past. What is apparent is that the constraints on government have shifted from the parliamentary arena to a set of extra-parliamentary arenas.

Table 8.1   Constraints on the core executive

	Social	*Institutional*	*Economic*
Domestic	Elections Pressure groups Media Social movements	Parliament Judiciary Policy networks Sub-government Parties	Domestic economy Economic interests
International	Media Pressure groups Other governments International policy communities	European Union International organisations Treaties Transnational policy networks Other governments	International economy Economic interests

FROM PARLIAMENTARY TO EXTRA-PARLIAMENTARY CONTROL

Traditional approaches to central government have paid scant attention to the impact of the outside world on the prime minister or the cabinet. Indeed, even Heclo and Wildavsky's seminal study of the Treasury ignores the wider economic context in which public expenditure decisions are made. This omission is largely a result of the themes outlined in Chapter 2. Parliamentary sovereignty and the Westminster model have resulted in analysts looking only at the internal workings of the system. This view may have been an accurate reflection of a limited period of the nineteenth century when Parliament was strong and the Empire large, but it has had little relevance throughout most of the twentieth century. This century has witnessed a shift of resources from the parliamentary to the extra-parliamentary arena. A simple historical schema would suggest the period from 1832 to 1865 was one of parliamentary government; that the era from 1880 to the 1970s was one largely executive government, or 'elective dictatorship', and that in the period from the 1970s to the present day decision-making has moved increasingly into extra-parliamentary arenas such as policy networks, the European Union and the global economy. How realistically does this schema reflect the reality? The following section will evaluate the changing role of Parliament.

The decline of the parliamentary arena

Constitutionally, power resides in the 'Crown in Parliament', and therefore the most important check on the executive is Parliament. All legislation has to receive parliamentary approval and Parliament can, through a vote of no confidence, force the government to resign. However, this formal position has been undermined by party discipline, which has effectively produced party government and in Hailsham's (1978) famous term an 'elective dictatorship'. The debate concerning the role and influence of Parliament again falls generally into the stale zero-sum conceptions of the Westminster model and tends to revolve around whether Parliament has been completely subsumed by the power of the executive or if it still retains important functions. However, there are two levels on which this issue should be considered. First, what is the nature of the relationship between the executive and the legislature? Second, to what extent is the parliamentary arena still significant in the decision-making process?

The idea of 'parliamentary government', where Parliament approves the government and accepts or rejects policy, is now a chimera, having existed in reality only during a very particular period of the mid-nineteenth century. Parliamentary government arose partly with the crystallisation of the commercial classes. During the eighteenth century, commercial interests became increasingly strong, exacerbating the conflicts between the landed classes and commercial ones. Commerce supported an aggressive foreign policy in pursuit of raw materials and new markets, while the landed classes were not prepared to pay the extra taxes that imperialism required. At the same time, radical voices called for the overhaul of an antiquated and corrupt Parliament. By the end of the eighteenth century, the landed classes had passed the zenith of their power and were finally forced to make concessions to the capitalist class with the 1832 Reform Act (Moore 1967).

After 1832, Parliament consciously used its power. MPs were able to force governments out of office and reject budgets, for example, Lord Althorp's in 1833. MPs were in control, and the government could not be certain of outcomes in the division lobby. Between the 1830s and 1880s, parties were amorphous organisations and MPs voted on party lines on less than 30 per cent of all issues. Consequently, legislation was made on the floor of the Commons, and Parliament controlled its own timetable (Lenman 1992).

Although this system of parliamentary government became established as constitutional myth, by the late nineteenth and early twentieth centuries party discipline and executive dominance had started to shift power away from the parliamentary arena into the executive. Economic, social and political reasons were behind this change. First, the growth of large-scale industrial capitalism created corporations and unions with significant economic muscle, which were incorporated into the policy process, often bypassing Parliament. Middlemas (1979) demonstrates how the unions and business were transformed into 'governing institutions', and incorporated into government following events such as the General Strike in 1926 (see also Raison 1979). Second, as we saw in Chapter 3, the growing complexity of society and the growth of expertise meant that decision-making was increasingly undertaken by professionals rather than by Parliament. Third, pressure groups have increasingly sidelined Parliament as sources of advice and as legitimisers of policy decision. Fourth, the growth of international organisations means decisions are often made at the international level, with little or no reference to Parliament.

Perhaps the most significant factor was the growing strength of parties. The period from 1868 witnessed the development of party discipline. With a wider franchise, and the introduction of the secret ballot, parties became essential to the running of elections and of government. In order to be elected, candidates needed a party label that established executive control over MPs. Gladstone was particularly effective at using parties to execute executive dominance in Parliament. According to Lenman (1992: 18):

> The reassertion of executive control over the legislature came with the rise of organized mass parties in the later nineteenth century, starting with the final coming together of various groups under the leadership of William Gladstone to form the Liberal party in 1867–8. Of this event, John Vincent has shrewdly said: 'Oratory apart, Gladstone did not so much create the circumstances of the 1860s as make good administrative use of the opportunities given by popular support, to reassert the authority of the State over Parliament.

The role of parties greatly increased in the twentieth century for the following reasons:

- *The media* have focused more attention on party leaders, and are prepared to pick up and magnify any dissension, thus making parties concerned with controlling internal dissension. The Labour Party introduced a new offence of 'bringing the party into disrepute' in 1997, thus enabling the leadership to punish any form of dissent it chose.
- *The rise of the career politician* has created a cadre of individuals whose sole career is in politics and therefore their own success is seen in terms of ministerial preferment (Riddell 1993). As a result, they are unlikely to rebel against the party leadership.
- *The whips' offices* have grown significantly in the twentieth century. They provide an important information service to MPs, informing them when and how to vote. This dependence increases their disciplinary influence. With strong parties and stiff electoral competition, MPs without a whip are in the wilderness. However, as Norton (1985) points out, for MPs unconcerned with promotion,

the whips have few powers except persuasion (although the unambitious are few in number). Nevertheless, there were reports at the time of the votes to ratify the Maastricht treaty that whips could be very persuasive and often backed persuasion with threats of leaking personal information and, apparently, physical and sexist abuse (Baker *et al.* 1993).

- *Increased prime-ministerial patronage* has increased the incentives for party discipline.

Consequently, Parliament has lost influence over the executive. Power and decision-making have shifted from Parliament to other arenas such as the executive, policy networks and the international level. In a sense, there has been a 'hollowing out' of Parliament more than of the state. The professionalisation of politics, with more MPs concerned with developing a ministerial career, and increased party discipline, means that even where Parliament retains capabilities it is increasingly unwilling to defy the executive or party. The loss of parliamentary influence over the core executive was illustrated by the Thatcher government (see Box 8.1).

BOX 8.1
Thatcher and the elective dictatorship

Thatcher rhetorically expressed a belief in parliamentary sovereignty. However, the Thatcher governments won large majorities with a relatively small percentage of the vote. She, and her government, were able to push through major legislative change often with little popular support because of the executive's control over Parliament. Butler *et al.* (1994: 227) have illustrated the failings of Parliament in attempting to block the poll tax despite considerable opposition among Conservative MPs:

> an executive less dominant within the legislature than Britain's would almost certainly not have introduced the poll tax – nor been able to implement it. Without the full exertions of the whips, backed by the bloated pay roll vote embracing more than a third of all Tory MPs, the Mates amendment would probably have been carried; and that would have gone far towards transforming the poll tax into a local income tax.

The poll tax was approved without an inquiry by select committees in either the Lords or the Commons, and 'The procedure of
the Commons itself was careful manipulated by the government to
ensure that the poll tax legislation emerged unscathed.'

The poll tax is indicative of the extent to which the executive
came to dominate the legislative process in the 1980s. Despite
Norton's (1980) claims of increasing dissension from the 1970s
onwards, the Thatcher period demonstrates the impotence of
Parliament when faced with a large government majority. Policy
was made almost exclusively within government, with Parliament
having little role in the initiation or formulation of policy. The
Thatcher government was almost never defeated on the floor of
the House. Indeed, the 1986 Shops Bill is only the third occasion
this century that a government with a majority has been defeated
on second reading – 95 per cent of government legislation gets
through (see Norton 1985) – and the government was still able to
liberalise shopping hours eventually. It has been argued that the
lack of parliamentary scrutiny of legislation has led to a number
of poor bills becoming law and then unravelling during implementation such as the Dangerous Dogs Act 1991 and the Child
Support Act 1991 (Marr 1996, Mather 1994).

Even Parliament's ability to scrutinise government seems to have
declined. Ministers' questions are generally about political point-scor-
ing, and there are a number of occasions when ministers have deliberately misinformed Parliament, for example, over the sale of arms to
Iraq and the sinking of the Belgrano during the Falklands War.
Despite the new powers of select committees, the role of MPs in
scrutiny is relatively limited. The strength of party discipline prevents
committees producing unanimous and critical reports. Moreover, the
committees have no executive power, and there is little that they can do
if their recommendations are ignored. Select committees and their
reports rarely have any impact on government, unless there are wider
pressures affecting executive decisions. Often they are under-resourced
and ill-informed, and it is relatively easy for departments to withstand
their scrutiny. With the establishment of executive agencies, lines of
accountability have become less clear (Barker 1998) and select committees have, to date, paid little attention to agencies (Natzler and Silk
1995).

Does Parliament matter?

Despite the apparent evidence of the decline of Parliament, two authors have suggested that Parliament continues to exercise considerable influence over the executive. For Norton (1993), although Parliament may have lost its role in initiating legislation, it continues to perform a number of significant functions: recruiting and training ministers; influencing legislation; scrutinising the administration of government; representing citizens; and, perhaps most importantly, ensuring the legitimacy of government.

The legitimising function highlights what Judge sees as the central role of Parliament. For Judge (1993: 2):

> Historically, parliament fused the principle of consent with that of representation and served to legitimate government polices and changes of government itself. Throughout, however, representative government in Britain has placed the emphasis upon *government*, with parliament acting as a two-way conduit between 'political nation' and the executive. In this process of transmission, government has been limited, its actions controlled and authorised by representatives of the political nation (however constituted in any particular period), and the political regime itself legitimised.

Judge is making an important and subtle point. The British state is a parliamentary state, and therefore the actions of the executive are conceived of, and executed, within a parliamentary framework. The parliamentary system creates the boundaries of executive activity and requires the legitimacy of the system; the executive cannot afford to break its convention because it would delegitimise its actions.

The problem is whether Judge mistakes the legitimising role of the constitutional myth for a real constraint on the executive. Judge sees Parliament, or more particularly the House of Commons, as a defining institution of the modern state. While it is true that ministers and officials continually justify their behaviour in terms of Parliament, and frequently behaviour deemed unacceptable by the Commons can lead to resignation, it is still questionable whether the Commons has any real impact. The Scott report revealed that ministers did not feel the need to inform Parliament of the changes in the guidelines on arms sales. Ministers are prepared to make policy without reference to Parliament, to lie to Parliament and, on many occasions, to elude, and redefine, responsibility. Ministers are constrained by the need to maintain legitimacy, but their autonomy within that constraint is great.

Government does need the legitimacy of Parliament, and in particular it needs the support of its backbenches. Consequently, there is dependency in the relationship between the core executive and Parliament. MPs want jobs, and they want their government to be successful and to defeat the opposition. The core executive needs votes and legitimacy. However, government needs *party*, rather than Parliament. As King (1990) points out, it is a simplification to separate the legislature and executive into two distinct bodies, because a crucial model of executive–legislative relations is intra-party relations. Ministers need the support of their own backbenchers, and there are continuous formal and informal interactions between backbenchers and ministers. These links occur in the Conservative Party through the 1922 Committee and for Labour through the Parliamentary Labour Party, and there is a continual flow of communication between the whips, the MPs and the government (Andeweg and Nijzink 1995). Whips play a crucial role in informing government of the boundaries of the possible. Consequently, the power of government backbenchers is not in stopping legislation once it has been announced, but in preventing it before it is put to the House. The executive may be able to overrule MPs once or twice, but continual insensitivity to the wishes of loyal MPs will cause party problems. Resource-exchange relationships exist between government backbenchers and the government, but not between the opposition and the government, 'The government fully expects the opposition to make hostile speeches. It does not need, or want, the opposition's moral support. It does not need the opposition's votes' (King 1990: 217). Jones (1995) sees backbench dissatisfaction, which was partly derived from the poll tax, as a key factor in explaining Thatcher's resignation.

Nevertheless, the influence of backbenchers is variable and depends crucially on the overall position of the party and the government. If the government has a large majority and is doing well in the opinion polls then dissent is likely to be less and to have little impact. When the government is unpopular or the majority is low, the leverage of backbenchers is much greater. The effect of a small majority on government policy can be seen in the example of the Major government's policy on Europe (see Box 8.2).

The example in Box 8.2 suggests that parties, if not Parliament, can, on particular occasions, constrain the core executive. However, the problem with this approach is that it assumes that in other

---

BOX 8.2
Backbenchers and European Policy

A survey of Conservative MPs conducted by Baker *et al.* (1995) in 1994 on attitudes to Europe suggested a high degree of euroscepticism among backbenchers with the majority opposing further integration. Throughout his period in office, 'Major suffered most of the serious forms of rebellion to a degree unprecedented since the war' (Ludlam 1996: 98) over the European issue and was eventually forced to offer himself for re-election in an attempt to end the continual backbench hostility (see Chapter 4). The degree of Euroscepticism expressed within his party forced Major to a Eurosceptical position. When Major first became Prime Minister he abandoned Thatcher's confrontational position and suggested that Britain should be at the heart of Europe (George and Sowemimo 1996). However, by the end of Major's period in office the government was taking an increasingly Eurosceptical line, rejecting the social chapter and taking an extremely cautious position on monetary union. His small majority resulted in a number of concessions to the Eurosceptical wing of the party.

---

circumstances Major would have acted differently. In the case of Europe there is evidence that the Eurosceptical policies he followed were the ones that he preferred and not policies that were imposed on him by backbenchers (Ludlam 1998).

The Major government faced a number of significant problems at the end of its term, owing to a lack of a majority and a high degree of dissension. A former minister, Lord Wakeham, said in an interview that the government behaved as if it did have a large majority and therefore tried to push through policies that did not have sufficient support:

> I thought that 20 was not a working majority and that the best thing we could do to support the causes we all believed in was to make sure that we won the next election by a bigger majority. My colleagues took no notice. In fact they thought that if the majority was 20 and it was going to slip so 'lets get our legislation through fast' . . . They set about trying to run the government the wrong way – at least in my view.

Nevertheless, it is rare for a government to lose a major piece of legislation. Even after Major lost the vote on Maastricht, he forced it through by putting a confidence motion before the House of Commons. Backbenchers may on occasions prevent the government introducing a measure, but their impact on the core executive is generally limited. In that sense, they are part of the context within which the core executive operates. However, their impact is intermittent. For Marr (1996: 115),

> Government backbenchers can, at rare moments, exercise some leverage on the general drift of executive policy which can, from time to time, help change the world beyond Westminster. But most of the time, frankly, its more like children shouting at passing aircraft.

The loss of parliamentary control raises important questions: if power is not in the parliamentary arena, then where is it, and to what extent has it shifted to extra-parliamentary institutions?

THE EXTRA-PARLIAMENTARY ARENA

The arguments behind globalisation and the 'hollow state' suggest that government has lost powers to higher and lower authorities with decisions being made in alternative arenas. Consequently, government is now only one actor among many in the decision-making process. This implies that a range of institutions other than Parliament are constraining the core executive. In this section we will examine the actors and/or institutions that constrain the core executive.

Pressure groups and policy networks

The role of pressure groups in the policy process is well documented (see Grant 1989, Jordan and Richardson 1987, Smith 1995). Despite attempts by the Thatcher administration to resist the pressure of lobbyists, pressure groups can stop governments taking certain actions and push new issues on to the agenda. Pressure groups have been effective in raising environmental issues, for example, the anti-road lobby forced the Major government into significantly reducing its roads programme. Pressure groups have also had an impact on issues such as VAT on fuel, water quality and food issues.

Increasingly, pressure groups are organised at the international level and are concerned with raising issues which cross national boundaries. Many of the environmental concerns that have affected government policy in recent years are a result of pressure applied at the international rather than the domestic level. In particular, pressure groups and NGOs (non-governmental organisations) have forced governments to at least consider environmental issues like global warming and acid rain and aid issues such as Third World famines.

Perhaps the greatest constraint from pressure groups occurs when they form policy networks with government departments, again placing the decision-making process outside the parliamentary arena, and often beyond the control of the coordinating elements of the core. There is a large amount of literature covering the impact of policy networks on the core executive (see Rhodes and Marsh 1992a, Smith 1993, Richardson and Jordan 1979, Marsh and Smith 1998, Marsh 1998) and therefore they will be discussed only briefly in this chapter. Marsh and Rhodes (1992b) have demonstrated that even when a government has a relatively distinct agenda, policy goals can be thwarted by decisions being made within discrete policy networks beyond the control of the core executive. More importantly, it is often policy networks which are responsible for the implementation of policy and therefore can ensure the goals ministers intended to achieve have a very different impact on the ground (Hu 1995).

Networks are becoming increasingly transnational, and therefore even more difficult for national governments to control. One obvious example of a transnational network is the agricultural policy network, which is now made up of DG-VI of the European Commission, national ministries of agriculture, national and European farms groups, and to some extent the World Trade Organisation. Similarly, the regional policy network, although largely dominated by central government, stretches from local authorities to the EU (see Rhodes 1997a).

Subgovernment

The issue of implementation is further complicated by the existence of a range of subgovernment organisations such as local authorities and quangos. Rhodes (1988) highlights the lack of executive capability within the state, which forces it to rely on subgovernment organisations for service delivery (health authorities, education authorities, local authorities and increasingly a range of quangos). Consequently, there is a high degree of resource dependency between the core and subnational government, resulting in a further constraint on the activities of the centre (see also Gray 1994).

The judiciary

The large Conservative majority under Thatcher, and a greater quantity of legislation led to more judicial activism under the Conservative administration than ever before. The last Conservative Home Secretary, Michael Howard, lost a number of cases in the domestic courts, the European Court of Human Rights and the European Court of Justice. According to Flinders (1997: 16), 'Judges have sought to control and limit the powers of ministers while ministers attempt to undermine the traditional discretion enjoyed by the judiciary.' The judiciary has taken on a role in holding the executive to account through public inquiries and tribunals. Some of the most thorough examination of the operations of ministers, officials and MPs have come within the auspices of the Scott (on arms to Iraq), Nolan (on standards) and Learmont (on prisons) inquiries (see Flinders 1998, Thompson 1996a, Barker 1998).

There has also been a significant increase in the amount of judicial review undertaken by the courts. Judicial review is where decisions can be challenged in the courts because they are 'illegal, unreasonable or unfair'. In the 1940s and 1950s judicial review was rare, but in 1994 there were 3 200 reviews (James 1996: 614). For James, judicial review has four important affects on administrative behaviour:

a *cancelling effect*, striking down individual decisions;
a *corrective effect*, making administrators review or reverse the policy or procedure underlying the decisions struck down;
a *restrictive effect*, trammelling future policy developments or use of government powers;
an *inhibitive effect*, compelling authorities, when taking decisions or developing new policies, to trim their sails in apprehension of judicial challenge (James 1996: 617).

Intervention of this kind will increase with the incorporation of the European Convention on Human Rights into British law.

The international arena

The globalisation debate, despite its problems (see Chapter 2), has focused attention on the growing role of international organisations in the domestic policy process. The core executive is now involved in making decisions through a range of international fora which limit the range of actions of ministers and departments. Most defence decisions are now made within the context of NATO or the West European Union. Many environmental issues are perceived as transnational problems and, hence, the site of solutions is the international level. A range of treaties on acid rain, whaling, CFCs and global warming have been made internationally rather than nationally (see Camilleri and Falk 1992). Economic decisions have to be taken increasingly in international organisations including the Group of Seven, the IMF and the World Bank. For example, in 1987 the Group of Seven agreed to coordinate exchange rate and interest rate policy in order to prevent the world slipping into recession. The Louvre Accord set a central rate for the dollar and the yen that was protected by a central fund by Group of Seven members (Lawson 1992: 554) The effect was that an international economic decision had a major impact on domestic policy-making.

The World Trade Organisation also acts as an international constraint. It is responsible for regulating trade throughout the world. The EU and Britain accept its adjudication on trade issues and this has important domestic implications. For example, the EU has banned the importing of beef from the United States that has been treated with growth hormones. The WTO argues that this is a restraint on trade and therefore has ruled that the EU must accept imports of US beef. Consequently a policy made on health grounds is being overturned by an international trade organisation, demonstrating the way in which international organisation and treaties increasingly affect what appears to be domestic policy.

Baker (1997), following Cox (1992), points to indications that the state is becoming increasingly transnational:

The co-existence of territorial configuration of political authority with international patterns of élite interaction between business, state officials, bureaucrats and members of international organisations and the strengthening of these transnational networks have given rise to the notion of the 'transnationalisation of the state'.

In other words, state actors are increasingly interacting with personnel from other states, and are constrained more by international forces than by domestic ones. Baker suggests that in Britain the Treasury is linked into a close network of international organisations and actors in making economic decisions.

In response to the globalisation literature, it should be remembered that international constraints on the core executive are not new. Britain has been highly constrained at least since the Second World War. In 1956, for instance, the British government was more or less forced to retreat from Suez because of financial pressure from the US (Sanders 1990). Nearly all post-war British military activity has either been underwritten or supported by the US. Even the Falklands War, which was an apparently exclusively British affair, could not have been won without US support.

According to much of the globalisation literature, the strongest impact of recent changes is in the restructuring of global markets, which has weakened the ability of states to control their domestic economies. With the globalisation of economic activity, the government's room for manoeuvre in economic, and by extension social policy, is becoming increasingly limited as nations are forced to compete in the world economy. Open markets and the massive capital flows that shift between states mean that currency values and interest rates are no longer controlled by domestic economies. The world foreign exchange markets deal with over $1 trillion a day, which is much more than the foreign exchange holdings of the world's wealthiest nations. Multinationals account for 25 to 33 per cent of world outputs and 70 per cent of world trade (McGrew 1997: 6). Not even the world's strongest economies can compete. For Perraton *et al.* (1997: 267):

Contemporary financial globalisation has transformed the framework for national economic policy. Global market evaluations of national economic policy are reflected in risk premia on national interest rates and, in the case of developing countries, credit rationing. Standard economic analysis since Mundell-Fleming indicates that in the absence of capital controls, countries can choose between fixing their exchange rate or pursuing an independent monetary policy. However, this is ceasing to be an accurate representation of the policy choices available to national authorities. Financial globalisation has rendered fixed exchange rates systems unsustainable over the longer term . . . The logic of this is that countries choices are now limited to floating rates or monetary union. However globalisation has also weakened countries' abilities to pursue independent monetary policies with floating exchange rates.

The impact of globalisation has informed the economic policy of the Labour government (Kenny and Smith 1997). Blair has demonstrated considerable awareness of the economic constraints that his government faces and therefore, rather than resist external pressures, he has attempted to incorporate the constraints into policy. Blair and Brown have explicitly stated the need, for a flexible labour force to compete in the world economy, to restrict public expenditure and to control public borrowing. Increasingly, it seems that the Labour government will bow to what Perraton *et al.* see as the inevitable and commit Britain to monetary union.

Nevertheless, the impact of globalisation should not be exaggerated. Marxist and neo-pluralist analysts have always seen capital as being a constraint on the state. Lindblom (1977) and Offe (1984) have highlighted how the economic imperative of a successful economy means that business is privileged in the policy process. Ministers cannot afford to make decisions which threaten the profitability of capital. Coates (1980) sees the economic power of domestic and international capital as a key explanation for the policy changes of the 1974–9 Labour government.

Hirst and Thompson (1996: 4) have provided significant evidence, despite the degree of international trade, that there is scant indication of a truly global economy. National governments still matter:

> While national governments may no longer be 'sovereign' economic regulators in the traditional sense, they remain political communities with extensive power to influence and sustain economic actors within their territories. Technical top-down macroeconomic management is now less important. However, the role of government as a facilitator and orchestrator of private economic actors has become far more salient as a consequence. The *political* role of government is central in the new forms of economic management.

While internationalisation affects the resources and constraints that core executives face, international economic pressures are still mediated by national states. For Milner and Keohane (1996: 21), 'Government policies and institutions may serve as a "wall" between the domestic economy and the international.' Changing economic relations internationally and nationally affect the structural context within which states operate but actors within the core executive have not been deprived of choice. Their actions are rarely solely determined by economic pressures.

In recent years, the greatest international constraint on the British core executive has been the European Union. A whole range of policies – industrial, regional, agricultural and trade – are almost completely European rather than domestic. Despite Menon and Hayward's (1996) claim that there is still a high degree of national autonomy in industrial policy, the European context does frame many policy decisions. Consequently, the EU has had an important impact on the organisation of the British core executive, and therefore in the remainder of this chapter I will look at the way the EU has reshaped the institutions of the core executive.

THE CORE EXECUTIVE AND THE EUROPEAN UNION

In assessing the relationship between Whitehall and Europe, there are two countervailing tendencies that are indicative of the British core executive. On one hand, the strong centripetal forces of departments, with their own separate histories and departmental interests, result in particular relationships with Europe. On the other hand, there are strong centralising tendencies emanating from the Cabinet Office and the Foreign and Commonwealth Office (FCO), which attempt to control and standardise responses to Europe. One change of recent years is that, as departments have become more adept and better resourced in dealing with Europe, they have relied much less on either Cabinet Office or FCO support. As a result, the role of the coordinating bodies has become less important.

After the establishment of the Single European Market and the signing of the Maastricht Treaty, an increasing number of departments are involved in EU business. When Britain originally joined the EEC, in 1973, membership only had implications for a handful of departments. The Foreign and Commonwealth Office (FCO) was thought by many to have had a new lease of life from membership after the shock of the decline of Empire. Another Department immediately affected was MAFF, which was dealing with the most comprehensive European policy, the Common Agricultural Policy (CAP). Finally, the DTI was soon dealing with the implication for British industry of the developing common market and the Community's trade policy *vis-à-vis* third countries.

By the mid-1990s, every department was affected by the plethora of decisions taken at the Community level. The EU imposes new burdens of work on ministers and their civil servants. Often, directives passed by Brussels do not correspond precisely with existing British law. This leads to the formulation of new legislation, which has to be passed at Westminster, and this can have the effect of reopening policy issues at a domestic level that governments have previously tried to close (Bender 1991, Toonan 1991: 109).

The increased European activity and the ever increasing directives from Europe has elicited the need for all European governments to invest more in coordination of the national decision-making machinery. In Britain this has occurred with limited formal institutional change at the centre. However, what has also happened is the rise of an informal, yet powerful, élite comprising of Number 10, the FCO, the Cabinet Office and the UK permanent representative (UKREP). Burch and Holliday (1996) point to the existence of a European network with the task of managing EU policy formation centring on: one ministerial committee – the Overseas and Defence Committee (OPD(E)) – which is chaired by the Foreign Secretary; the relevant official committee; and the European Secretariat in the Cabinet Office (Burch and Holliday 1996: 88).

In principle, the role of the European Secretariat is to coordinate the responses of Whitehall to the EU. Therefore, it convenes meetings to ensure that: the British government has a response to all new developments at the European level; the objectives of departments do not conflict; policy is consistent with the government's wider objectives; and there is proper implementation of EU decisions (see Spence 1992). In the view of the Cabinet Office, their role is: 'to be the neutral umpire, the dispassionate chairman of meetings' and therefore to resolve conflicts between various departmental interests (interview with Cabinet Office official).

The FCO also has a coordinating function. According to Spence (1992: 60): 'The FCO provides the institutional framework for the day to day coordination of EC policy through the Permanent Representative in Brussels.' The FCO monitors information from Brussels, prepares briefs for the Council of Ministers and has responsibility for political cooperation (Spence 1992). While the coordinating role of the Foreign Office is important, other departments are aware that it has its own departmental interests and so the rest of Whitehall is perhaps more wary of its advice.

On the whole, departments are happy with the process of coordination at the centre. An official in the Treasury described it as 'excellent', and the view from the DTI was 'to the outsider the structure looks very complicated and to some extent duplicatory . . . But actually it works quite well because we all know one another . . . and so a lot of it is done very informally'. Despite the division of functions between the FCO and the European Secretariat, there seems to be little overlap. The departments find the FCO and Cabinet Office knowledge of the EU useful, and there is a constant process of consultation between the departments and the coordinating machinery. Key policy papers have to go through the Foreign Office and the Cabinet Office, and then on to UKREP. The Cabinet Office coordinates within Whitehall, but the FCO instructs the British Ambassador at UKREP. Every Friday there is a meeting involving the FCO, a senior Cabinet Office official, the Ambassador and the relevant departments. The purpose is to iron out any problems or conflicts, and any unresolved issues go to the relevant cabinet committee.

Nevertheless, it is clear that the role of the coordinators has changed. To some extent the FCO believes (according to an interviewee) that it still controls contact with Brussels:

> any input that a UK government department wants to make into the system in Brussels goes through the UK permanent representative in Brussels. They are the people who talk to the Commission, talk to other member states and so on.

The reality, however, is that as EU business increases, the FCO and the Cabinet Office are losing control, and departments are increasingly conducting business with the Commission, and other member states, directly. Clearly, departments with continual EU contact, like the DTI and the MAFF, are competent at conducting their own negotiations. For the Department of the Environment (DoE), except for major issues of legislation:

> the majority of our links are bilateral . . . There is a continuous process of consultation and communication on a bilateral basis . . . We also have a lot of direct bilateral contact with officials in DG 11 in the Commission who are dealing with the areas that we are

concerned with. We also have a lot of bilateral contact with our opposite numbers in the environment ministries in other member states.

The preferences of officials in relation to Europe have been influenced by the process of integration. The FCO and the Cabinet Office have adapted well to the need to coordinate European policy. Individual departments are increasingly developing close relationships with both the Commission and their opposite numbers in other member states.

Institutional Interests

While for some departments the EU is viewed as a constraint, for others Europe provides an opportunity for increasing their role and autonomy. According to a senior official in the Cabinet Office:

> Departments tend to have a view of Europe which at least in part reflects the nature of the impact of Europe on their work. MAFF, because the impact of Europe has made the department more important and determines its policy, finds itself very closely involved. Whereas the Treasury, because it is such a bloody nuisance for them, tends to find itself rather irritated.

For some departments, Europe has been integrated into their work for a long period, and it provides new opportunities and enhances their functions. Consequently, they tend to be positive in their approach. For two departments at least, the DTI and the Ministry of Agriculture, Europe has given the departments an important *raison d'être* without which they may well have disappeared.

The Ministry of Agriculture is a small department in terms of budget, economic importance, political weight and size. Despite the logic of Thatcherism, which was to end agricultural subsidies and to abolish the department, the Ministry has outlived departments with larger budgets such as Employment and Energy. To a large extent, EU membership has saved the Ministry of Agriculture and has probably increased its autonomy (Smith 1993). There is no national agricultural policy, and MAFF officials spend much of their time in Brussels. Officials within MAFF acknowledge the CAP's problems, but are generally pro-European. The impact of the European agricultural policy has been to save their department and at a time of economic retrenchment to ensure that farmers' subsidies are protected. Effectively, membership of the EU has meant that agricultural expenditure is not subjected to Treasury control, and while the Council of Agricultural Ministers remains pro-farmer, it is unlikely that MAFF expenditures can be radically reduced. The department has been able, to some extent, to resist Treasury calls for the reform of the CAP. Despite several rounds of reform, farmers still receive large subsidies, and the CAP continues to take 50 per cent of the EU budget (Grant 1995), maintaining a crucial role for MAFF.

The DTI has faced similar questions over its existence. The logic of Thatcherism was to abolish the DTI. With privatisation, and the end of many industrial subsidies, questions were often raised over its existence (Purnell 1995). However, the DTI sees significant benefits in EU membership:

> [T]he DTI has always had positive objectives in Europe. We have had some defensive ones too but there have always been things that we have wanted to achieve, and those things on the whole have been less controversial in party political terms.

The DTI has had three important reasons for seeing Europe as beneficial. First, the EU provides the DTI with a significant amount of work. Issues relating to the single European market, regulation, monopolies and mergers, technology, trade and industrial subsidies are key aspects of EU policy that are dealt with by the DTI. Luckily for the DTI, to paraphrase Margaret Thatcher, while the state has been rolled back at the national level, it has been extended at the EU level and thus provided new functions for the department.

Second, a theme throughout the history of the DTI is support for free trade. Trade issues are best resolved at the multinational level, and therefore the DTI is one of the few departments that actually believes in the need for a strong Commission. As a DTI official commented:

> I think that the department has consistently been in favour of: a Europe that is open to the outside world; a Europe that creates an effective internal market that is tough on state aids, on monopoly practices; has effective competition policy; and looks at the regional dimension; that spends money wisely . . . We have also become one of the departments that has been arguing for deregulation in Europe,

or at least better regulation . . . All of which leads us in institutional terms to favour on the whole a strong Commission which is capable of policing single market, policing state aids and which is capable of devising and seeing through an effective liberal trade policy.

The DTI's EU activism has even led to the department accepting the need for qualified majority voting, despite the implied loss of national sovereignty.

Third, unlike other departments, EU policies have complemented DTI domestic policy, and it has been a way of achieving domestic policy goals. The view in the DTI is that ' in the areas that are core to the DTI, trade policy and single market policy, we are closer to the Commission probably than any other member state'. This is not to say that the DTI is a Euro-federalist department.

The DoE increasingly finds much of its work deeply enmeshed in the EU level. The EC Council of Ministers has agreed over 300 items of legislation affecting the environment in the past twenty years. For example, 'the extent to which one can consider what is done in the UK in terms of controlling pollution, as being separate from European legislation, the distinction is almost non-existent'. The EU provides opportunities and constraints for the DoE. On the one hand, the EU enables the DoE to press environmental legislation on other departments, in particular MAFF and the DTI, which would have been opposed if determined at the domestic level. On the other, nearly all environmental legislation is decided at the EU level, restricting what DoE can do on its own in this area.

For the Foreign Office, the EU is important because it is effectively the lead department on European policy, and as Britain's world role has declined the FCO has managed to maintain its status as a central negotiator in key European issues. As a Foreign Office official maintained, the FCO is conscious that 'Britain's involvement in Europe is central to its future as an international power . . . and I think we may be particularly conscious in the Foreign Office that the UK's future on the international stage is very much bound up with its being a major player in Europe'.

Departments that have only recently become involved in Europe tend to be more sceptical about its involvement in domestic policy. A Cabinet Office official suggested:

I think it is certainly true that departments like the DSS or the Department of Health or the Department of National Heritage, all of which over the last few years have found European policies intruding on their areas, are still largely operating on the basis of a discreet and hermetically sealed groups of people who deal with Europe. And they see it as an imposition and a difficulty. At the same time, the rest of the department, which goes on creating domestic policy, thinks that the European aspect is a distraction.

The DSS finds the EU is adding both legislative and expenditure burdens, with the EU increasingly attempting to harmonise social policy despite Britain's opt out from the social chapter. The DSS has a team of lawyers continually examining and contesting EU regulations. For the DSS, the EU is a burden rather than an opportunity. For the Home Office, the relationship is more ambivalent. In certain policy areas, such as drugs, the EU is a useful level for organising and cooperating on policy. On others, such as immigration, the relationship has been more problematic. In some senses, the Home Office is the least integrated department, coming very late to Europe. It is also apparent, when one is talking to Home Office officials, that the third pillar of the Union, being intergovernmental, operates very differently from business conducted within the Community institutions. To a large extent, the Home Office is still concerned with limiting EU competence, maintaining sovereignty and protecting national interests. The Home Office does not see it as in its interest to lose control of immigration, law and order or criminal justice issues, especially as these have such domestic political importance.

But scepticism does not only exist in newly integrated departments. The Treasury has always been involved in European policy. As a Treasury official admitted: 'There are no bits of Treasury work now that don't have some kind of European dimension.' Nevertheless, the relationship with the EU is somewhat ambivalent. The EU is frustrating for the Treasury, because it reduces its autonomy – economic policy is no longer purely a domestic concern. 'There is more attempt by Europe to try and dictate the way that financial and monetary policy is run,' and while the Treasury accepts the convergence criteria it does have to submit to EU pressures. As Thain and Wright (1995: 550) point out, the implications of the free movement of capital and labour are 'a convergence of regulations and payments in social security and income maintenance' which will constrain further Treasury control. However, in the area of economic policy Treasury superiority remains. According to one official:

I don't think that membership of the European Union has changed the Treasury much. I think it's more the other way around, in the sense that the UK thinks that it can try and persuade the Europeans that its approach to economic policy is the sensible one.

In terms of public expenditure, the EU has presented particular challenges to Treasury officials. From the initial period of membership until the mid-1980s, the size of the British financial contribution was a problem, and it created an area of public expenditure outside Treasury control. In addition, the EU can impose expenditure in a number of areas that the Treasury cannot control and would probably prefer did not exist. This has become increasingly apparent in the area of regional spending, where the EU has provided funds to Britain on the grounds that there would be additionality (that is, the subsidies would be additional to, not a replacement of, existing expenditure). However, the Treasury has continually sought ways of circumventing the additionality requirement (Bache 1996).

In sum, for the Treasury, the EU creates problems. As a Cabinet Official explains:

> Their more sceptical approach derives from their lack of control over allocation of resources, which they find difficult to accept. Together with the fact that there is a budgetary procedure, and an auditing procedure, which the Treasury will feel is less effective than domestic equivalents and it must be rather frustrating for them.

The Treasury's domestic instinct is to say no to new legislation, on the basis that it will increase public expenditure, and this scepticism continues at the EU level. This is confirmed within the Treasury, where an official suggested that the Treasury goes to a whole range of meetings covering even issues like home affairs because of potential expenditure increases: 'I suppose the Treasury is very suspicious and doesn't think that it can trust anybody.' Even with a pro-European Chancellor, the Treasury will try to slow up integration measures if it thinks they will result in increased costs.

How EU membership has restructured the core executive varies according to the ways in which the departments perceive membership. The attitude of departments and the way they relate to Europe, varies greatly. Civil servants do not have a set of endogenously determined preferences. Instead, their preferences are institutionally determined.

For some departments, Europe creates new opportunities and may increase autonomy in relation to the Cabinet or the Treasury. For others, it clearly indicates a loss of control. In such cases, the tendency is to attempt to slow further integration.

Departmental coordination

Departments' relations with Europe has affected the process of co-ordination within departments. In August 1993, John Gummer min-uted John Major saying that the only way of guaranteeing 'the political objective of placing the United Kingdom at the heart of Europe is delivered in practice [is] by seeing to it that Whitehall Departments become, and remain, truly European, professionals in the ways of Brussels.' Yet different departments organise in a range of ways. Nevertheless, in the post-Maastricht era there seems to be a concerted effort to integrate Europe much more into the everyday operations of departments.

The Treasury provides a good example of how intra-departmental coordination has changed:

> Five years ago, all the relations with Europe were handled by the Europe Division in the International area. Whereas now what happens is that every team that deals with a particular policy domestically also deals with it at an international and European level. So for example, the team that dealt with MAFF expenditure also deals with CAP (interview with Treasury official).

So, rather than relying on EU specialists, all officials within the Treasury have some EC competence. In addition, there is a small coordination team – EU Coordination and Strategy – which ensures that a unified departmental line is maintained and deals with issues where a domestic section does not have departmental expertise. The coordinating division also plays a role at the external level and represents the department in Cabinet Office meetings. Nevertheless, there is still an impression in the Treasury that Europe is not, as yet, that important or central to its work. A Cabinet Office official suggested that there are a number of Treasury officials closely involved in EU work, but:

> There is a culture within the Treasury, there is a smallish cadre of people who have made their careers dealing with EU matters . . .

And perhaps the vast majority of Treasury officials do see European issues as something not to be touched with a bargepole.

Even in the Foreign Office, which has been centrally involved in the EU since the beginning, there has been a change in the way that EU business is integrated into the department. Developments such as the collapse of communism in Eastern Europe, greater European political cooperation and a common security policy

> mean that there is virtually nobody in any corner of the Foreign Office used not sometime to having to go off to attend a working group in Brussels . . . There is generally a far greater consciousness of the European dimension of business all through the office.

In formal organisational terms, the FCO has a European Union command with three departments: European Union Department External, which deals with external economic policy of the European Union; EU Department Internal, which is concerned with EMU, the IGC and all the institutional questions, while also dealing with shadowing the work of domestic departments; and the Common Foreign and Security Policy Department, which deals with briefing the political director and with all the second-pillar work.

Likewise, the DTI, which again has been closely involved in European policy, has always had a European division. Now, however, 'we have concluded that the only way you can now run EU policy in reality is by letting the individual experts get on with it', and so, while there is some central coordination there is a range of policy areas, such as telecommunications or consumer protection, on which the department does not coordinate. Now the role of the European Division is to try to keep an overview of what is going on in the department in relation to Europe, to provide advice on the working procedures of the EU and in some senses to act as a European secretariat for the department. Much of the contact with the EU is now bilateral, with officials consulting directly with people in the EU and the governments of other member states.

It is the Department of the Environment that has been the most active in establishing new procedures. The department has undertaken a review of how it handles European business. One of the problems for the DoE is that while some of its responsibilities are almost completely European, such as water, others like Housing and Local Government have little contact with the EU. Therefore, there has not been an attempt to force all divisions into adopting similar approaches to the EU. Rather, there is a high level European Strategy Group, which brings together grade 2 officials from different policy areas every three to six months to review the department's European strategy. In addition, there is a European Division within the Environmental Protection Group for dealing with day-to-day European issues and providing expertise for the whole of the Department on Europe. In areas where there is a high European content, contact is bilateral rather than through a coordinating body.

In recent years, most departments have made significant organisational changes in order to adapt to the requirements of the EU. It is interesting that in most cases, departments have attempted to integrate the EU throughout the department rather than to concentrate it within a European coordination body as used to be the case. However, there are still some departments, notably the Home Office and the DoE, where large parts of the department have little EU relevance. In these cases, the European Division takes on a much more central role. There are significant differences in the way that Departments deal with the EU, in the sense that some like the DTI and DoE seem to have come to terms with the importance of the EU and see the relevance of intimate and regular contacts. Others, like the FCO and Treasury, still tend to see the EU as external and more of an aspect of foreign policy than of domestic policy, and their role as that of protecting national interests. These differences can again be very much related to institutional interests. For the DoE, there is some evidence that EU engagement is a way of obtaining more rigorous environmental regulation than would be the case in a purely domestic context. For Departments like MAFF, the DTI and DoE, Europe increases their scope and they have adapted well to developing transgovernmental links.

Conclusion: is Britain a hollow state?

The thrust of this chapter and the previous one is that the core executive has lost capacity because of reform and the shifting of power out of the parliamentary and executive arenas. Does this now mean Britain is a hollow state? The hollowing out of the state 'refers to the loss of functions upwards to the European Union, downwards to special purpose bodies and outwards to agencies' (Rhodes 1997a: 17). For Rhodes, the polity has become more differentiated, and as a consequence the role of the core executive has become less one of direction and more one of coordination. This raises important questions concerning what the state can do and the extent to which political leadership can be effective.

Before jumping to apocalyptic conclusions about the future of the core executive, it is worth considering a number of points. First, the state has always been constrained, and the question of whether the government makes a difference is an old one. Second, Saward (1997: 26) suggests 'the state is being redefined or reshaped, not hollowed out, at least on the internal dimension'. Rhodes's notion of subgovernment raises the question of whether government ever really controlled the implementation process, and therefore the creation of agencies and regulatory bodies may be a more effective means of executive coordination than traditional hierarchy. There is a high level of dependency between agencies and departments (see Gains 1998), and government has the ability to increase the powers of regulatory bodies.

However, Saward (1997: 32) also argues that at the international level there is evidence that national governments are more vulnerable to outside pressures and events and are 'becoming local governments'. Again, it is important to be cautious. The balance of resources between the national arena and the international one has changed, and the relationships of dependency may have altered. But, as we have seen with dependency throughout the book, it is two-way, and international actors depend on nation-states. The EU, in particular, can achieve little without the support of national governments.

Consequently, although power has shifted from the parliamentary arena, the executive arena still retains significant and important resources. There is a continuing role for national leadership. Leadership may be more concerned with managing networks than simply directing (Rhodes 1997b), but leaders often have the legitimacy, and the electoral and parliamentary support, to take authoritative decisions and therefore to orient the policy direction of networks. Moreover, when leaders are in a particularly strong position they have the ability to bypass networks. Leadership is constrained by institutions (Elgie 1995) and by the available resources, state capabilities and external constraints. But within these – admittedly severe – confines, leaders can make choices about policy goals and tactics. When presented with particular 'windows of opportunity', leaders who make the right choices can have a significant impact on institutional structures and policy.

9 Constitution, State and Core Executive

The study of the core executive in Britain has been skewed by the focus of media, constitutional myth and behavioural studies. The media, through their concentration on personalities, have contributed to an excessive focus on the Prime Minister and increasing presidentialism. The constitution locates power in the upper echelons of the executive, and behaviourism, with its methodological individualism and belief in observation, has led to a focus on principal actors and the question, 'Who gets what?'. This book has drawn upon realist epistemology. In other words, its concern is not with the observable behaviour of actors but with the underlying structures that create the institutional arena within which people act. For example, a behaviourist examining power and European Monetary Union would examine the preferences of the key actors such as the Chancellor and the Prime Minister. If the Chancellor favoured joining and the Prime Minister was opposed to membership and the final decision was to join, the behaviourist would see the Chancellor as winning and, therefore, having power. For the realist, however, these are second-order questions that derive from understanding why EMU is so important. Instead, the focus would be on how structures constrain and facilitate the decision-makers. The key question would be whether the decision to join was a result of the Chancellor's power or of the structural pressures deriving from the City's needs to have access to European financial markets. Therefore, while we have to examine behaviour, we also have to understand structure and context and how they constrain, facilitate and shape the decisions of policy-makers.

The methodology that derives from a realist epistemology is essentially historical, contextual and institutional. Actors have to be analysed within their structural contexts, and we need to examine the terrain on which they operate and, within that context, the choices they make. This book has been about three sets of actors: Prime Ministers, ministers and civil servants. Each operates on a different structural terrain. The terrain of the Prime Minister is the apex of government and the resources at his or her disposal derive from the office. The constraints are those of cabinet, party and the outside world. The terrain of the minister is the department and the constraints are departmental rules, values and institutions, and cabinet colleagues, in addition to constraints imposed by the Prime Minister and the outside world. Both ministers and Prime Ministers exist on terrains where they are expected to act, to make choices about policy and the rules of government. But they make choices within varying contexts, structures and resource dependencies. Personality may be one of the factors affecting choices, but it should not be seen as the key factor. Prime Ministers have different styles, and they are in a position to affect the structure of government, but their style is also shaped by the context and their dependencies. It may help to view the Prime Minister as an institution of government as well as a personality.

The terrain of officials is very different. They operate in a context where the rules of the game of the official world are essentially set by a constitution that the officials maintain through their actions and their beliefs. For example, if we compare the guidelines for the procedures of ministers written in 1992 and 1997, we can see that little has changed, because it is based on official advice on the nature of the constitution. The rules of ministerial behaviour are formally set down on paper by the Prime Minister, but contain much official advice on what the constitutional position is in relation to the role of ministers. Through this document, and others, and their behaviour, officials maintain the constitution. The constitution, or more accurately the constitution and its enveloping myths, set the limits of official behaviour, and to that extent officials are much more the bearers of structure than are ministers. If a permanent secretary in the Treasury changes then the impact is generally small (although it did have some affect on the Treasury views of Next Steps agencies). However, if Gordon Brown were to be replaced by a left-winger such as Ken Livingstone, for example, there would be changes in policy, even if they were effectively constrained by the wider context. This is not to say that officials do not act (or are powerless), but that their terrain of action differs from that of ministers. Officials are concerned with interpreting their freedom of manoeuvre within the confines of loyalty to ministers. Indeed, much of their action is interpreting what is a loyal action. As we saw in the case of the Scott report in Chapter 5, this leeway can often be considerable, because the constitution is largely mythical and it is officials who interpret the myth.

This point illustrates the duality of structure and agency. At one level, actors reproduce their own structures. It is officials who reproduce the rule of the game, such as loyalty to the minister, that constrains their actions. The structures are created by human agency, and so there are occasions when officials directly counter the wishes of ministers (one example was an official who persistently opposed Norman Tebbit's regional industrial policy), but in most cases officials accept the constraint of ministerial loyalty. Their success is judged in terms of their ability to meet the minister's needs, questioning rational choice approaches that see officials as largely concerned with their own material interests. Similarly, Prime Ministers reproduce the rules of prime-ministerial behaviour. At the same time, however, there are structures – for example, events in the world economy – over which officials or the Prime Minister can have little control. This demonstrates that actors within the core executive operate on several different structural terrains simultaneously.

The point of highlighting structural terrains is to illustrate that ministers, Prime Ministers and officials are not in competition with each other for power. In terms of achieving policy goals, they bring different things to the equation. Consequently, they are all dependent on each other. This book has traced the lines of dependency that exist between these actors and that go from Prime Minister to ministers to officials in a process of exchange. In order to achieve their goals, Prime Ministers have to make exchanges with ministers, and ministers have to exchange resources with officials. On their own they cannot make policy.

Actors in themselves do not have power but resources. Resources are usually structurally determined, but the use of resources depends on the context and the choices of strategies and tactics. In certain contexts, actors have more freedom to use resources than others. Sometimes they are more dependent on other actors. The key to success is knowing what tactics to use in any particular context. Thatcher's tactic of domination and isolation was perhaps right (or more properly, executable) in 1987, following electoral and economic success, but inappropriate in the context of the highly unpopular poll tax and the recession of the late 1980s.

The book also stresses how the choices and tactics of actors within the core executive are also limited by the wider politico-economic context. Jessop (1990) and Hay (1996) have emphasised the structural selectivity of the state: 'Its structures, practices and *modus operandi* are more amenable to some types of political strategy and certain types of intervention than others' (Hay 1996: 7). In 1979, the DTI had the machinery to make relatively detailed interventions into the economy; in 1998 much of that capability has disappeared, and if government were to develop an interventionist industrial policy then it would require the rebuilding of administrative and financial machinery. Consequently, there is an institutional bias against the Secretary of State choosing such a strategy. This point illustrates the need to relate the core executive to wider theories of the state.

THE CORE EXECUTIVE AND THE STATE

It is crucial to remember that neither the structure of resources nor the structures of dependency are immutably fixed. The role of the state, the core executive and the resources of actors are related to wider social, political and economic change. Indeed, for Hay (1996: 8), the state is a series

of dynamic and complexly interwoven *processes* and practices (occurring within specific institutional settings), and hence . . . a dynamic and evolving system. Accordingly, we must reject the prevalent notion that the direction of the state may be used to 'fix' and thereby render static what is, in fact, a constantly changing network of relationships and institutional practices and procedures.

This view of the state creates problems for actors within the core executive. The core executive, through elections, the constitution and the establishment of bureaucratic capabilities, developed the legitimacy and the ability to be the key authoritative actor within the British political and social system. However, it is not clear what the core executive has power over; the lines of dependency are constantly changing, and it faces both external and internal threats to its position. The core executive makes decisions and, through official processes, the decisions are implemented, but it has great difficulty in controlling outcomes. The Education Secretary may decide to raise standards, but he or she does not control the teaching or, more importantly, the learning process. The Chancellor may decide not to join EMU, but speculative attacks on an isolated pound may force Britain into the haven/clutches of the Euro.

The problem for the core executive is that the nature of the state is elusive. Ministers can see what needs to be done – defeat crime, control inflation – but can they find the means to do so? As we have seen, because of the distribution of resources controlling the core executive is complex as centres compete for dominance and departments fight to retain autonomy. Controlling the wider state is even more difficult, and controlling civil society barely possible. Consequently, some commentators (Dunsire 1990, Kickert 1993) see the social world as autopoietic – self-regulating – with the changing whims of the state having little impact on the everyday organisation of society.

As we saw in Chapter 3, the nature of the core executive cannot be isolated from the wider socio-economic context. Large-scale social, economic and political change affects the form and function of the core executive. Indeed, many non-behavioural approaches suggest that the core executive is the wrong focus because decisions are made elsewhere. However, the core executive is where crucial actors within the state operate, and it is important to understand the processes whereby wider social forces are translated into policy.

From 1945 until the 1980s, the core executive was a reflection of the post-war settlement, with its concomitant commitment to full employment and the welfare state, and the post-war world of economic boom and the cold war. These events and decisions structured the choices of actors within it and to some extent affected the resources they had available. The belief that the welfare state could reduce injustice, and that Keynesianism could produce full employment, led state actors to believe that they could set and achieve social goals. Consequently, the core executive was to some extent concerned with controlling a large bureaucratic machine so that officials and politicians could affect the social order. It was a rejection of both the anti-rationalism of traditional conservatism and the anti-statism of the liberalism. In addition, with the post-war boom and rising prosperity, the financial resources available to the core executive seemed ever-expanding and, indeed, during particular spells in the 1950s to 1970s there was little rigorous financial control on departmental expenditure. The cold war increased the perception of states being concerned with protecting their national boundaries and sovereignty from external threats. Consequently, the core executive, legitimised by parliamentary sovereignty, was in charge of the political system and, to a significant degree, the social one also.

The core executive of the post-war settlement was concerned with controlling a particular form of state. Its features were:

- a high degree of state control – the result of policies such as nationalisation;
- a large bureaucratic machine;
- legitimacy to undertake large-scale intervention in society;
- the incorporation of key economic groups into the policy process;

- a high degree of consensus between official and politicians over their role in governing and decision-making.

The nature of the post-war state was essentially hierarchical and élitist. The public sector ethos, the electoral cycle and ministerial accountability provided the legitimising codes for a closed system of policy-making. The presumption was that Whitehall knew best – officials were imbued with the public service ethos and therefore could work in the public interest with little external oversight (Richards and Smith 1998). Control of officials was in the hands of elected politicians who were accountable for what occurred in their government (collective responsibility) and in their departments (ministerial accountability). The whole process was essentially one of internal regulation; officials were controlled by their own codes and ministers; ministers were controlled by Parliament, and Parliament was made up of MPs who were representatives not delegates.

This hierarchical, closed, élitist and self-regulating governing system was first systematically questioned in the 1970s. The perception developed that politicians and officials could no longer deliver what they promised, either in programmatic terms or in the quality of government that was supposed to emanate from the Whitehall–Westminster model. As Hay (1996) highlights, the 1970s saw the disintegration of the post-war state regime in Britain. The combination of the end of the post-war boom and Britain's relative economic decline led to an economic and political crisis. In order to retain legitimacy, the post-war state had incorporated key economic actors and used the public sector ethos as a mechanism for obtaining the trust of the people. With economic crisis, the incorporated actors were beginning to feel that they were receiving little for their troubles. In addition, the welfare state had not greatly reduced the levels of relative poverty, and with increasingly regular public expenditure crises (at least from 1968) welfare policy was under greater restraint. As unemployment rose, Keynesianism no longer appeared to be delivering. Consequently, voters had less reason to trust the rulers, and indeed, with events like the Fulton report, it seemed some of the rulers were increasingly distrustful of other ruling élites. The contradictory elements of the post-war settlement could be papered over for much of the period, but the continual accumulation of unresolved crises led to a crisis of the state regime (Hay 1996: 96).

This structural crisis, which was manifested most clearly in the Winter of Discontent in 1979 (although with hindsight it was also evident in the collapse of the Heath Government in 1974, the high inflation of 1975–6, and the IMF crisis of 1976), created the space for the Thatcherite restructuring of the state. For Hay, the parameters of the Thatcherite state regime are: a dismantling of corporatism and weakening of the unions; abandonment of the commitment to full employment; a shift away from the public towards the private sectors; the marketisation of the welfare state and the centralisation of state power (Hay 1996: 151–2). This reconstruction of the state regime has, as we saw in Chapter 7, had significant implications for the nature of the core executive.

The Thatcher government rhetorically rejected the legitimisation of the public sector ethos by elevating the importance of managerial and private sector values and introducing much greater levels of audit. Managerialism led to changing relations between politicians and officials, and between the core executive and the wider state. Officials have become increasingly concerned with managerialism and delivering services for ministers, while the establishment of agencies and privatisation have changed the relationship between the core and the wider state from one of direction to one of contract and regulation. There is a sense in which the fingers of officials and politicians were burnt by the degree of blame they received for the problems of the 1970s, and therefore the strategy has been to unload potentially problematic issues such as the nationalised industries and wage restraint. The core executive lost legitimacy by its failure to steer the wider state, and therefore has taken on a new role, coordinating the shift from government to governance.

Consequently, in contrast to the post-war period the key characteristics of the core executive are:

- a shift from bureaucratic management towards decentralised and delayered management;
- a tendency to set the overall direction of policy rather than the detail of policy – a lack of detailed intervention;
- control over a much smaller public sector;
- the exclusion of economic groups from the policy process;
- less consensus between official and politicians;
- concern with managing networks rather than directing state bureaucracies.

If we see the core executive as operating within a system of governance then the focus of analysis should shift away from formal institutions to networks that operate within and between various elements of the state and civil society. Networks are a useful tool for understanding the operation of the core executive, because they can be conceived as more flexible than traditional organisations. Networks exist at a range of levels: within the core executive; between the core executive and civil society; within civil society; and at the international, transnational (above states) and global levels (see Mann 1997). Thus the core executive has to operate at numerous levels and often in relationships of high dependence where it has little impact on the final outcome. Moreover, there are a number of networks, within civil society and at the transnational level, where the core executive is excluded from the decision-making process. The concept of networks may be limited as a theory of power, but it sensitises the researcher to the need to see the policy process as complex and as existing outside formal institutions. It therefore highlights the multiple dependencies that exist for actors and institutions within the core executive.

It is important to note that the types of networks that exist within the core executive are very different from those that exist between the state and outside groups. When we are analysing a closed policy community between a department and a pressure group, we are often looking at a particular power relationship. This type of network is a mechanism for excluding certain groups and defining a policy issue in a particular way. Therefore, the policy community is constituting a particular power relationship and the nature of the relationship can explain policy outcomes (see Marsh and Smith 1998). The use of networks within the core executive is more descriptive. They describe the relationships of dependency that exist between various actors and institutions within the central state. Because the actors within the core are playing by certain rules of the game, they cannot, within this universe, be excluded from the network. Therefore, the networks are less often about power relationships. In these circumstances, the nature of power is analysed not through the network but through the degree of resource dependency between actors, because in most cases actors cannot be removed from networks. What is important is not who is or who is not in a network, but what is the nature of the dependency between actors within the network. Therefore, networks within the core executive tend to be highly fluid. They are created to deal with particular problems and often actors can enter or exit at will.

The nature of the core executive has been greatly affected by wider social, economic and political changes. Even if we reject the more extreme claims of some of the globalisation literature, it is clear that the integration of Britain into the EU has affected the balance of resources within the core executive. Moreover a shift to a macroeconomic policy that is concerned with financial stringency and low inflation means that the goals of the core executive are much more limited.

Recent years have witnessed changes in the structural resources of actors within the core executive. The resources of the Prime Minister's Office appear to have increased as it has taken on a greater policy and coordinating role. The resources of officials have become fewer in relation to ministers as they have been constrained by the rhetoric of management, external audit, a decreasing policy role and a reduction in their numbers. The impact of the EU has been contradictory. For instance, it has increased the resources of the Cabinet Office and the Foreign Office and made some departments more autonomous over particular issues. However, the EU has reduced the control of the Treasury over particular financial items.

With the reforms of the core executive and changes in the wider world the structures of dependency have changed. The core executive has increased its dependence on international organisations; ministers are more dependent on the Prime Minister; new exchange relationships have developed between agencies and departments and the Treasury is increasingly dependent on departments and, to some extent, on the role the Prime Minister ascribes to the Treasury. The Prime Minister and the Treasury retain advantages over other institutions within the core executive. Both have high levels of authority, both have resources that other actors need and both are networked to the whole core executive. They, however, need each other and need departments. Consequently, the particular nature of the relationships between the Treasury, the Prime Minister and the rest of the core executive, and the process of exchange, depend on the context and within that context the choices of the key actors.

As a result of these changes, the core executive is increasingly concerned with governance rather than government (see Rhodes 1997a and 1997c, Peters 1997). The core executive is no longer sovereign (if it ever was), but it is at the centre of a network of different organisations that it does not directly control such as agencies, privatised utilities, the EU, international bodies, voluntary agencies and quangos. The world of government was always more complex than the constitutional model implied, but it is now *recognised* as complex. In a sense, the capabilities that the core executive developed in the twentieth century have to some extent been given up. It has exchanged direct control through nationalisation and bureaucratisation for indirect control through markets, regulation and contract. This is seen as making government easier by reducing responsibility, but it also makes government more difficult by limiting the levers of control for the core executive. However, it has to be remembered that the core executive continues to be more highly resourced in terms of authority, finance, and control over coercion than any other domestic institution. Therefore, its centrality and control of resources means it continues to have dominance over other organisations and networks.

THE CONSTITUTIONAL IMPLICATIONS

A theme of this book has been to analyse how the British constitution has framed the way both academics and political actors understand the operation of the state. To some extent they have believed the unwritten propaganda that they have also propagated. The core executive approach to central government, and many of the empirical changes of recent years, highlights the questionable assumptions of the constitutional focus. The constitution assumes parliamentary sovereignty, but decision-making has moved beyond the parliamentary arena. Both the sovereignty of Parliament and the sovereignty of the nation are questionable.

The constitution also assumes ministerial responsibility. There is a time-honoured tradition of ministers attempting to elude responsibility. But this notion has become even more contestable when we consider the significant role of officials in policy-making and the fragmentation of the state through the establishment of quangos, agencies and privatised bodies with public functions. The creation of agencies, in particular, has created a new set of relationships and roles but without any conscious or explicit change in the constitutional values that govern the relationships (Gains 1998). Therefore, it is important to create some constitutional procedures that recognise it is not only ministers who make decisions.

The third constitutional assumption is collective responsibility, but, again, the processes of collective decision-making are extremely unclear. The cabinet is now almost universally accepted as nothing more than a rubber stamp; it has almost become a dignified part of the constitution. The forum for collective decision-making is either cabinet committees or the relationship between the Prime Minister and the Chancellor. Both of these processes are *ad hoc* and neither is collective. Therefore, there is a need to explicate the nature of the

Chancellor—Prime Minister axis in order to clarify their position in relation to the rest of the cabinet. The contingent nature of these relationships highlights the difficulty of coordinating government – a process that has become more difficult – in what is a highly personalised system. Thatcher effectively bypassed the formal processes of coordination by personal intervention, but if coordination is individual rather than institutional then it depends almost solely on the whims, abilities and strength of the individual. Such a system is bound to fail, because no Prime Minister can oversee all that goes on in government. Moreover, if Cabinet is largely dignified, it raises the question of what collective responsibility departmental ministers can have.

If we are in a world of governance rather than government, what are the constitutional principles that underpin it? At least with parliamentary sovereignty, Parliament was the decision-maker, and those who made decisions could be removed with election. But what is the status of the new decision-makers? Government and officials maintain the fiction that ministers are still responsible, but it is clear that quangos, private companies and even agencies are also making decisions that affect the public good. If ministerial accountability is not working satisfactorily, how are the decision-makers held to account? New forms of accountability have been brought into being through the media, the use of audit, and the judicial process but, again, their roles have developed in an *ad hoc* way, without any clear idea about what they are supposed to achieve (see Flinders 1998). While the media have been important in raising issues of accountability, in the cases of particular individuals such as Neil Hamilton and in some policy areas such as arms to Iraq, they have no formal constitutional role. The argument for an unwritten constitution has always been that it is flexible, that it can change without going through a complex legislative procedure. What the last twenty years have demonstrated is that it has no flexibility, because no one knows how to change it. The constitution has not kept pace with the changes that have occurred in government, and hence its legitimacy has been undermined, raising considerable questions concerning its legitimising role. The structures of government have changed, and the values system governing those structures need to change with them. There is a need for an explicit constitutional framework to govern the operation of the reformed core executive. This is not to say that a written constitution will necessarily solve the problems. Written constitutions are only as good as the people who use them, and therefore real constitutional change comes only with changes in attitudes among the rulers. The importance of a written constitution is that it may assist the necessary cultural change and provide some external controls on state actors.

CONCLUSION

This book has highlighted three points. First, in understanding central government it is wrong to focus too much on personality, or on the role of the Prime Minister and key ministers. They may be important, but other actors within the core executive are also crucial. Second, while actors are central, so are structures, and therefore we need to understand the structural and historical context within which the core executive operates. Third, one way of doing this is to have an explicitly analytical framework, which focuses on the context, resources, structures and choices of the institutions and actors within the core executive, and to underpin this with a theory of power that is relational and based on dependency rather than dominance. The way in which this framework can be taken forward is to apply it to particular case studies of core executive policy-making in the hope that this highlights the complex nature of power within the central state.

Bibliography

Addison, P. (1975) *The Road to 1945*. London: Cape.

Ahn, M. S. (1995) 'Administrative Reform in Kim-Young Sam's Government', *Proceedings of the International Seminar on Governmental Reform Policy*, Korean Association of Policy Studies.

Alderman, K. and Carter, N. (1991) 'A Very Tory Coup: The Ousting of Mrs Thatcher', *Parliamentary Affairs*, 44, 125–39.

Anderson, B. (1983) *Imagined Communities*. London: Verso.

Anderson, B. (1991) *John Major: The Making of a Prime Minister*. London: Fourth Estate.

Anderson, J. (1946) 'The Machinery of Government', *Public Administration*, 24, 147–56.

Anderson, P. (1964) 'Origins of the Present Crisis', *New Left Review*, 23, 26–53.

Anderson, P. (1987) 'The Figures of Descent', *New Left Review*, 161, 20–77.

Andeweg, R B. and Nijzink, L. (1995) 'Beyond the Two-Body Image: Relations Between Ministers and MPs in Western Europe', in H. Doring (ed.), *Parliament and Majority Rule in Western Europe*. Frankfurt: Campus-Verlag.

Armstrong, R. (1988) 'Taking Stock of our Achievements', in Peat Marwick McLintock, *Future Shape of Reform in Whitehall*. London: Royal Institute of Public Administration.

Armstrong, R. (1994) 'Cabinet Government in the Thatcher Years', *Contemporary Record*, 8, 447–52.

Bache, I. (1996) 'EU Regional Policy: Has the UK Government Succeeded in Playing the Gatekeeper Role Over the Domestic Impact of the European Regional Development Fund?', unpublished PhD thesis, University of Sheffield.

Baker, A. (1997) 'The Transnationalisation of the Core Executive in the UK: The Case of HM Treasury's International Finance Directorate', paper presented at the European Consortium for Political Research Joint Sessions of Workshops, Bern, 27 April to 4 March.

Baker, D., Gamble, A. and Ludlam, S. (1993) '1847 . . . 1906 . . . 1996? Conservative Splits and European Integration', *Political Quarterly*, 64, No. 4.

Baker, D., Gamble, A. and Ludlam, S. (1995) 'Backbench Conservative Attitudes to European Integration', *Political Quarterly*, 66, 221–33.

Baker, K. (1993) *The Turbulent Years: My Life in Politics*. London: Faber & Faber.

Barber, J. (1984) 'The Power of the Prime Minister' in Borthwick, R. L. and Spence, J. E. (eds), *British Politics in Perspective*, Leicester: Leicester University Press.

Barber, J. (1991) *The Prime Minister since 1945*. Oxford: Blackwell.

Barberis, P. (1997) 'An Era of Change', in Barberis, P. (ed.) *The Civil Service in an Era of Change*, Aldershot: Dartmouth.

Barberis, P. (1994) 'Permanent Secretaries and Policy Making', *Public Policy and Administration*, 9, 35–49.

Barker, A. (1998) 'Political Responsibility for UK Prison Security – Ministers Escape Again', *Public Administration, 76,* 1–23.

Barnett, C. (1986) *The Audit of War.* London: Macmillan.

Battista, R. (1994) *Servicing the Stigma; the Implementation of AIDS policy,* unpublished MA thesis, University of York.

Bauman, Z. (1989) *Modernity and the Holocaust.* Oxford: Polity.

BBC (1994) *Newsnight,* 13 September.

Beer, S. (1982) *Britain Against Itself.* London: Faber.

Bender, B. (1991) 'Governmental Processes: Whitehall, Central Government and 1992', *Public Policy and Administration,* 6, 13–29

Benn, T. (1981) *Arguments for Democracy.* London: Cape.

Berger, P. and Luckman, T. (1967) *The Social Construction of Reality.* Harmondsworth: Penguin.

Birch, A. (1984) 'Overload, ungovernability and deligitimation: the theories and the British Case', *British Journal of Political Studies,* 14, 135–60.

Blackstone, T. and Plowden, W. (1988) *Inside the Think Tank: Advising the Cabinet 1971–1983.* London: Heinemann.

Blitz, J. and Adonis, A. (1995), 'Inside Whitehall: Time for the Deputy to Make His Mark', *Financial Times,* 27 July.

Broadbent, J. and Laughlin, R. (1997) 'Evaluating the "New Public Management" Reforms in the UK: A Constitutional Possibility', *Public Administration,* 75, 487–507.

Brown, A. H. (1968) 'Prime Ministerial Power (Part I), *Public Law,* Spring, 28–56.

Brown, G. (1972) *In My Way.* Harmondsworth: Penguin.

Bulpitt, J. (1986) 'The Discipline of the New Democracy: Mrs Thatcher's Domestic Statecraft', *Political Studies,* 34, 19–39.

Burch, M. (1988) 'British Government: a Residual Executive', *Parliamentary Affairs,* 41, 34–47.

Burch, M. and Holliday, I. (1996) *The British Cabinet System.* Hemel Hempstead: Prentice-Hall.

Burk, K. (1982a) 'Editor's Introduction', in Burk, K. (ed.), *War and the State: The Transformation of British Government, 1914–1919.* London: Allen & Unwin.

Burk, K. (1982b) 'The Treasury from Impotence to Power' in Burk, K. (ed.), *War and the State: The Transformation of British Government, 1914–1919.* London: Allen & Unwin.

Burnham, J. and Jones, G. W. (1993) 'Advising Margaret Thatcher: The Prime Minister's Office and the Cabinet Office Compared', *Political Studies,* 41, 299–314.

Burns, T. (1995) 'The Management of Economic Policy', Eleanor Rathbone Memorial Lecture, University of Manchester, 28 March.

Butcher, T. (1993) 'Whitehall's Managerial Revolution', *Public Policy Review,* 1, 51–5.

Butler, D., Adonis, A. and Travers, T. (1994) *Failure in British Government: The Politics of the Poll Tax.* Oxford University Press.

Butler, H. (1997) 'Dependency in Prime Minister – Foreign Secretary Relations', in Stanyer, J. (ed.), *Contemporary Political Studies 1997,* vol. II. Belfast: Political Studies Association.

Butler, H. (1998) 'Dependency in Prime Minister/Foreign Secretary Relations.' Unpublished PhD, University of Sheffield.

Butler, R. (1971) *The Art of the Possible*. London: Hamish Hamilton.

Butler, R. (1993) 'The Evolution of the Civil Service – A Progress Report', *Public Administration*, 71, 395–406.

Butler, R. (1994) 'Reinventing British Government', *Public Administration*, 72, 263–70.

Byrne, T. (1986) *Local Government in Britain*. Harmondsworth: Penguin.

Cabinet Office (1992) *Questions of Procedure for Ministers*. London: Cabinet Office.

Cabinet Office (1997a) *Ministerial Code: A Code of Conduct and Guidance on Procedures for Ministers*. London: Cabinet Office.

Cabinet Office (1997b) *1997 Departmental Plan*. London: HMSO.

Cabinet Office/OPS (1997) 'Civil Service Numbers Decline', Press Office, CAB 19/97, 5 June.

Callaghan, J. (1987) *Time and Chance*. London: Collins.

Callaghan, J. (1988) *Time and Chance*. London: Fontana.

Camilleri, J. and Falk, J. (1992) *The End of Sovereignty*, Aldershot: Elgar.

Campbell, C. and Wilson, G. (1995) *The End of Whitehall: Death of a Paradigm*. Oxford: Blackwell.

Campbell, J. (1993) *Edward Heath: A Biography*. London: Cape.

Castle, B. (1980) *The Castle Diaries 1974–76*. London: Weidenfeld and Nicolson.

Cerny, P. (1990) *The Changing Architecture of Politics*. London: Sage.

Chapman, L. (1979) *Your Disobedient Servant*. Harmondsworth: Penguin.

Clarke, J. and Newman, J. (1997) *The Managerial State*. London: Sage.

Clarke, R. (1975) 'The Machinery of Government', in Thornhill, W. (ed.), *The Modernisation of British Government*. London: Pitman.

Cloonan, M. (no date) *The Westland Affair: Constitutional or Conspiratorial Government?*, Case Studies for Politics, Case Study 4, University of York.

Cmnd 8616 (1982) *Efficiency and Effectiveness in the Civil Service*. London: HMSO.

Cm 1599 (1991) *The Citizen's Charter*. London: HMSO.

Cm 2627 (1994) *The Civil Service: Continuity and Change*. London: HMSO.

Cm 3579 (1996/7) *Next Steps Agencies in Government: Review 1996*. London: HMSO.

Coates, D. (1980) *Labour in Power?*. London: Longman.

Cockerell, M. (1988) *Live from No. 10*. London: Faber.

Collins, B. (1987) 'The Rayner Scrutinies' in Harrison, A. and Gretton, J. (eds), *Reshaping Central Government*. Oxford: Transaction Books.

Connolly, M., McKeown, P. and Milligan-Byrne, G. (1994) 'Making the Public Sector More User Friendly? A Critical Examination of the Citizen's Charter', *Public Administration*, 72, 23–36.

Cope, S., Leishman, F. and Starie, P. (1995) 'Hollowing Out and Hiving Off: Reinventing Policing in Britain', in Lovenduski, J. and Stanyer, J. (eds), *Contemporary Political Studies*, vol. II. Belfast: Political Studies Association.

Cortell, A. P. (1997) 'From intervention to disengagement: domestic structure, the state and the British information technology industry, 1979–1990', *Polity*, 24, 1–30.

Cortell, A. P. and Peterson, S. (1998) 'Altered states: explaining domestic institutional change', *British Journal of Political Science*, forthcoming.

Cox, R. (1992) 'Global Perestroika' in Miliband, R. and Panitch, L. (eds), *Socialist Register 1992*. London: Merlin.

Crewe, I. (1994) 'Electoral Behaviour', in Kavanagh, D. and Seldon, A. (eds), *The Major Effect*. London: Macmillan.

Cronin, J. E. (1991) *The Politics of State Expansion*. London: Routledge.

Crossman, R. H. J. (1963) 'Introduction', in W. Bagehot, *The English Constitution*. London: Fontana.

Crossman, R. H. J. (1972) *Inside View*. London: Cape.

Crossman, R. H. J. (1975) *The Diaries of a Cabinet Minister*, volume 1, Minister of Housing (London: Hamilton and Cape).

Daalder, H. (1963a) *Cabinet Reform in Britain 1914–63*, California: Stanford University Press.

Daalder, H. (1963b) 'The Haldane Committee and the Cabinet', *Public Administration*, 41, 117–35.

Daniel, C. (1997) 'May the Task Force Be With You', *New Statesman*, 1 August.

Day, P. and Klein, R. (1992) 'Constitutional and Distributional Conflict in British Medical Politics: The Case of General Practice, 1911–1991', *Political Studies*, 40, 462–78.

Deakin, N. and Parry, R. (1996) 'Images of the Treasury', paper presented at the Conference on the Economic and Social Research Council Whitehall Programme 'Understanding Central Government: Theory into Practice', University of Birmingham, 16–18 September.

Dell, E. (1991) *A Hard Pounding: Politics and Economic Crisis, 1974–76*. Oxford University Press.

Dell, E. (1994) 'The Failings of Cabinet Government in the Mid to Late 1970s', *Contemporary Record*, 8, 453–72.

Dell, E. (1997) *The Chancellors*. London: HarperCollins

Doern, G. B. (1993) 'The UK Citizen's Charter: Origins and Implementation in Three Agencies', *Policy and Politics*, 21, 17–29.

Doherty, M. (1988) 'Prime Ministerial Power and Ministerial Responsibility in the Thatcher Era', *Parliamentary Affairs*, 41, 49–67.

Donoughue, P. (1987) *Prime Minister: The Conduct of Policy Under Harold Wilson and James Callaghan*. London: Macmillan.

Dowding, K. (1991) *Political Power and Rational Choice*. London: Elgar.

Dowding, K. (1995) *The Civil Service*. London: Routledge.

Dowding, K. (1996) *Power*. Milton Keynes: Open University Press.

Draper, D. (1997) *Blair's Hundred Days*. London: Faber.

Drewry, G. and Butcher, T. (1991) *The Civil Service Today*. Oxford: Blackwell.

Dudley, G. and Richardson, J. J. (1996) 'Promiscuous and Celibate Ministerial Styles: Policy Change, Policy Networks and UK Roads Policy', *Essex Papers in Politics and Government*, no. 107, Colchester: University of Essex. Department of Government.

Dunleavy, P. (1985) 'Bureaucrats, Budgets and the Growth of the State: Reconstructing an Instrumental Model', *British Journal of Political Science*, 15, 299–328.

Dunleavy, P. (1989a) 'The United Kingdom: The Paradoxes of Ungrounded Statism', in Castles, F. (ed.), *The Comparative History of Public Policy*, Cambridge: Polity.

Dunleavy, P. (1989b). 'The Architecture of the British Central State, part I, Framework for Analysis', *Public Administration*, 67, 249–75.

Dunleavy, P. (1990) 'Reinterpreting the Westland Affair: Theories of the State and Core Executive Decision Making', Public Administration, 68, 29–60.

Dunleavy, P. (1991) *Democracy, Bureaucracy and Public Choice*. Hemel Hempstead: Harvester Wheatsheaf.

Dunleavy, P. (1994) 'Globalization of Public Service Production: Can Government Be "Best in World"?', *Public Policy and Administration*, 9, 36–64.

Dunleavy, P. (1995) 'Estimating the Distribution of Positional Influence in Cabinet Committees under Major', in Rhodes, R. A. W. and Dunleavy, P. (eds), *Prime Minister, Cabinet and Core Executive*. London: Macmillan.

Dunleavy, P. and Francis, A. (1990) 'Memorandum to the Treasury and Civil Service Select Committee', in HC 496 (1990/91), *The Next Steps Initiative*. London: HMSO.

Dunleavy, P. and Jones, G. (1995) 'Leaders, Politics and Institutional Change: The Decline of Ministerial Accountability to the House of Commons, 1868–1990', in Rhodes, R. A. W. and Dunleavy, P. (eds), *Prime Minister, Cabinet and Core Executive*. London: Macmillan.

Dunleavy, P. and O'Leary, B. (1987) *Theories of the State*. London: Macmillan.

Dunleavy, P. and Rhodes, R. A. W. (1990) 'Core Executive Studies in Britain', *Public Administration*, 68, 3–28.

Dunsire, A. (1990) 'Holistic Governance', *Public Policy and Administration*, 5, 4–19.

Dynes, M. and Walker, D. (1995) *The New British State*. London: Times Books.

Eccleshall, R. (1984) 'Conservatism', in Eccleshall, R., Geogheyn, V., Jay, R. and Wickford, R. *Political Ideologies*. London: Hutchinson.

Edgerton, D. (1991) *England and the Aeroplane*. London: Macmillan.

Efficiency Unit (1988) *Improving Management in Government: The Next Steps*. London: HMSO.

Efficiency Unit (1991) *Making the Most of the Next Steps: The Management of Ministers' Departments and Executive Agencies*. London: HMSO.

Efficiency Unit (1994) *Next Steps: Moving On*. London: HMSO.

Elgie, R. (1995) *Political Leadership in Liberal Democracies*. London: Macmillan.

Flinders, M. (1997) 'Judicial Accountability: Quis Custodiet Custodes?', mimeo, University of Sheffield.

Flinders, M. (1998) 'The Politics of Accountability', unpublished PhD thesis, University of Sheffield.

Flinders, M. and Smith, M. J. (1998) *The Politics of Quasi-Government*. London: Macmillan.

Foley, M. (1992) *The Rise of the British Presidency*. Manchester University Press.

Foster, C. and Plowden, F. (1996) *The State Under Stress*. Milton Keynes: Open University Press.

Foster, C. D. (1997) *A Stronger Centre of Government*. London: Constitutional Unit.

Foucault, M.(1980) *Power/Knowledge*, Brighton: Harvester.

Fowler, N. (1991) *Ministers Decide*. London: Chapman.

French, D. (1982) 'The Rise and Fall of Business as Usual' in Burk, K. (ed.), *War and the State: The Transformation of British Government, 1914–1919*. London: George Allen & Unwin.

Fry, G. (1979) *The Growth of Government*. London: Cass.

Fry, G. (1981) *The Administrative Revolution in Whitehall*. London: Croom Helm.

Fry, G. (1990) 'The Fulton Committee and the 'Preference for Relevance' Issues', *Public Administration*, 68, 175–90.

Fry, G. (1993) *Reforming the Civil Service: The Fulton Committee in the British Home Civil Service 1996–98*, Edinburgh University Press.

Fry, G. (1995) *Policy and Management in the British Civil Service*. Hemel Hempstead: Harvester Wheatsheaf.

Fry, G. (1997) 'The Conservatives and the Civil Service: 'One Step Forward, Two Steps Back'?' *Public Administration*, 75, 695–710.

Gains, F. (1998) 'Resource Dependency between Departments and Next Steps Agencies', unpublished PhD thesis, University of Sheffield.

Gamble, A. (1974) *The Conservative Nation*. London: Routledge & Kegan Paul.

Gamble, A. (1981) *Britain in Decline*. London: Macmillan.

Gamble, A. (1988) *The Free Economy and the Strong State*. London: Macmillan.

Gamble, A. (1990) 'Theories of British Government', *Political Studies*, 38, 404–20.

Gamble, A. and Payne, T. (1996) *Regionalism and World Order*. London: Macmillan.

Garfinkel, H. (1967) *Studies in Ethnomethodology*. Polity: Cambridge.

Geelheod, E. B. (1991) *Margaret Thatcher in Victory and Defeat*. New York: Prager.

Geertz, C. (1973) *The Interpretation of Culture*. New York: Basic Books.

George, S. and Sowemimo, M. (1996) 'Conservative Foreign Policy Towards the European Union', in Ludlam, S. and Smith, M. J. (eds), *Contemporary British Conservatism*. London: Macmillan.

George, S. (1996) 'The European Union, 1992 and the Fear of Fortress Europe', in Gamble, A. and Payne, T. (eds), *Regionalism and World Order*. London: Macmillan.

Giddens, A. (1985) *The Nation-State and Violence*. Oxford: Polity.

Giddens, A. (1986) *The Constitution of Society*. Oxford: Polity.

Gilmour, I. (1978) *Inside Right*. London: Quartet Books.

Gilmour, I. (1992) *Dancing with Dogma*. London: Pocket Books.

Gowan, P. (1987) 'The origins of the administrative elite', *New Left Review*, 162, 4–35.

Grant, W. (1982) *The Political Economy of Industrial Policy*. London: Butterworths.

Grant, W. (1987) *Business and Politics in Britain*. London: Macmillan.

Grant, W. (1989) *Pressure Groups, Politics and Democracy in Britain*. London: Phillip Allan.

Grant, W. (1995) *Pressure Groups, Politics and Democracy in Britain*, 2nd edition. London: Harvester Wheatsheaf.

Gray, A. and Jenkins, W. (1987) 'Public Administration and Government in 1986', *Parliamentary Affairs*, 40, 299–317.

Gray, A. and Jenkins, W. (1991) 'Public Administration and Government in 1990', *Parliamentary Affairs*, 44, 21–39.

Gray, A. and Jenkins, W. (1993) 'Public Administration and Government in 1991–2', *Parliamentary Affairs*, 46, 17–37.

Gray, C. (1994) *Government Beyond the Centre*. London: Macmillan.

Gray, J. (1993) *Beyond the New Right*. London: Routledge.

Greenaway, J., Smith, S. and Street, J. (1992) *Deciding Factors in British Politics: A Case-studies Approach*. London: Routledge.

Greenleaf, W. H. (1973) 'The Character of Modern British Conservatism', in Benewick, R., Berki, R. N. and Parek, B. (eds), *Knowledge and Belief in Politics*. London: George Allen & Unwin.

Greenleaf, W. H. (1983a) *The British Political Tradition: Volume 1, The Rise of Collectivism*. London: Methuen.

Greenleaf, W. H. (1983b) *The British Political Tradition: Volume 2, The Ideological Heritage*. London: Methuen.

Greenleaf, W. H. (1987) *The British Political Tradition: Volume 3, A Much-Governed Nation, Part One*. London: Methuen.

Greer, P. (1994) *Transforming Central Government*. Milton Keynes: Open University Press.

Hailsham, Lord (1978) *The Dilemma of Democracy*. London: Collins.

Haines, J. (1977) *The Politics of Power*. London: Jonathon Cape.

Hall, J. A. (1994) *Coercion and Consent: Studies in the Modern State*. Oxford: Polity.

Hall, P. (1986) *Governing the Economy*. Oxford: Polity.

Hall, S. and Schwarz, B. (1985) 'State and Society, 1880–1930', in Langan, M. and Schwarz, B. (eds), *Crises in the British State 1880–1930*. London: Hutchinson.

Hamilton, H. (1955) 'Treasury Control in the Eighties', *Public Administration*, 33, 13–17.

Harden, I. (1992) *The Contracting State*. Milton Keynes: Open University Press.

Harris, J. (1990) 'Society and State in Twentieth Century Britain', in Thompson, F. M. L. (ed.), *The Cambridge Social History of Modern Britain, 1750–1950: volume 3, Social Agencies and Institutions*, Cambridge University Press.

Harris, M. and Kelly, G. (1995) 'Rethinking Preferences in Public Choice' in Lovenduski, J. and Stanyer, J. (eds), *Contemporary Political Science*, vol. 2. Belfast: PSA.

Hart, D. (1972) 'The Genesis of the Northcote–Trevelyan Report', in Sutherland, G. (ed.), *Studies in the Growth of Government*. London: Routledge & Kegan Paul.

Hay, C. (1995) 'Structure and Agency' in Marsh, D. and Stoker, G. (eds), *Theory and Method in Political Science*. London: Macmillan.

Hay, C. (1996) *Re-Stating Social and Political Change*. Milton Keynes: Open University Press.

Hay, C. (1997) 'Political Time and the Temporality of Crisis: On Institutional Change as Punctuated Evolution', paper presented at the Institute on Western Europe, Columbia University. New York, 3 January.

Hay, C. and Wincott, D. (1997) 'Interrogating Institutionalism Interrogating Institutions: Structure, Agency and Institutionalist Theory', mimeo, University of Birmingham.

HC 313–II (1996/7) Public Service Committee, *Ministerial Accountability and Responsibility: vol. II, Memoranda of Evidence*. London: HMSO

HC 390–1 (1992/3) The Treasury and Civil Service Committee, *The Role of the Civil Service Interim Report*. London: HMSO

HC 390–i (1992/3) The Treasury and Civil Service Committee, *The Responsibilities and Work of the Office of Public Services*. London: HMSO.

HC 390–II (1992/3) Treasury and Civil Service Committee, Sixth Report, *The Role of the Civil Service: Interim Report*. London: HMSO.

HC 390–iv (1992/3) Treasury and Civil Service Select Committee, *The Role of the Civil Service: Minutes of Evidence*. London: HMSO.

HC 481 (1989/90) Treasury and Civil Service Select Committee, *Progress in the Next Steps Initiative*. London: HMSO.

HC 496 (1990/91) Treasury and Civil Service Select Committee, *The Next Steps Initiative*. London: HMSO.

HC 550–i (1990/91) Social Security Committee, *The Organisation and Administration of the Department of Social Security*. London: HMSO.

Headey, B. (1974) *British Cabinet Ministers*. London: George Allen & Unwin.

Healey, D. (1989) *The Time of My Life*. London: Michael Joseph.

Healey, D. (1990) *The Time of My Life*. Harmondsworth: Penguin.

Heclo, H. and Wildavsky, A. (1981) *The Private Government of Public Money: Community and Policy Inside British Politics*. London: Macmillan.

Heiser, T. 1994. 'The Civil Service at a Crossroads', *Public Policy and Administration*, 9, 14–26.

Henderson, N. (1993) *The Private Office*. London: Weidenfeld & Nicolson.

Hennessy, P. (1986) *Cabinet*. Oxford: Blackwell.

Hennessy, P. (1990) *Whitehall*. London: Fontana.

Hennessy, P. (1994) 'Cabinet Government: A Commentary', *Contemporary Record*, 8, 484–94.

Hennessy, P. (1995) *The Hidden Wiring: Unearthing the British Constitution*. London: Gollancz.

Hennessy, P. (1998) 'The Blair Style of Government: An Historical Perspective and an Interim Audit', *Government and Opposition*, 33, 3–20.

Hirst, P. and Thompson, G. (1992) 'The Problem of Globalization: international economic relations, national economic management and the formation of trading blocs', *Economy and Society* 21, 357–96.

Hirst, P. and Thompson, G. (1995) 'Globalization, Foreign Direct Investment and Economic Governance', *Organization*, 1, 277–303.

Hirst, P. and Thompson, G. (1996) *Globalisation in Question*, Cambridge: Polity.

HL 55 (1997/8) House of Lords Select Committee on the Public Services, *Report*. London: HMSO.

HM Treasury (1994) *Civil Service Staffing 1979–1994*, Treasury Occasional Paper no. 1. London: HM Treasury.

Hogg, Q. (1947) *The Case for Conservatism*. Harmondsworth: Penguin.

Hogg, S. and Hill, J. (1995) *Too Close to Call*. London: Little, Brown.

Hogwood, B. (1992) *Trends in British Public Policy*, Buckingham: Open University Press.

Honderich, T. (1990) *Conservatism*. Harmondsworth: Penguin.

Hood, C. (1995) 'Contemporary Public Management: A New Global Paradigm', *Public Policy and Administration*, 104–17.

Hood, C. and James, O. (1996) *Bureaucratic Gamekeeping: the Regulation of UK Public Administration*, Project Discussion Paper no. 1. London School of Economics.

Hood, C. and James, O. (1997) 'The Central Executive', in Dunleavy, P., Gamble, A., Holliday, I. and Peele, G. (eds), *Developments in British Politics 5*. London: Macmillan.

Hood, C., James, O., Jones, G., Scott, C. and Travers, T. (1998) 'Regulation inside Government: Where New Public Management meets the Audit Explosion' *Public Money and Management*, April–June 1998, 61–7.

Howe, G. (1994) *Conflicts of Loyalty*. London: Macmillan.

Hu, K.-C. (1995) 'Policy Networks in Democratic and Authoritarian Regimes', unpublished PhD thesis, University of Sheffield.

Hutton, W. (1995) 'Myth that Sets the World to Right', *Guardian*, 12 June.

Jackson, P. (1992) 'Economic Policy', in Marsh, D. and Rhodes, R.A.W. (eds), *Implementing Thatcherite Policy*. Milton Keynes: Open University Press.

James, O. (1995) 'Explaining the Next Steps in the Department of Social Security: The Bureau-shaping Model of Central State Reorganization', *Political Studies*, 43, 614–29.

James, S. (1992) *British Cabinet Government*. London: Routledge.

James, S. (1996) 'The Political and Administrative Consequences of Judicial Review', *Public Administration*, 74, 613–37.

Jenkins, P. (1989) *Mrs Thatcher's Revolution*. London: Jonathan Cape.

Jenkins, S. (1996) *Accountable to None*. Harmondsworth: Penguin.

Jennings, I. (1966) *The British Constitution*. Cambridge University Press.

Jessop, B. (1990) *State Theory*, Blackwell. Oxford.

Jessop, B. (1994). 'The Transition to Post-Fordism and the Schumpetarian Workfare State', in Burrows, R. and Loader, B. (eds), *Towards a Post-Fordist Welfare State*. London, Routledge.

Jessop, B. (1995) 'The Regulation Approach, Governance and Post-Fordism', *Economy and Society*, 24, 307–33.

Jones, G. (1975) 'Development of the Cabinet', in Thornhill, W. (ed.), *The Modernisation of British Government*. London: Pitman.

Jones, G.W. (1985) 'The Prime Minister's Power' in A. King (ed.) *The British Prime Minister*, 2nd edn. London: Macmillan.

Jones, G.W. (1995) 'The Downfall of Mrs Thatcher' in Rhodes, R. and Dunleavy, P. (eds), *Prime Minister, Cabinet and Core Executive*. London: Macmillan.

Johnson, B. (1998) 'Tony Has the Smile, but Gordon Has the Brains', *Daily Telegraph*, 14 January.

Jordan, A. G. and Richardson, J. J. (1986) *British Policy and the Policy Process.* London: Allen & Unwin.

Jordan, A. G. and Richardson J. J. (1987) *Government and Pressure Groups in Britain.* Oxford: Clarendon.

Jordan, G. (1994). 'From Next Steps to Market Testing: Administrative Reform as Improvisation', *Public Policy and Administration*, 9, 21–33.

Judge, D. (1993) *The Parliamentary State.* London: Sage.

Kaufman, G. (1997) *How to Be a Minister.* London: Faber.

Kavanagh, D. (1990) *Thatcherism and British Politics.* Oxford University Press.

Keegan, W. (1989) *The Battle of Downing Street.* London: Hodder & Stoughton.

Kellner, P. and Crowther Hunt, L. (1980) *The Civil Servants: An Enquiry into Britain's Ruling Class.* London: Macdonald.

Kelly, R. (1989) *Conservative Party Conferences.* Manchester University Press.

Kemp, P. (1990) 'Memorandum to the Treasury and Civil Service Select Committee' HC 496 (1990/91) *The Next Steps Initiative.* London: HMSO.

Kemp, P. (1993) *Beyond Next Steps: A Civil Service for the 21st Century.* London: Social Market Foundation.

Kennedy, P. (1988) *The Rise and Fall of the Great Powers.* London: Fontana.

Kenny, M. and Smith, M. J. (1997) '(Mis)understanding Blair', *Political Quarterly*, 68, 220–30.

Kickert, W. (1993) 'Autopoiesis and the Science of (Public) Administration: Essence, Sense and Nonsense', *Organization Studies*, 14, 261–78.

King, A. (1975) 'Overload: Problems of Governing in the 1970s', *Political Studies*, 23.

King, A. (1985a) 'Introduction: The Textbook Prime Minister' in King, A. (ed.), *The British Prime Minister.* Basingstoke: Macmillan.

King, A. (1985b) 'Margaret Thatcher: The Style of a Prime Minister', in King, A. (ed.), *The British Prime Minister.* Basingstoke: Macmillan.

King, A. (1990) 'Modes of Executive-Legislative Relations: Great Britain, France and West Germany', in Norton, P. (ed.), *Legislatures. Oxford University Press.*

Klein, R. (1989) *The Politics of the NHS*, London: Longman.

Kogan, M. (1971) *The Politics of Education.* Harmondsworth: Penguin.

Kooiman, J. (1993) *Modern Governance.* London: Sage.

Lash, S. and Urry, J. (1987) *The End of Organized Capitalism*, Cambridge: Polity.

Lawson, N. (1992) *The View from No. 11.* London: Bantam Press.

Lawson, N. (1994) 'Cabinet Government in the Thatcher Years', *Contemporary Record*, 8, 440–7.

Lee, J. M. (1977) *Reviewing the Machinery of Government: 1942–1952: An Essay on the Anderson Committee and Its Successors.* London: Social Science Research Council.

Lee, S. (1996) 'Manufacturing', in Coates, D. (ed.), *Industrial Policy in Britain.* London: Macmillan.

Lenman, B. P. (1992) *The Eclipse of Parliament*. London: Edward Arnold.

Lent, A. (1997) 'Transforming the Labour Party 1983–1989', unpublished PhD thesis, University of Sheffield

Leys, C. (1989) *Politics in Britain*. London: Verso.

Lindblom, C. E. (1977) *Politics and Markets*. New York: Basic Books.

Linklater, M. and Leigh, D. (1986) *Not with Honour: The Inside Story of the Westland Affair*. London: Observer.

Loughlin, M. and Scott, C. (1997) 'The Regulatory State', in Dunleavy, P., Gamble, A., Holliday, I. and Peele, G. (eds), *Developments in British Politics 5*. London: Macmillan.

Lowe, R. (1997) 'The Core Executive, Modernization and the Creation of PESC, 1960–64', *Public Administration*, 75, 601–15.

Ludlam, S. (1992) 'The Gnomes of Washington: Four Myths of the IMF Crisis of 1976', *Political Studies*, 40,

Ludlam, S. (1996) 'The Spectre Haunting Conservatism: Europe and Backbench Rebellion' in Ludlam, S. and Smith, M. J. (eds), *Contemporary British Conservatism*. London: Macmillan.

Ludlam, S. (1998) 'The Cauldron: Conservative Parliamentarians and European Integration', in Baker, D. and Seawright, D. (eds), *Britain: For and Against Europe*. Oxford University Press.

Ludlam, S. and Smith, M. J. (1996) *Contemporary British Conservatism*. London: Macmillan.

MacDonagh, O. (1958) 'The Nineteenth-Century Revolution in Government: A Reappraisal', *Historical Journal*, 1, 52–67.

Mackintosh, J. P. (1963) *The British Cabinet*, 1st edn. London: Stevens.

Mackintosh, J. P. (1977a) *The Politics and Government of Britain*. London: Hutchinson.

Mackintosh, J. P. (1977b) *The British Cabinet*, 3rd edn. London: Stevens.

Madgwick, P. (1991) *British Government: the Central Executive Territory*. London: Philip Allen.

Major, J. (1994) 'The Role and Limits of the State', Speech to the European Policy Forum QE11 Conference Centre. London, 27 July.

Mandelson, P. and Liddle, R. (1996) *The Blair Revolution: Can New Labour Deliver?* London: Faber.

Mann, M. (1984) 'The Autonomous Power of the State', *Archives Européennes de Sociologie*, 25, 185–213.

Mann, M. (1986) *The Sources of Social Power, volume one: A History of Power from the Beginning to AD 1760*. Cambridge University Press.

Mann, M. (1997) 'Has Globalisation Ended the Rise and Rise of the Nation-State?', *Review of International Political Economy*, 4, 472–96.

Marquand, D. (1988) *The Unprincipled Society*. London: Fontana.

Marr, A. (1996) *Ruling Britannia: The Failure and Future of British Democracy*. Harmondsworth: Penguin.

Marsh, D. (1991) 'Privatisation under Mrs Thatcher', *Public Administration*, 69, 459–80.

Marsh, D. (1998) *Comparing Policy Networks: Policy Networks in Theoretical and Comparative Perspective*. Milton Keynes: Open University Press.

Marsh, D. and Rhodes, R. A. W. (1992a) *Policy Networks in British Government*. Oxford University Press.

Marsh, D. and Rhodes, R. A. W. (1992b) *Implementing Thatcherite Policies*. Milton Keynes: Open University Press.

Marsh, D. and Smith, M. J. (1995) 'The Role of Networks in Understanding Whitehall', paper presented at the annual conference of the Political Studies Association, University of York, April.

Marsh, D. and Smith, M. J. (1998) 'Policy Networks: Towards A Dialectical Approach', mimeo, University of Birmingham.

Martinez Lucio, M., Noon, M. and Jenkins, S. (1997) 'Constructing the Market: Commercialization and Privatization in the Royal Mail', *Public Administration*, 75, 267–82.

Massey, A. (1995) *After Next Steps*, a report to the Office of Public Service and Science. University of Portsmouth.

Masujima, T. (1995) 'Administrative Reform in Japan', *Proceedings of the International Seminar on Governmental Reform Policy*, Korean Association of Policy Studies.

Mather, G. (1994) 'The Market, Accountability and the Civil Service', paper presented at the Public Administration Conference, University of York, 5–7 September.

Maxwell, S. (1996) 'Apples, Pears and Poverty Reduction: An Assessment of British Bilateral Aid', *IDS Bulletin*, 27, 36–51.

McEachern, D. (1990) *The Expanding State: Class and Economy Since 1945*. Hemel Hempstead: Harvester Wheatsheaf.

McGrew, A. (1997) 'Globalization and Territorial Democracy: An Introduction', in McGrew, A. (ed.), *The Transformation of Democracy?* Milton Keynes: Open University Press.

Meacher, M. (1982) *Socialism with a Human Face*. London: George Allen & Unwin.

Meadowcroft, J. (1995) *Conceptualising the State: Innovation and Dispute in British Political Thought 1880–1914*. Oxford University Press.

Mellon, E. (1990) 'Memorandum to the Treasury and Civil Service Select Committee' HC 496 (1990/91) *The Next Steps Initiative*. London: HMSO.

Middlemas, K. (1979) *Politics in Industrial Society*. London: André Deutsch.

Middlemas, K. (1983) *Industry, Unions and Government: Twenty One Years of NEDC*. London: Macmillan.

Middlemas, K. (1986) *Power, Competition and the State: Volume 1, Britain in Search of Balance*. London: Macmillan.

Middlemas, K. (1990) *Power, Competition and the State: Volume 2, Threats to the Postwar Settlement, Britain 1961–74*. London: Macmillan.

Middlemas, K. (1991) *Power, Competition and the State: Volume 3, The End of the Postwar Era*. London: Macmillan.

Miliband, R. (1969) *The State in Capitalist Society*. London: Quartet.

Milner, H. and Keohane, R. (1996) 'Internationalization and Domestic Politics', in Keohane, R. and Milner, H. (eds), *Internationalisation and Domestic Politics*. Cambridge University Press.

Moore, B. (1967) *Social Origins of Dictatorship and Democracy*. Harmondsworth: Penguin.

Mottram, R. (1994) 'A Future Shape for the Civil Service – The Position of HM Government', paper presented at the Queen Mary and Westfield Public Policy Seminar, A Future Shape for the Civil Service. London, 7 June.

Mountfield, R. (1997) 'Organisational Reform Within Government: Accountability and Policy Management, *Public Administration and Development*, 17.

Mueller, H. (1984) *Bureaucracy, Education and Monopoly: Civil Service
Reforms in Pressure and England*, Berkeley: University of California Press.

Mulgan, G. (1994) *Politics in an Antipolitical Age*, Cambridge: Polity.

Murdoch, J. (1995) 'Governmentality and the Politics of Resistance in UK
Agriculture: the Case of the Farmers' Union of Wales', *Socioligica Ruralis*,
35, 187–205.

Natzler, D. and Silk, P. (1995) 'Departmental Select Committees and the Next
Steps Programme', in Giddings, P. (ed.), *Parliamentary Accountability*.
London: Macmillan.

Niskanen, W. A. (1971) *Bureaucracy and Representative Government*. Chicago:
Aldine-Atherton.

Niskanen, W. A. (1973) *Bureaucracy: Servant or Master?* London: Institute of
Economic Affairs.

Norgaard, A. (1994) 'Rediscovering Reasonable Rationality in Institutional
Analysis: a Weberian Perspective', paper presented to the European
Consortium for Political Research Joint Session of Workshops, Madrid,
17–22 April.

Northcote, S. and Trevelyan, C. (1954) 'The Northcote–Trevelyan Report',
reprinted in *Public Administration*, 32, 1–16.

Norton, P. (1980) *Dissension in the House of Commons 1974–79*. Oxford
University Press.

Norton, P. (1985) 'Behavioural Changes; Backbench Independence in the
1980s', in Norton, P. (ed.), *Parliament in the 1980s*. Oxford: Blackwell.

Norton, P. (1988) 'Prime Ministerial Power', *Social Studies Review*, 3, January.

Norton, P. (1991a) 'Introduction', in Norton, P. (ed.), *New Directions in British
Politics,* Aldershot: Elgar.

Norton, P. (1991b). 'In Defence of the Constitution', in Norton, P. (ed.), *New
Directions in British Politics,* Aldershot: Elgar.

Norton, P. (1992) 'The Conservative Party from Thatcher to Major' in King,
A. (ed.), Britain at the Polls 1992, New Jersey, Chatham House.

Norton, P. (1993) *Does Parliament Matter?* Hemel Hempstead: Harvester
Wheatsheaf.

Oakeshott, M. (1962) *Rationalism in Politics*. London: Methuen.

Offe, C. (1984) *Contradictions of the Welfare State*. London: Hutchinson.

Osborne, D. and Gaebler, T. (1992) *Reinventing Government,* Wokingham:
Addison-Wesley.

Oughton, J. (1994) 'Market Testing and the Future of the Civil Service', paper
presented at the Public Administration Conference, University of York, 5–7
September.

Owen, G. (1995) 'Simple Theories and Complex Policies: Linking Policy
Network Theory and Complexity Theory', in Lovenduski, J. and Stanyer, J.
(eds), *Contemporary Political Science*, vol. 3. Belfast: PSA.

Painter, C. (1989) 'Thatcherite Radicalism and Institutional Conservatism',
Parliamentary Affairs, 42, 463–84.

Painter, C. (1994) 'Public Service Reform: Reinventing or Abandoning
Government?', *Political Quarterly*, 65, 242–62.

Parker, G. (1995) 'Heseltine Sets Limits to his Power', *Financial Times*, 10 July.

Parkinson, C. (1992) *Right at the Centre*. London: Weidenfeld & Nicolson.

Parkinson, M. and Duffy, J. (1984) 'Government's Response to Inner City Riots: The Minister for Merseyside and the Task Force', *Parliamentary Affairs*, 37, 76–96.

Parris, H. (1960) 'The Nineteenth-Century Revolution in Government: A Reappraisal Reappraised', *Historical Journal*, 3, 17–37.

Parry, R., Hood, C. and James, O. (1997) 'Reinventing the Treasury: Economic Rationalism or Econocrat's Fallacy of Control', *Public Administration, 75*, 395–415.

Pattie, C. and Johnson, R. (1996) 'The Conservative Party and the Electorate', in Ludlam, S. and Smith, M. J. (eds), *Contemporary British Conservatism*. London: Macmillan.

Payne, A. P. (1993) 'Westminster Adapted' in Dominguez, J. (ed.), *The Future of Democracy in the Caribbean*, Baltimore: Johns Hopkins University Press.

Peacock, A. T. and Wiseman, J. (1967) *The Growth of Public Expenditure in the United Kingdom*. London: George Allen & Unwin.

Peden, G. C. (1991) *British Economic and Social Policy: Lloyd George to Margaret Thatcher*. London: Phillip Allan.

Perkin, H. (1977) 'Individualism Versus Collectivism in Nineteenth Century Britain: A False Antithesis', *Journal of British Studies*, 17, 105–118.

Perkin, H. (1989) *The Rise of Professional Society*. London: Routledge.

Perraton, J., Goldblatt, D. Held, D. and McGrew, A. (1997) 'The Globalisation of Economic Activity' *New Political Economy*, 2, 257–78.

Perrow, C. (1970) *Organizational Analysis*. London: Tavistock.

Petch, L. (1951) 'Changes in the Machinery of Government Since 1945', *Public Administration*, 29, 383–92.

Peters, B. G. (1997) 'Shouldn't Row, Can't Steer: What's a Government to Do?' *Public Policy and Administration, 12*, 51–61.

Pliatsky, C. (1989) *The Treasury Under Mrs Thatcher*. Oxford: Blackwell.

Pollard, S. (1982) *The Wasting of the British Economy*. London: Croom Helm.

Pollard, S. (1992) *The Development of the British Economy 1914–1990*. London: Edward Arnold.

Pollitt, C. (1984) *Manipulating the Machine*. London: George Allen & Unwin.

Pollitt, C. (1990) *Managerialism and the Public Services*. Oxford: Blackwell.

Ponting, C. (1986) *Whitehall: Tragedy and Farce*. London: Hamish Hamilton.

Portillo, M. (1994) 'A Revolution in the Public Sector', *A Speech Delivered to Hertford College Deregulation Seminar*. Oxford, 7 January.

Price Waterhouse (1994) *Executive Agencies: Survey Report 1994*. London: Price Waterhouse.

Pryce, S. (1997) *Presidentializing the Premiership*. London: Macmillan.

Purnell, S. (1995) 'An Empire Falls Back', *Financial Times*, 16 October.

Radcliffe, J. (1991) *The Reorganisation of British Central Government*, Aldershot: Dartmouth

Raison, T. (1979) *Power and Parliament*. Oxford: Blackwell.

Ranelagh, J. (1991) *Thatcher's People*. London: HarperCollins.

Rhodes, R. A. W. (1981) *Control and Power in Central Local Relations*, Farnborough: Gower.

Rhodes, R. A. W. (1988) *Beyond Westminster and Whitehall*. London: Allen & Unwin.

Rhodes, R. A. W. (1992) 'Local Government Finance', in Marsh, D. and Rhodes, R. A. W. (eds), *Implementing Thatcherite Policies*. Milton Keynes: Open University Press.

Rhodes, R. A. W. (1993) 'The Changing Nature of the British Executive', report to the Economic and Social Research Council, May.

Rhodes, R. A. W. (1994) 'The Hollowing Out of the State', *Political Quarterly,* 65, 138–51.

Rhodes, R. A. W. (1995a) 'Introducing the Core Executive', in Rhodes, R. and Dunleavy, P. (eds), *Prime Minister, Cabinet and Core Executive*, Macmillan. London.

Rhodes, R. A. W. (1995b) 'From Prime Ministerial Power to Core Executive', in Rhodes, R. and Dunleavy, P. (eds), *Prime Minister, Cabinet and Core Executive*, Macmillan. London.

Rhodes, R. A. W. (1996a) 'Governing without Governance: Order and Change in British Government', Inaugural Lecture, University of Newcastle, 18 April.

Rhodes, R. A. W. (1996b). 'The New Governance: Governing without Government', *Political Studies*, 44, 652–67.

Rhodes, R. A. W. (1997a) *Understanding Governance*. Milton Keynes: Open University Press.

Rhodes, R. A. W. (1997b) ' "Shackling the Leader"? Coherence, Capacity and the Hollow Crown', in Weller, P., Bakvis, H. and Rhodes, R. A. W. (eds), *The Hollow Crown: Countervailing Trends in Core Executives*. London: Macmillan.

Rhodes, R. A. W. (1997c) 'From Marketization to Diplomacy: It's the Mix that Matters', *Public Policy and Administration,* 12, 31–50

Rhodes, R. A. W. and Dunleavy, P. (1995) *Prime Minister, Cabinet and Core Executive*. London: Macmillan.

Richards, D. (1997) *The Civil Service Under the Conservatives* Brighton: Sussex Academic Press.

Richards, D. and Smith, M. J. (1997) 'How Departments Change: Windows of Opportunity and Critical Junctures in Three Departments', *Public Policy and Administration*, 12, 62–79.

Richards, D. and Smith, M. J. (1998) 'Power, Knowledge and the Public Service Ethos', 'The Gatekeepers of The Common Good: Power and the Public Service Ethos', *EGPA Yearbook 1998*, European Group for Public Administration, Brussels.

Richards, S. (1987) 'The Financial Management Initiative', in Harrison, A. and Gretton, J. (eds), *Reshaping Central Government*. Oxford: Transaction Books.

Richards, S. (1996) 'The Civil Service Code' paper presented at the ESRC Whitehall Programme Workshop, University of London, 13 June.

Richardson, J. J. and Jordan, A. G. (1979) *Governing under Pressure*. Oxford: Martin Robertson.

Richardson, J. (1993) *Doing Less By Doing More: British Government 1979–93*, EPPI Occasional Papers, no. 93/2, University of Warwick.

Riddell, P. (1993) *Honest Opportunism*. London: Hamish Hamilton.

Roll, E. (1966) 'The Machinery for Economic Planning: 1. The Department of Economic Affairs', *Public Administration*, 44, 1–11.

Rose, R. (1984) *Do Parties Make a Difference?* London: Macmillan.

Rose, R. (1987) *Ministers and Ministries: A Functional Analysis.* Oxford: Clarendon.

Rose, R. (1991) *The Postmodern President,* New Jersey: Chatham House.

Rose, R. and Davies, P. (1994) *Inheritance in Public Policy.* New York: Yale University Press.

Rosenau, J. (1992) 'Governance, Order and Change in World Politics', in Rosenau, J. N. and Czempiel, E.-O. (eds), *Governance without Government.* Cambridge University Press.

Rosevere, H. (1969) *The Treasury: The Evolution of a British Institution.* London: Allen Lane.

Russel, T. (1978) *The Tory Party.* Harmondsworth: Penguin.

Russell, L., Scott, D. and Wilding, P. (1997) 'The Funding of Local Voluntary Organisations', *Policy and Politics,* 24, 395–412.

Sanders, D. (1990) *Losing an Empire, Finding a Role. London:* Macmillan.

Savage, G. (1996) *The Social Construction of Expertise.* University of Pittsburgh Press.

Saward, M. (1997) 'In Search of the Hollow Crown', in Weller, P., Bakvis, H. and Rhodes, R. A. W. (eds), *The Hollow Crown: Countervailing Trends in Core Executives.* London: Macmillan.

Schwarz, B. (1985) 'Conservatism and "Caesarium", 1903–1922', in Langan, M. and Schwarz, B. (eds), *Crises in the British State 1880–1930.* London: Hutchinson.

Scott, R. (1996) *Report of the Inquiry into the Export of Defence Equipment and Dual Use Goods to Iraq and Related Prosecutions.* London: HMSO.

Scruton, R. (1984) *The Meaning of Conservatism.* London: Macmillan.

Sedgemore, B. (1980) *The Secret Constitution.* London: Hodder & Stoughton.

Seldon, A. (1995) 'The Ethos of the Cabinet Office: A Comment on the Testimony of Officials', in Rhodes, R. A. W. and Dunleavy, P. (eds), *Prime Minister, Cabinet and Core Executive.* London: Macmillan.

Seldon, A. (1997) *Major: A Political Life.* London: Weidenfeld & Nicolson.

Skocpol, T. (1979) *States and Social Revolutions.* Cambridge University Press.

Skocpol, T. (1985) 'Bringing the State Back In: Strategies of Analysis in Current Research', in Evans, P. B., Rieschemeyer, D. and Skocpol, T. (eds), *Bringing the State Back In.* Cambridge University Press.

Skowronek, S. (1982) *Building a New American State: The Expansion of National Administrative Capacities.* Cambridge University Press.

Smith, B and Stanyer, J. (1976) *Administering Britain.* London: Fontana.

Smith, M. J. (1990) *The Politics of Agricultural Support in Britain: the Development of the Agricultural Policy Community.* Aldershot: Dartmouth.

Smith, M. J. (1991) 'From Policy Community to Issue Network: *Salmonella* in Eggs and the New Politics of Food', *Public Administration,* 69, 235–55.

Smith, M. J. (1993) *Pressure, Power and Policy.* Hemel Hempstead: Harvester Wheatsheaf.

Smith, M. J. (1994) 'The Core Executive and the Resignation of Mrs Thatcher', *Public Administration,* 72, 341–363.

Smith, M. J. (1995) *Pressure Politics.* Manchester: Baseline Books.

Smith, M. J. (1996) 'Reforming the State' in Ludlam, S. and Smith, M. J. (eds), *Contemporary British Conservatism*. London, Macmillan.

Smith, M. J., Marsh, D. and Richards, D. (1993) 'Central Government Departments and the Policy Process', *Public Administration*, 71, 567–94.

Smith, M. J., Richards, D. and Marsh, D. (1998a) 'Ideological Ministers and Civil Servants: The Case of Tony Benn', mimeo, University of Sheffield.

Smith, M. J., Richards, D. Marsh, D. and Chapman, J. (1998b) 'Bureaucrats, Politicians and Reform in Whitehall: Analysing the Bureau-Shaping Model', mimeo, University of Sheffield.

Spence, D. (1992) 'The Role of British Civil Servants in European Lobbying: the British Case', in Mazey, S. and Richardson, J. (eds), *Lobbying in the European Community*. Oxford University Press.

Stephens, P. (1994) 'Vultures Gather Over Major' *Financial Times*, 7 April.

Stephens, P. (1995) 'Life after the Landslide', *Financial Times*, 6 May.

Stephen, P. (1996) *Politics and the Pound: The Conservatives' Struggle with Sterling*. London: Macmillan.

Stoker, G. (1998) 'Quangos and Local Democracy', in Flinders, M. and Smith, M. J. (eds), *The Politics of Quasi-Government*. London: Macmillan.

Stone, B. (1995) 'Administrative Accountability in Western Democracies: Towards a New Conceptual Framework', *Governance*, 8, 1995, 505–25.

Stones, R. (1990) 'Government–Finance Relations in Britain 1964–7', *Economy and Society*, 19, 32–55.

Street, J. (1988) 'British Government Policy on AIDS', *Parliamentary Affairs*, 41, 490–507.

Tant, A. P. (1993) *British Government: the Triumph of Elitism*. Aldershot: Dartmouth.

Tebbit, N. (1988) *Upwardly Mobile*. London: Weidenfeld & Nicolson.

Thain, C. and Wright, M. (1995) *The Treasury and Whitehall*. Oxford: Clarendon.

Thane, P. (1990) 'Government and Society in England and Wales, 1750–1914', in Thompson, F. M. L. (ed.), *The Cambridge Social History of Modern Britain, 1750–1950: volume 3, Social Agencies and Institutions*. Cambridge University Press.

Thatcher, M. (1993) *The Downing Street Years*. London: HarperCollins.

Theakston, K. (1987) *Junior Ministers in British Government*. Oxford: Blackwell.

Theakston, K. (1995) *The Civil Service since 1945*. Oxford: Blackwell.

Thomas, G. (1998) *Prime Minister and Cabinet Today*, Manchester: Manchester University Press.

Thompson, H. (1995) 'Joining the ERM', in Rhodes, R. and Dunleavy, P. (eds), *Prime Minister, Cabinet and Core Executive*. London: Macmillan.

Thompson, H. (1996a) 'Economic Policy under Thatcher and Major' in Ludlam, S. and Smith, M. J. (eds), *Contemporary British Conservatism*. London: Macmillan.

Thompson, H. (1996b) *The British Conservative Government and the European Exchange Rate Mechanism, 1979–1994*. London: Pinter.

Tilly, C. (1990) *Coercion, Capital and European States*. Oxford: Blackwell.

Tomkins, A. (1996) 'The Scott Report: The Hope and Failure of Parliament', *Political Quarterly*, 67, 349–53.

Toonen, A. J. (1991) 'Europe of the Administrations: the Challenges of '92', *Public Administration Review*, 52, 108–15.

Turner, J. (1982) 'Cabinets, Committees and Secretaries: The Higher Direction of War', in Burk, K. (ed.), *War and the State: The Transformation of British Government, 1914–1919*. London: George Allen & Unwin.

Wakeham, J. (1994) 'Cabinet Government', *Contemporary Record*, 8, 473–83.

Walker, P. (1991) *Staying Power*. London: Bloomsbury.

Walkland, S. and Ryle, M. (1977) *The Commons in the Seventies*. London: Fontana.

Wapshott, N. and Brock, G. (1983) *Thatcher*. London: Futura.

Ward, H. (1987) 'Structural Power – A Contradiction in Terms?', *Political Studies*, 35, no. 4, 223–41.

Warner, N. (1984) 'Raynerism in Practices: Anatomy of a Rayner Scrutiny', *Public Administration*, 62, 7–22.

Wass, D. (1984) *Government and Governed*. London: BBC.

Waters, M. (1993) *Globalization*. London: Routledge.

Watkins, A. (1991) *A Conservative Coup*. London: Duckworth.

Weirm M. and Skoclpol, T. (1985) 'State structures and the possibility of "Keynesian" Responses to the Great Depression in Sweden, Britain and the United States' in Evans, P. B., Rieschemeyer, D. and Skocpol, T. (eds), *Bringing the State Back In*. Cambridge University Press.

Weir, S. and Hall, W. (1994) *Ego Trip: Extra-governmental Organisations in their Accountability*. London: Democratic Audit and Charter 88.

Whitehead, P. (1985) *The Writing on the Wall*. London: Michael Joseph.

Willets, D. (1992) *Modern Conservatism*. Harmondsworth: Penguin.

Willson, F. M. G. (1955) 'Ministries and Boards: Some Aspects of Administrative Development Since 1832', *Public Administration*, 33, 43–57.

Wilson, H. (1974) *The Labour Government 1966–70*. Harmondsworth: Penguin.

Wilson, H. (1976) *The Governance of Britain*. London: Weidenfeld & Nicolson.

Woodhouse, D. (1994) *Ministers and Parliament*. Oxford: Clarendon.

Wright, M. (1972) 'Treasury Control 1854–1914' in Sutherland, G. (ed.), *Studies in the Growth of Government*. London: Routledge & Kegan Paul.

Wrong, D. (1988) *Power*. Oxford: Blackwell.

Young, D. (1990) *The Enterprise Years*. London: Headline.

Young, H. (1989) *One of Us*. London: Macmillan.

Young, H. and Sloman, A. (1982) *No, Minister*. London: BBC.

Young, H. and Sloman, A. (1984) *But Chancellor*. London: BBC.

Zifcak, S. (1994) *New Managerialism*. Milton Keynes: Open University Press.

Zysman, J. (1983) *Governments, Growth and Markets*. Oxford: Martin Robertson.

Index

BARNSLEY COLLEGE
EASTGATE
LEARNING CENTRE